Fast Media
Media Fast

How to Clear Your Mind and Invigorate
Your Life in an Age of Media Overload

Thomas W. Cooper, Ph.D.

AuthorHouse™
1663 Liberty Drive
Bloomington, IN 47403
www.authorhouse.com
Phone: 1-800-839-8640

Published by Gaeta Press, Boulder, CO, www.gaetapress.com
Gaeta Press and the circle G logo are trademarks of Gaeta IP, LLC

First published by AuthorHouse 10/13/2011

ISBN: 978-1-4520-8500-5 (sc)
ISBN: 978-1-4520-8501-2 (hc)
ISBN: 978-1-4567-3325-4 (ebk)

Printed in the United States of America

This book is printed on acid-free paper.

Edited by Shareen Ewing

Cover design: Jan Guarino
www.guarinographics.com

Copy Consultant: Michelle Molin
www.organiccommunications.com

ACCLAIM FOR
FAST MEDIA/MEDIA FAST

"In this century of media overload, I, like many others, find it crucial to find balance. *Fast Media/Media Fast* is an incredibly helpful guide toward personal balance and creating a consciousness for coping with one of the most pressing issues of our hyper-mediated society."

Jochen Zeitz, Chairman and CEO, Puma;
Leader in the Corporate Social Responsibility movement

"Few have stood firmer for ethical principles in the unremitting media wasteland than Tom Cooper. He is not a straw but a pillar for us all to grasp."

Robert Gardner, Film-Maker, Anthropologist;
Professor, Harvard University

"In this fascinating and original book, Tom Cooper shows us how to step outside of the media maelstrom and find a kind of peace and perspective that can transform our lives and the world. Both practical and visionary, he helps us redefine and reclaim connection and attachment and reap surprising rewards."

Jean Kilbourne, EdD, Creator of the Killing Us Softly:
Advertising's Image of Women *film series;*
Senior Scholar, the Wellesley Centers for Women

"Tom Cooper's *Fast Media/Media Fast* offers a stimulating, provocative and compelling account of the consequences, both personal and cultural, of freeing ourselves from, or at least controlling, the mediated world in which we live."

Theodore L. Glasser, Professor of Communication,
Stanford University

"*Fast Media/Media Fast* challenges us to look critically at the role of media in our lives…. Today we are told to value speed, that bigger is better, and that more should be our goal (Dr. Cooper speaks of the "triple ups"—speed-up, keep-up, and blow-up). He challenges us to slow down and be reflective and dare to be ourselves. 'What is present when my electronic programming is absent? I am.'"

Tara K. Giunta, International Communications and
Corporate Compliance Attorney, Washington, D.C.

"A clarion voice for consciousness. Here, a way forward is clearly laid out without being high-minded and formulaic. Dr. Cooper manages to present an impeccably-researched case that is inclusive, balanced and invites us to make the kind of changes that feel right in our lives and families. At first glance it may appear that this is a book about the media but in reality it is a path to connectedness, to our families and to ourselves."

Kim John Payne, M.Ed., Author of Simplicity Parenting;
Founding Director, The Center for Social Sustainability

"A feast on fasting from the most creative mind in our field. The intellectual and literary context is of Mt. Kilimanjaro magnificence, and its practical wisdom inspires our transformation."

Dr. Clifford Christians, Research Professor of
Communications Emeritus, University of Illinois

"Tom Cooper has the standing to write this original book: he's actually done what he's asking others to do. With a light touch, he sees the irony of using the media (a book) to help us shut off the media. Doing so, he's asking one of the profound moral questions of our age: how much is too much?"

Rushworth M. Kidder, Founder and President, Institute for Global
Ethics; author of Good Kids, Tough Choices

"Tom Cooper explores where few inhabitants of the 'developed' world dare to venture, escaping ever more intrusive media to discover the real world and real people (including ourselves) that are right here, hidden in plain sight. As he points out, there is a reason media companies refer to their shares of our space and time as 'penetration.'"

Adam Clayton Powell III, Director, Washington Policy Initiatives,
University of Southern California

"In this elegant book, Professor Cooper takes on the profoundly thorny problem of how best to live a life saturated by media. While one of the book's great strengths is the author's often brilliant reading of our media-soaked lives, he is after something larger. In language both elevating and grounding, and with surprising grace, the author offers us strategies about how we might make our own way through this ever-deepening media thicket."

Robb Moss, The Rudolf Arnheim Lecturer on Filmmaking,
Harvard University

"Media is like wine. Slowly sipping a glass of fine red wine with an evening meal can be beneficial to one's health and longevity. Quickly gulping down wine at all hours of the day can be extremely harmful. Dr. Thomas Cooper, in his latest book, *Fast Media/Media Fast,* shows how a steady diet of too much media can be and has been of harm, especially to children. *Fast Media/Media Fast* offers solutions to the problem: selecting and limiting media exposure, just as one would limit excessive drinking of bad wine. Dr. Cooper cites studies which show that the problem has become endemic and requires a special effort by all of us to ameliorate."

Robert L. Hilliard, Ph.D., Professor Emeritus, Emerson College;
Co-author, The Broadcast Century and Beyond

"Here is a timely, lucid and original book. *Fast Media/Media Fast* is a challenging invitation to inhabit the world differently. Creative and practical, this is well worth slowing down to absorb."

Dr. Jolyon Mitchell, Professor, New College,
The University of Edinburgh, Scotland

ALSO BY THOMAS COOPER

An Ethics Trajectory: Visions of Media Past, Present, and Yet to Come, co-authored with Anantha Babbili and Clifford Christians, Univ. of Illinois.

A Time Before Deception, Clear Light Publishing.

Natural Rhythms: The Indigenous World of Robert Gardner, Anthology Film Archives.

Communication Ethics and Global Change: International and National Perspectives (with C. Christians, F. Plude, and R. White), Longman.

Television and Ethics: An Annotated Bibliography (with R. Sullivan, P. Medaglia and C. Weir), G.K. Hall.

Media Ethics Summit Conference (with C. Christians and J.M. Kittross), Emerson College.

FAST MEDIA
MEDIA FAST

TABLE OF CONTENTS

PART I
Taking a Personal Media Fast or Diet

PART II
Learning from the Fast

FOREWORD

How much mainstream media have you been exposed to today? According to hundreds of serious studies on the subject and the everyday experience of most Americans, a whole lot, and far more than ever before.

In 20 years of clinical practice as a natural healthcare professional, I have seen the health effects of media overstimulation on thousands of patients of all ages—including anxiety, insomnia, depression, mental exhaustion, and attention deficit/hyperactivity syndromes. Nearly all of these patients did not connect these persistent complaints to their imbalanced media exposure, and felt a greater sense of calm and well-being when they became conscious of the choices they were making. This observation led me to explore the research published on the subject. I was amazed at what I found, and quite relieved at the practical perspectives on media oversaturation I discovered in a manuscript of Dr. Thomas Cooper's—*Fast Media/Media Fast*.

A Kaiser Family Foundation survey of 2,002 children between 8 and 18 (conducted between October 2008 and May 2009) discovered that today 8- to 18-year-olds devote an average of 7 ½ hours to using entertainment media across a typical day (more than 53 hours a week), up from about 6 ½ hours in 2004. And because they spend so much of that time "media multitasking" (using more than one medium at a time), they actually manage to pack a total of 10 hours 45 minutes worth of media content into those 7½ hours. This represents a 20% increase in five years.

The Kaiser survey results, published in January 2010, revealed that the average young person spends almost one hour daily on the phone, lives in a house with four TVs (71% have one in their bedroom), two computers and two video-game players; 67% have a cell phone and 75% have a media player, like an iPod. They spend an hour and a half daily sending 57 text messages. One third spend no time reading, other than schoolwork. The other two thirds spend an average of one hour reading. The 79% who watch TV watched an average of six hours. On the whole, young people spend three hours forty minutes each day watching TV. And 45% have a TV on in the house "most of the time," even if no one is watching; 64% have a TV on during meals. The 60% who play video games average two hours. The 85% who listen to music and other audio averaged three hours. Average computer use, other than schoolwork, is two and a half hours. *Fast Media/Media Fast* offers a range of practical answers and options for avoiding media overload.

During a recent visit to Chicago, my wife visited a small hotel we were walking by, to see if it might be a place to stay on a future visit. She learned that children were not allowed as guests, and asked why. "Oh, we're not set up to have children here. We don't have a TV." We suspected that noise concerns may have also been a factor in the hotel's policy, but the comment was telling.

We can only conclude that our children, whose life habits are formed in those critical years, will grow to be even more media-centric adults who will pass those habits along to their own children. But is unbalanced media exposure only an issue for our children?

For adults too, the data are clear and compelling. Nielsen's Three Screen Report for the first quarter of 2010—"a regular analysis of video viewing and related consumer behavior in the U.S."—reveals that Americans continue to view video at a record pace. Each week, the typical American continues to increase his/her media time, watching over 35 hours of TV, two hours of which is time-shifted TV, 20 minutes of online video and four minutes of mobile video, while also spending nearly four hours on the Internet. In addition, 59% of Americans surf the Internet and watch TV at the same time.

Is there a practical solution? Do I disconnect entirely from all media to avoid the overstimulation and pervasive marketing messages? Do I shrug my shoulders and accept the media barrage as an unavoidable consequence of the Information Age? I want to live a balanced and useful life in the world as it is. What to do?

In this book, Dr. Thomas Cooper, one of our world's best and brightest experts on media, ethics and culture, offers a perspective sourced in deep experience. In this timely book, he offers a clear and meaningful perspective that encourages conscious individual choices, rather than an all-or-nothing proposition. You and I can benefit from the unprecedented and immediate access we have to news and information, while staying heart-connected to our deeper purpose and the people we love. We can be, as Dr. Cooper writes, consumers of information without being consumed by it. Based on recent research, it will take deliberate action for that to happen.

Researchers from Yale University School of Medicine, National Institutes of Health, and California Pacific Medical Center reviewed 173 studies, examining the relationship between media exposure and seven health outcomes. This systematic review, reported by Common Sense Media, revealed that the average American child spends 45 hours per week with media, compared with 17 hours with parents and 30 hours in school. This remarkable meta-analysis of 28 years of research clearly shows the connection between media exposure and long-term negative outcomes, especially childhood obesity, tobacco use and sexual activity. One third of U.S. children and two-thirds of U.S. adults are now overweight or obese.

According to the Media Education Foundation, the average American child views up to 110 commercials per day, or 40,000 per year. Sweden, since 1991, has banned all advertising during children's prime time due to findings that children under 10 are incapable of telling the difference between a commercial and a program, and cannot understand the purpose of a commercial until the age of 12.

A review of hundreds of studies from the past 50 years and published in an early 2010 issue of *Pediatrics* reveals that:

- By age 18, the average adolescent will have seen an estimated 200,000 acts of violence on television alone, and depictions of violence are prevalent in video games. There is a significant connection between exposure to violence in media and real-life violent behavior.

- Youth exposed to sexual content are at moderately higher risk for early sexual behavior and unplanned pregnancy, particularly if exposed to pornography.

- More than $22 billion is spent each year marketing and advertising tobacco, alcohol and prescription drugs in the U.S. Portrayals of drug use, particularly tobacco smoking, are prevalent in both old and new media. Children's exposure to smoking in movies predicts the likelihood that they will start smoking within eight years.

- Media use clearly contributes to childhood obesity, but exactly how is unclear. Possible culprits include marketing of junk food and fast food, and a tendency to eat while viewing media.

- Studies have linked television viewing in early childhood with later development of attention deficit disorder (ADD) during the early school years, but experts disagree about the nature of this connection.

- Media can teach children and teenagers antiviolence attitudes, empathy, tolerance toward people of other races and ethnicity, and respect for their elders.

The authors of this landmark study in *Pediatrics* conclude that "To date, too little has been done by parents, healthcare practitioners, schools, the entertainment industry, or the government to protect children and adolescents from harmful media effects and to maximize the powerfully pro-social aspects of modern media. More research is needed, but sufficient data exist to warrant both concern and increased action."

Dr. Cooper emphasizes the irony that the more "connected" we are to media and the Internet, the less connected we are to each other. The more time teens spend watching television and using computers, the less likely they are to develop close relationships with parents and peers, a study of two New Zealand teen groups separated by 16 years found. For every hour adolescents spent watching television, there was a 13% increased risk of low attachment to parents and a 24% increase in the risk of having low attachment to peers, according to a report on one of the groups published online in the *Archives of Pediatrics & Adolescent*

Medicine. "Screen time was associated with poor attachment to parents and peers in two cohorts (study groups) of adolescents 16 years apart," Rosalina Richards, Ph.D., of the University of Otago in New Zealand, and colleagues wrote. "Given the importance of attachment to parents and peers in adolescent health and development, concern about high levels of screen time among adolescents is warranted."

Educational systems like Waldorf education, perhaps the fastest-growing educational approach in the world, offer a refreshing and much-needed media-free environment for our children's open minds to grow and thrive, unmolded by marketing-driven values and media overstimulation.

By all accounts, we live in a media-soaked culture that diminishes, rather than adds to, our quality of life and health. We scurry to "get connected," meaning the Internet, but have become less connected to what counts—other people, the natural world, and a deep inner life—in which we are spiritually connected to a pattern of life larger than ourselves.

At every turn of the eye or ear, our attention is sought by innumerable sources of carefully filtered information ("news") and marketing messages that emphasize what is apparently wrong with us and what we don't, but should, have. Our children are more stimulated and distracted, yet less emotionally intelligent and confident.

In this cacophony of fast media, which make for superficial lives, comes Dr. Cooper's learned voice, speaking words of wisdom and balance. Brilliant academics are at times disconnected from most people's daily life experience, preferring complex theoretical frameworks to wisdom sourced in authentic experience. Dr. Cooper is remarkable in that his impeccable academic credentials are balanced by a heart-filled, spiritual, and eminently practical perspective, based in deep life experience.

Having stepped back from the incessant noise and superficial chatter that define modern mainstream media and culture, Dr. Cooper has led hundreds on media fasts and diets. After spending months living with cultures without media, Dr. Cooper blended his stellar academic background with direct experience to offer this practical guide to making conscious choices about our relationship to mass media.

As a father of two young children, I have personally benefited from this work by creating a more balanced and harmonious home and family life. As an acupuncturist and clinical nutritionist, I incorporate the wisdom of this timely book when I guide adults through three-week detoxification programs. Many patients report that the media fast was their favorite component of their transformational cleanse.

Balance in our relationship to mass media deepens us and frees our precious time and energy so we can be more available as a positive and helpful presence in the lives of others. I welcome you to savor the deep wisdom contained in this timely text and find your life richer and more fulfilling.

Michael Gaeta, D.Ac., M.S., C.D.N.
Loveland, Colorado

PREFACE

At last we have an incisive treatise on a dimension of self-expansion which comes about in the absence of the media. Tom Cooper explores the world of "fast media" (the hurried and superficial hawkers of this-and-that snippet of information vying for our attention) and discusses the benefits of media fasting for our mental, psychological and spiritual health.

We must all despair on occasion of our media habits that decrease our freedom, limit our direct connection with the "real" world, beckon us to accept secondhand opinions, take media "personalities" seriously, and disconnect us from serious concern and conversations with our friends and family. Certainly we spend more time with the media and their disjointed messages than we do with people, with natural wonders, and with intrapersonal communication.

Tom Cooper, initially for a month, determined to disengage himself from the media, to substitute for this experience a "fast" by which he would try to better know himself as he faced reality directly. He gave up the pseudo-reality of the media world and lived existentially. In essence, he saw the trees, smelt the flowers, felt the sand trickling through his fingers, and listened to the sounds of his wife and child.

In this book he details his experiences during his fasting and also explains how each of us might take our own media fast, should we choose. I must admit that the prospect is compelling, as I have long found in existentialism and in Zen Buddhism a transcendent confrontation with a reality sadly missing in the insistent expositions, admonitions and superficial gossip of the mass media. I have known instinctively that the vast barrage of messages pouring in upon us are, by and large, useless, and that we would be better off with less, not more, interpersonal communication.

It is important to stress that Tom Cooper is not *against* mass media, no more so than a *food* faster is *against* food. He simply bemoans our increasing habituation to them. This is not a negative book: it is indeed positive, since the author stresses the wisdom of selectivity and moderation, rather than our normal tendency to overindulgence in media fare.

Messages in great proliferation insistently demand our attention. And it is upon this problem of communication overload that Tom Cooper puts his sensitive finger. Ignorance may not be bliss, but knowledge of helter-skelter media facts is certainly not conducive to personal equilibrium or group harmony.

Media tend to trivialize our worlds. Our interpersonal and intrapersonal orientations are destroyed in the cacophony of public messages. It is the nature of media to invade our privacy, usurp our freedom, influence our values, sensationalize everything from sex to politics, and go far in stereotyping others, lobotomizing us, and creating an unreal world. Not everyone would agree with the above picture of the media, but this may be because not everyone takes a "fast" from time to time so as to obtain a better perspective.

Tom Cooper is a modern-day Thoreau, living for a month in the peacefulness and silence of a media-less Walden, where he could rest his senses and find in himself a more natural and genuine self. And without Thoreau's bitter anti-media bias, we are treated to some of his conclusions. He shares his experiences with us in a calm and sensible way. I would wager that many of the readers of this book, after seriously considering their less than nourishing media diet, will be tempted to begin some fasting of their own.

"Fast media," much like fast food, gives us information faster than we can digest it. This media diet is not very nourishing, to say the least. And, as Dr. Cooper points out, it can very likely do us harm.

The author draws on thinkers like Sartre and Pascal, as well as Oriental sages, to support his advocacy of a more direct approach to the world around us, without the intervention of media personalities and secondhand inferences. He presents the benefits of being devoted to being, to the concept of merger with one's surroundings, to "going with the flow."

We are not Buddhist monks, of course, and must live in the hurried, peer-pressured pragmatic world, where media provide us with the grist for our daily interpersonal mills. It would be abnormal and unreasonable for us to hide from media for long. Tom Cooper is not suggesting that we do that. What he is saying is that a fast from time to time will do much to restore meaning to our lives and expand our self-awareness to deeper levels. Such fasts, he believes, might very well lead us to more sensible and selective media exposure.

Beyond the glare of the television set and the redundant squawk of commercials, beyond the insistent doom-saying of news and views mouthed by funereal anchorpersons, and beyond the glitzy sitcoms and pseudo-worlds of the "soaps" is the real world "out there," waiting to be discovered. There are also family and friends needing the touch of a human hand and the smile of affection. But, as Tom Cooper shows in this fascinating little book, the media world is simply too much with us; too little we see beyond the page and tube that we can make ours.

Why, I have often asked myself, should I let some TV personality hold my attention for hours? Why should I spend hours reading about every little political expression from camera-hungry politicians? Why should I spend my few days here on earth flitting among recycled episodes, thinking all the while that news incidents are really important and I should know about them?

Would it not be better, as this book suggests, for me to break out of my practice of media "gluttony" and come to know myself, others, and the sights and sounds of the real world around me?

Tom Cooper has done us all a real service with this book, as he turns our attention from the media and their messages to the individual and direct transcendence of personhood. This is a most worthy goal, and one which has been admirably achieved.

John C. Merrill, Ph.D.
Professor Emeritus of Journalism
University of Missouri—Columbia

ACKNOWLEDGMENTS

When I began this book, for once my former wife Nancy and child Angelica could say I wrote a book which delighted them. Usually, writing a communication book involves my watching, listening to or reading so much media that family life is reduced to rare days deliberately spent together. However, one great benefit of fasting was that much more time was spent with people. In a way, Nancy and Angelica co-authored this book, and certainly shared the fast experience, with me. No husband and father could be more fortunate.

In 2010, when I rewrote this volume, and expanded it from a short classroom workbook to a larger volume for the public, I was married to Eileen Flanagan. Always supportive and inspiring, Eileen is my wonderful co-author, not only of these pages but also of life itself. I feel most privileged and thankful for her love, care and inspiration. Here's to Eileen and her wonderful family of Flanagans.

Over the years, many of the best-known researchers and thinkers in communication have taken me or one of my projects under their wing. George Gerbner, Marshall McLuhan, Clifford Christians, Bob Gardner, Vlada Petric, Brenda Dervin, Yassen Zassoursky, Bob Hilliard, Kaarle Nordenstreng and many others have contributed considerably to my education. Library researchers such as Robert Sullivan and Bob Roberts have located many obscure references and added to my memory banks considerably. Colleagues such as Kathleen Jamieson, Tom Gordon, Mike Kittross, Don Fry, Claire Andrade-Watkins, Jan Roberts-Breslin, Jane Shattuc, Shujen Wang, Tom Kingdon, Eric Schaefer and Bob Picard have often seen the best in my work and encouraged its refinement and publication.

In 1982 I began workshops and seminars with friends like Alan Hammond, Bill Porter, Gary Diggins and my wife for many professionals in various fields of mass communication and the performing arts. Eventually, what was originally intended to support individuals of integrity in communication became an organization known as the Association for Responsible Communication. One fringe benefit of founding ARC was that many of its leaders—friends like Barbara Coffman, George Hanson, Bill Wilkinson, Bill Becker, Paul Luft, Barbara Lourgos and many others—became very supportive of my work. Local ARC colleagues, like Jeff Volk, Carol Procter, and especially Ron Kertzner, so effectively picked up administrative leadership of ARC's New England activities that my time for fasting was considerably expanded.

Emerson College has also been a family of backers. It was helpful to have a Department Chair, in this case David Gordon, who, when told I would be attempting a media fast, did not say "...a what?" or "You're not paid for that!" but immediately saw the implications for our field and said, "Great idea!" My other former chairs, Michael Selig, Rob Sabal, Arthur Barron, Eric Schaefer, and my current Chair, Jonathan Wacks, have also been fine friends and solid backers of creative research.

I will always be grateful to Emerson's administration, at first John Zacharis, and later Jackie Liebergott, Phil Amato, Dorothy Aram, Mary Harkins, Linda Moore, Anne Doyle, and others for supporting my better ideas and teaching me theirs. In recent years, when the book itself has come to fruition, new friends have joined the leadership team, such as Grafton Nunes, Janis Andersen, Richard Zauft, Amy Ansell, Dan Tobin, and Richard West. Their strong, positive support has been invaluable.

For those who detect or suspect a philosophic, religious or spiritual component to this book, no doubt I was initially influenced to some degree by the strong Protestant upbringing of my loving parents, the convert's Catholicism of McLuhan, the Judaism of my first wife's family, the atheistic explorations of my college years at Harvard, and the Eastern religions I discovered during graduate school at the University of Toronto. However, it is a more recent association with The Emissaries that has led me neither to chose nor reject any single religion or philosophy, but rather to look for what is "right" behind each of them. If that appreciation for integrity, wherever it may be found, can be read between the lines of this book, I have Martin and Michael Exeter, their families, David and Joyce Karchere, Jim Wellemeyer, Vicki Tweiten, David and Sue Washington, Patricia Gursu, Alice Penfield, Virginia Morrison and many others to thank for it. Currently, the seven Emissary Trustees—Jane Anetrini, Ruth Buckingham, Hugh Duff, David Karchere, Rich Kenny, Phil Richardson and Maureen Waller—have been enormously supportive.

I am also most grateful to my Baptist friends at Union University, my Unitarian friends here in Swampscott, my close friend in spirit, Rabbi Al Axelrad, and so many others who have inspired me.

My parents, Margaret and David Cooper, and Eileen's parents, Larry and Eileen, and many other relatives (Coopers, Pardues, Isaacs, Abels, et al) have been generous in providing moral support and great friendship.

During my 2000 sabbatical, when the first version of this text was written, I was warmly welcomed as a Young Fellow at Elizabethtown College in Pennsylvania and as a guest scholar at the East-West Center in Honolulu. I am beholden to David Eller, Steve Scott, Nancy Lewis, and Meheroo Jussawalla for extremely collegial hospitality.

Although some may view this book as a departure from my research in media ethics, ethical considerations (as much as any others) are central to its scope. Many friends from the media ethics "team"— Barney, Black, Bowen, Capo, Christians, Dennis, Elbot, Elliott, Fackler, Gillmor, Glasser, Hodges, Jaksa, Lambeth, Linsky, Marks, Merrill, the Poynter group, Wilkins and others—have been creative contributors and sparring partners in the formulation of my thought. As co-publisher and editor of *Media Ethics* magazine, respectively, Manny Paraschos and Mike Kittross have been especially creative partners in surveying the ethics landscape together.

Writing a book is a collective process. I credit people like Gary Diggins, Terry Turowski, Henry David Thoreau, Ralph Waldo Emerson, Gandhi, Hugh Malafry, Richard Heinberg and many others whose thinking or experimentation in some way sparked mine about this fast. Others, like Roger de Winton, David Patrick, Joseph Antell, Jr. and Deb Reichlin, in assisting my increasingly good health, have also assisted in increasing my writing clarity and accuracy. Michael Gaeta, who is instrumental in publishing and distributing the book, is a current guide in the world of health and nutrition.

During my sabbatical new friends, such as Pat and Terry Amig, and old friends, such as Judd and Gloria Watkins, provided just the right accommodation at just the right time for the atmosphere needed by a writer. The many Amish, Mennonite, Rapa Nui, and other "no media" groups and individuals I have come to know and with whom I have sometimes lived, have taught me immeasurably.

No treasure could sparkle more brightly for a professor than his students. Teaching assistants, such as Florin Talos, Catherine Carey, Jennifer Kelley, E.J. Massa, and many others provided the skillful surround that allowed me to keep research momentum intact. Each student has been my valued teacher.

The notion of "best friends" is a wonderful one—there are people who see one through rough passages and rites of passage—as well as people who intuitively know when to offer enfoldment and when to offer complete space. Over the years I have been blessed with many such friends and mentors—Grace Van Duzen, Arnie and Susan Servais, Yujin Pak, Charlie Parker, Lem Marshall, Lucy Ferguson, Roger de Winton, Laurel Cox, Ron Kertzner, Bruce Allyn, Shannon Bowen, Bob Colby, David Smith, Bob and Shareen Ewing, the Sunrise "family," Ted and Claudia Black, Ricky and Eva Reynolds, Michael and Deanna Gaeta, David and Joyce Karchere—all of whom were there to share the work, the intensity, the rewards and the turbulence of life at one stage or during many. My first wife, Nancy Cooper, gave both me and our daughter, Angelica, the best years of her life and often cared for both of us through thick and thin. For these and many others, I am most grateful.

Michael Gaeta and Shareen Ewing have been invaluable and talented partners in the final editing and rewriting of this book. None of the best friends listed above have been more supportive, catalytic or generous, even when I was miles away, during the writing of this book than these three—Eileen Flanagan, Angelica Cooper and Charlene Hunter. To these three, and to Shareen and Michael, and to all those who hold the light high everywhere, this book is fondly dedicated.

Dr. Thomas Cooper
Swampscott, Massachusetts

INTRODUCTION

Has it ever seemed to you that "life is moving too fast"? For example, in the world of constant software updates, 1000 TV channels, satellite radio, iPods and iPads, do there seem to be too many changes, programs, upgrades, Web sites, attachments, servers and software packages to keep up? Or perhaps you have experienced what Richard Wurman calls "information anxiety"—too many e-mails, faxes, memos, text messages, beeper calls, pieces of junk mail, iTunes, Twitters, books, YouTube URLs, magazines, and voice mails—to be on top of it all? We live in an age of fast and faster media—faster downloads, editing, music, innovation, transmission, streaming and change—coming from more signals, channels, devices, stations, Web sites, broadcasts and locales than ever before.

One way to gain a perspective on this world of blurring speed-up is to take occasional *fasts* from or diets when using mass media. Just as Thoreau temporarily abandoned society for Walden Pond to gain fresh insights about life, now it is the electronic environment one must vacate to better understand our e-culture and ourselves.

I first abstained from all mass media—from books to films to computers—in 1989 and have led thousands of students and groups on media fasts and diets ever since. Although a few people have found that fasting is not for them, literally thousands of people have returned to their lives *after* fasting as more conscious, creative, deliberate and purposeful people.

Some people have undertaken a full media *blackout*—attempting to remove *all* media from their lives—and others have taken *practical* fasts (removing only those media their careers and responsibilities would allow) or media *diets* (narrowing or removing only those media with which they are obsessed). A full discussion of the types and methods of fasting, dieting and blackout is available in the opening chapters to follow.

This book serves multiple purposes: If you would like to participate in a media fast (or diet or blackout), no matter what the length or approach, this text can be your guide with tips on how to prepare, experiment and learn during the process. If you are sitting on the fence about fasting, you can read about what I and others I have supervised have learned and make your own informed decision. If you are a concerned parent or teacher who wishes to make informed choices about how much and what kind of media programming is healthy for children, you may well wish to read about how to take your family or class on a media fast. Or perhaps as a civic, religious or organizational leader you are interested in taking your group on a media fast or diet (such as no TV during National TV-Turnoff Week). Or perhaps you are just curious about either fast media or media fasting. If so, some chapters acquaint you with why some groups—such as the Amish and Kogi people—never use media. Other pages document the trail of speed-up and what is to come in the fastest future ever.

At the heart of our adventure there are fascinating questions about thinking and identity. "Is original thinking possible?" "What do I truly know when I can hear myself think?" "Underneath all the ads, programming and noise swimming in my subconscious mind, who am I, where am I going, and with what purpose?" "Which media intake enhances and dissipates my life energy and goals?" "When I eliminate artificial sounds and images in my world, what can and should I do for or with other people?" "If machines do not curtail my freedom, what can I productively and creatively accomplish with my time and my life?"

There are many other fascinating questions. Although I can provide some of my own personal answers, the unique and real answers reside inside each reader...so potentially this book is also about *you*. Only you can decide, based upon your own media intake and attitudes, who you are and what you know in the absence of recycled electronic signals.

After your fast, only you can know upon reentry into society if you wish to downsize, upgrade or transform your relationships with machines and people. That is part of the magic of this adventure—it is customized by and for each reader. Your storyline, plot and outcome could vary greatly from even your next-door neighbor, parent or spouse.

As you read, you will discover *many* benefits of taking a media fast—these include saving time, money, resources and energy; rediscovering one's passions; goals, hobbies, creativity, original thinking, nature, friends, family, relationships, performance, travel; enhancing perception, self-awareness and sensation; leading a conscious, aware, awakened life; gaining perspective upon and selectivity about media consumption and society; regaining freedom over one's thought, schedule, action, feelings and spirit; and many more benefits unique to each individual.

If you wish to fast or diet, I will offer myself to be your guide or facilitator in the days or weeks to come, as you read this book. Naturally, I cannot assume liability (nor accept my 15% as your agent if you win any awards) since I am only a surrogate guide and not there with you in your office, classroom or home. What I can do is try to anticipate the questions and circumstances you will face and provide a menu of suggestions. I can also tell you my own story, as follows, about how this novel experiment began.

THE BIRTH OF A QUEST

On June 30, 1989, for the first time in my life I stopped watching television and movies, listening to radio and CDs, and reading newspapers, books and magazines. Web sites and the flurry of new media were not yet in the picture. For over a month I deliberately conducted a "media fast" for reasons people often conduct food fasts: I wished to take responsibility for what I consumed rather than be controlled by habits; I was curious to see what, if any, effects mass media had upon me, which might be more noticeable in their absence; as a composer, father, husband, author, sports fan, etc., I was keen to move from the viewer role back to the active participant—from consumer to creator.

Moreover, as a professor of communication I was interested in sharing my "findings" with students and colleagues, and in urging them to conduct and compare fasts of their own. At a deeper level, I was only secondarily interested in what would be *absent* during the fast—direct encounters with mass media. Of far greater interest was who would be *present*—me. Increasingly devoid of programming and secondhand experience (including stereotypes, media illusions, artificial environments, etc.), I would be potentially more aware of firsthand reality, being, and my identity.

In the two decades which have followed, I have guided or assisted thousands of students, groups and colleagues with their own media blackouts (*no* media), practical fasts (as little media as is practical), and media diets (highly selective media intake). In recent years I have also personally tried different types of fasting and dieting, such as living among the Rapa Nui on Easter Island, who have only one television station, and living near (and later with) the Old Order Amish, who ban all electronic media. Many such adventures are included in the pages that follow.

THE ATTITUDE

During my first fast I heard from other people who had distanced themselves from mass media, some of them permanently. Many felt media were wrong, evil, shallow or socially destructive. Having studied and taught media criticism courses for many years, I understood and appreciated many of their positions. On the other hand, I have enjoyed thousands of programs, books, essays, articles, records and other forms of media culture. My interest was not in eliminating media but in how I and we approach them. This book is, after all, a form of media.

So my concern was much more with "How much?" "What kind?" "In what situations?" "With whom at the controls?" "For how long?" "With what attitude?" and similar questions—rather than "To use or not to use?" One of the primary purposes of a food fast is to initiate changes in eating immediately *following* the fast—to be more selective, moderate, conscious and in control of what one eats. Similarly, I was not interested in making a statement *against* all media (imagine making a statement against all food!), but rather in being more selective, balanced, conscious and in control of what I ingested. I intended to become more conscious as consumer *and* creator, as citizen and communicator, as student and teacher. As a human being, I aspired to be more alive and alert, more aware of my own senses and perceptions, and sensitive to other living beings. Of equal interest was the *origin* of my thoughts and actions.

Humility was a key requirement. After all, this experiment involved only one person for one month. There were no control groups and, from a scientific standpoint, there could be no binding findings. To generalize about personal experience can be highly subjective and is often the basis for gross inaccuracy. So this experiment would not conclusively *prove* anything arguably "objective."

Over time, however, I did develop more controlled, albeit informal, experiments. In some of my classes, for example, one third of the class would take a practical fast, one third would chose their diet menu, and one third would serve as a control. Comparing notes among the three groups was truly educational and will add to the insights that follow.

When I initiated the first fast, I realized that others had been there before me. Indeed everyone who lived prior to Gutenberg's printing press experienced a perpetual media fast. For over four centuries after that, the vast majority of human beings were illiterate and still "fasting." To this day, entire subcultures—tribes, religious sects, hermetic cults, social dropouts—downplay, ignore, stonewall or denounce mass media (see Chapters Seven and Eight). I was neither original nor alone.

THE INSPIRATION

Existence of "no media" pockets of society had always provoked my curiosity. When I discovered that my long-time friend Terry Turowski and his family (Patti, Todd and Sage) had lived in a self-reliant, isolated community in Missouri for several years, I asked him about his seven-year withdrawal from mass media, which had culminated in a three-year total fast. Turowski responded:

"There was nothing really valuable in living that I missed out on."

"But what about major news stories?" I responded.

"Well, when I had to fly out to an event in Florida, I was pretty surprised to hear about Three Mile Island and to realize I had missed hearing about it before." He was referring to a major incident at a nuclear power plant.

"Aha," I thought to myself, "here is a great use of news media—to alert people to danger and disaster."

But Terry continued: "But when you think about it, there's not much you can do if something like that happens anyway."

I began to question my previous assumption, then continued:

"And apart from Three Mile Island, you really didn't think you were missing anything?"

"Nothing of real importance," he mused. "And, if it is of *real* importance, you eventually hear about it anyway."

I continued to examine my assumptions. It occurred to me that I might test these assumptions by reading the available literature about media deprivation. Better yet, I thought, if my media fast objective is to *regain* firsthand experience, why not conduct a media fast *firsthand*?

THE SILENT MINORITY AND THE SILENT MAJORITY

Terry Turowski had *consciously* chosen to abstain from media consumption. Others, like Stan Zaroda, had subconsciously drifted in that direction without ever using the term *fast*. During the first week of my fast, I was on the faculty of Summer Concordia Institute at Colorado State University. After Kristy Clark, Director of the Institute, had mentioned my experiment to the group, Stan identified himself as the owner of an automobile maintenance shop in Palo Alto, California, who "at a certain point just stopped watching TV...it seemed shallow and artificial and uninteresting. Over the years, I've paid less and less attention to most media, except for books. I like to select and read a good book now and then."

Stan was typical of what I called "the silent minority"—people who had either overdosed on or never become infatuated with some or all mass media. Many of these had silently turned off or sold their TVs, laptops and radios, and canceled subscriptions. Unlike those in Terry Turowski's community, people like Stan Zaroda decided to remain within mainstream society—to ignore mass communication rather than escape it. Both groups—those who leave society and those who simply amputate their media pipelines—are virtually invisible to mainstream "users." Although I do not feel that people should permanently abandon mass media to understand themselves or society, it is important to note that many people are increasingly adopting a nineteenth-century lifestyle (see Chapter Seven).

Polls have often shown that in some countries there is also a silent consumer *majority*. This majority of the general public consists of people who, although in some way disgruntled with their mass media (not enough quality, too much advertising, too much government control, too much hype, etc.), consume media anyway. "Escape," "habit," "therapy," "convenience," "keeping up with my friends," "to be informed" are among the reasons frequently given.

I began to wonder about the size of this majority and minority, and if any research could demonstrate their makeup. One irony I discovered is a major reason we know so little about such people: for the most part, they would be very unlikely to approach or trust mass media to tell their story. So they seem all but invisible within society. However, there is a large body of research about some of the more fascinating media blackout groups, such as the Old Order Amish and Old Order Mennonites, and I have included special chapters on such groups to inspect whether the absence of media contributes to their social health or to their problems.

Based upon my pre-fast reading, such as Toffleresque future-casting books, I noted that "information overload," "data saturation," "paper-pushing burnout," etc., had been cited as major concerns of Western (and now Eastern) society. Was mine really a *personal* fast or was I somewhat representing a silent minority *in most if not all of us* that longs for greater simplicity and economy in the runaway information society? Were Terry and Stan really isolated eccentrics? Or were they part of a larger, early warning signal that indicates a coming flip-point in our lifestyle? Would many people, having reached their media saturation point, return to nature? culture? family? religion? spirituality? fitness? sports? roots? community? politics? all of the above?

PARENTING THE MEDIA

One group interpenetrating all societies seems obsessed with the fasting of *other* people, their children. This ubiquitous subculture, *parents*, confront spreading implementation of new and old media daily, even in the rural areas of developing countries, where portable radio and newspapers, and some televisions, are increasingly available.

As both a parent and a teacher in touch with many parents, I know how passionately many of them feel about what their children watch on television, about the music to which they listen, and about a growing addiction to video games and the Internet. Often parents will impose a "mini-fast" ("No TV tonight!") or larger blackout ("That's it. I've had it—*no* media until the weekend!") as a form of punishment or as a safeguard to insure completed homework. Others use "granny" or "nanny" software to steer young "inquiring minds" away from literally thousands of enticing porn sites.

In the United States alone, numerous organizations—Peggy Charron's Action for Children's Television, various PTAs, the Waldorf schools, and others—have also taken stands on the nature of children's media consumption. Media industries have responded to parental concerns by developing the V-chip, ratings systems, filtering software, and a host of warnings and labels.

I personally advocate taking the entire family or class on occasional media fasts, although one must remain sensitive to the reality that fasting is not for everyone. If a parent suddenly terminates media or, for example, TV in a child's life as a form of punishment following a burst of anger, far less is accomplished than when a blackout or fast establishes a positive learning environment. A shared experience affords everyone, adults and children alike, the opportunity to discuss pros and cons and expand together. Often families discover group activities that overcome, rather than reinforce, the generation gaps of target-niche programming. Chapter Six presents a guide for family, class and other group fasting.

FAST MEDIA TODAY

It is entirely possible that by now you are wondering whether a media fast is actually possible for your family, group or self. After all, the average U.S. household consumes over eight hours of daily television in the twenty-first century…while we are also texting, Twittering, or online on our laptop. The typical U.S. family owns more than six radios. You and I, if average, will have seen over two million ads before we die. If you are Chinese, only the numbers, not the phenomenon, will be different: China had one hundred eighteen TV sets in 1964; fifteen years later it owned three million. Why should it not be fully "TV homogenized" within this century? Even secluded Trappist monks now feast upon the Internet (Hart, 1999) and information reportedly *doubles* every eighteen months. (Olafsen, 2000) A majority of teens now report that, more often than not, they consume two or more media concurrently.

As a professor of communication, I am not blind to these trends of acceleration. Indeed, I am aware that far more learning goes on *via* electronic communication than about it. In 1997 I calculated that, in a lifetime, the average human being will absorb and possibly learn at least one thousand times more *from* the mass media *outside* the classroom than *about* mass media *within* the classroom. Of course much of this learning (what is sold at Burger King, how the Obamas talk, what type of makeup the ideal woman wears, etc.) is subconscious. Even learning to use media for educational purposes (i.e., knowing that weather information is broadcast *after* the news; a follow-up on the murder story will occur at 6 p.m.) is often picked up through subconscious learning patterns.

Former *U.S. News and World Report* editor and White House spokesman David Gergen reported that there are now over seventeen hundred news correspondents with White House press credentials. He further noted that foreign policy is increasingly determined by opinion polls and that opinion is increasingly influenced by mass media. One running joke in U.S. political circles is that there are now five political parties—ABC, CBS, NBC, Fox and CNN.

The implication of such innuendo is that media are often considered, as in the title of a Tony Schwartz book, a "second God." Schwartz argues in *Media: The Second God* that, like deity, media seem "omniscient, omnipresent, and omnipotent." A space alien observing our behavior might think that, given the hours we spend reverently in front of picture tubes, we worship televisions and computers.

Neal Postman, in *Amusing Ourselves to Death*, claims that media have trivialized not only politics (as Gergen noted) but every other important social sector—education, religion and public discourse, to name a few. Meyrowitz goes further in *No Sense of Place* to argue that even our spatial and interpersonal orientation are dislodged by television—roles and identities become scrambled as privacy and personal space are erased.

Nicholas Negroponte, Sherry Turkle and others continue to examine how our wired womb of cyber-rhythms completely transforms self and society. Moreover, for children now in school, thin handheld devices with their avatars and chat rooms *are* self and society.

In cataloging another one thousand media commentaries for a lengthy bibliography on TV ethics, I noted similar themes throughout hundreds of articles and books. Researchers and thinkers as different as Gerbner, Friendly, Berger, Matusow, McLuhan, Tuchman, Mander, Christians, Jamieson, and dozens of others, agree that media are neither neutral nor trivial. Annotations within other research bibliographies suggest similar aggregate findings. Ethicists are persistently concerned that media and media professionals invade privacy, violate confidence, sensationalize sex and violence, deceive children, lobotomize the public, perpetrate stereotyping, and create an unreal world we confuse with the real one. And each new medium, such as the Internet, which is supposed to be a solution to previous problems, brings with it a host of new challenges—cyberporn, super-viruses, cookies, carpal tunnel keyboard syndrome, Trojan horses, Wikipedia as "truth," and monitor radiation poisoning.

If media dominate our lives and consciousness as much as research suggests, why imagine that leaving media behind for only one week or month will make any difference whatsoever? Isn't it *impossible* to leave behind the background sounds of music, the frequent surround of billboards and printed ads, and the memory vault of stored programming—which comes to mind without notice—in any event? In an age in which fast media already seem to control society, isn't such a fast—one person for one month—too little or too late or both? Why bother?

NOT AN ISOLATED EXPERIMENT

Such overbearing questions could make a "one-man fast" seem minuscule, if not irrelevant. However, Thoreau seemed alone when fasting from the urbane at Walden. Most hunger-fast martyrs (Bobby

Sands of Ireland, Gandhi of India, etc.) seem alone when fasting from the violent. Many people who leave the media behind when they take a vacation also think they are alone.

However, the silent minorities and majorities have been slowly surfacing in recent decades. Perhaps a decade ago I saw three books that were selling well, side by side in a large bookstore—*Unplugging the Plug-in Drug*, by Marie Winn; *What to Do After You Turn Off the TV*, by Frances Moore Lappé; and *Media Speak: How Media Makes Up Your Mind*, by Donna Cross. Even more extreme stances have been taken, the most striking of which is *Four Arguments for the Elimination of Television*, by Jerry Mander, who also wrote *Four Arguments for the Elimination of Advertising* and later wrote about eliminating the computer (see Chapter Nine).

In taking my fast action, I did not wish to speak in the protesting voice of Mander or Sands. Rather, I sought to draw attention to the many who ask: "Do I wish to remain a couch potato or do something worthwhile with my life?" "What aspects of life, feeling and thought are we suffocating with media overkill?" "What is the authority of firsthand experience?" "If media are like mood-altering drugs, how are my moods altered?" "What are the positive features of each medium?" "How do we isolate these from the whirling dervish of runaway programming and paper?" "How much is too much?" "Are *1984, Brave New World, Gattaca, The Paper, The Insider, Brazil, Fahrenheit 451, Rollerball, Network, Broadcast News, Being There, The Imagemaker, Primary Colors, and Wag the Dog* merely entertainment or are they statements about *my* relationship to mass media?" "If so, who is home beneath my programming?"

Innumerable people have asked some of these, or similar, questions. Probably most media users briefly entertain at least one. Remember, virtually every significant thinker has in some way questioned the conventional wisdom and the primary sources of knowledge in his or her time. The key sources that carry the status-quo thinking of our day are popular media. Plato pointed out that writing would place us in an unfortunate position: we would read *about* objects and then think that we understood them; we would read *about* subjects and then imagine that we *knew* them, as if from firsthand experience.

Aristotle, Mohammed, Kant, Joan of Arc, Moses, Chief Seattle, Jesus, Buddha, Marx, Augustine, Elizabeth I, Confucius, and the great sources of wisdom and leadership of most cultures, largely derived their inspiration from other than mass communication. Therefore, for homogenized communication, via textbooks as much as via TV and newspapers, to become a major source of knowledge and folk wisdom—rather than only of entertainment, events and art—is a relatively new phenomenon, worthy of close inspection.

THE INVITATION

What, then, has one to lose by taking a brief media fast? I invite you to experience my fast vicariously by reading this book and thinking about, rather than blindly accepting, these observations. You may prefer to put down the book, which is itself a mass reproduced artifact, and design your own fast—one that is meaningful and practical for you.

Why not take your class on a media fast? Or your organization or group? Clearly you would wish to think about some practical guidelines for the experience (see Chapters One and Six). For example, what should you, your students (or colleagues) do if their/your parents or friends turn on a CD or DVD player in your presence? Should diaries be kept daily? After each observation? At all? What if some members of the group wish to break their fast? What is the ideal length of the experiment? Should the group divide into subgroups, one of which serves as a control? The variations and questions are endless. The central idea not to be lost among all these questions is that each person should be given the option to have the experience and reach his or her own conclusions. Following the collective fast, a lengthy group session comparing and collating observations can be extremely valuable.

I intend to take a monthly fast once per year, when practical (I cannot fast too frequently if I intend to responsibly teach communication!), and eventually to fast for several months to see how the experiment, experience and outcome change. I will also be keeping tabs on new scientific research about media deprivation and reading your letters/ reports about your own fasts.

One final note, before you begin your fast. Remember, you picked up this idea from a book and may consequently want to challenge or ignore my invitation, so as not to be persuaded by *this* medium. If I am truly concerned about media influencing our behavior, then this book must genuinely encourage creative thought and freedom of choice. What are the pros and cons of my own arguments? Only you know which path is right for you.

SPEED-UP VS. SLOW-DOWN

One advantage of momentarily leaving the world of "speed-up" is that you can slow down to take personal inventory, taste the lobster and smell the honeysuckle. Taking time to enjoy the moment and oneself brings forth a different interplay of senses and perceptions. Ultimately one's lifestyle and thoughtscape change.

Books such as *Faster*, by James Gleick, and *Warp Speed*, by Bill Kovach and Tom Rosenstiel, are among those who demonstrate how the acceleration of virtually all human processes in postmodern society create a world of greater shortcuts, disorientation, error, stress, inaccuracy, burnout, confusion, sleep deprivation, and the compression or elimination of ethical considerations during decision-making. Slowing down can provide restored homeostasis, healthy overview, greater effectiveness, and more space for the contemplative, balanced lifestyle. The concluding chapters will provide an assessment of the lessons of speed-up vs. slow-down.

A GUIDE TO CONTENTS

The first part of this book, "Taking a Personal Media Fast or Diet," is a straightforward aid to selecting, designing and conducting your own media fast. Within that section, Chapter One helps understand more the "what" and "why," while Chapter Two gives emphasis to the "when" and "how."

Part Two considers the many important lessons that can surround and inform your experiment. Each significant lesson area provides the focus for a chapter. For example, Chapter Three considers the differences between *firsthand* experience and the secondhand illusion and stereotype-filled world of mass communication. Chapter Four considers the ratio, quality, enjoyment and originality of what one ingests (consumer) vs. what one expresses (creator). The ancient debate about whether we are enslaved by our environment or free takes a new twist in considering *media addiction and habituation* in that chapter.

In Chapter Five the macro, or *largest context* of what is happening to the earth—omni-pollution, ozone holes, vanishing resources, nuclear waste, oxygen depletion, etc.—is related to our omnivorous consumption of the same mass media that report these bleak conditions. Are we killing ourselves with too much communication?

Part Three provides a perspective on *group* fasting. If you wish to take a citizens group, business, class or family on a media fast, or if you are a concerned parent or teacher, read Chapter Six. If you are interested in why the Pennsylvania Plain People maintain a *permanent* media fast, read Chapter Seven. A fascinating moment in the history of any people is when they break their fast to introduce, perhaps only momentarily, media into their society. Chapter Eight is the telling of this story about such different groups as the Kogi, Dani, Rapa Nui peoples, as well as natives of obscure Pacific Islands and of Essex, California.

Part Four examines the pinnacles vs. perils of speed-up vs. slow-down for each of us and for society writ large. After an examination of the effects of speed-up on the external world in Chapter Nine, the final chapter (ten) strips all such externals away to inspect *the individual devoid of artifice.*

At the end of my first fast I was learning so much that I decided to push fasting to its peak—I spent an additional week of not speaking (except, as a practical matter, when I was spoken to). Hence the final chapter addresses silence, stillness, listening, and the deeper levels of personal and interpersonal communication. What type of thought and action originates when programming, noise, mindless chatter, and copied images recede? Who am I underneath? Have I learned, changed or known anything in silence that may be applied and communicated when I return to the world of discourse and mass information? Do I, and does communication, have purpose? Meaning? Are there any ultimate discoveries or findings about communication and self? When the artificial is *absent*, what or who is *present*? Chapter Ten plays for all these marbles.

Two appendices, designed for the personal-fast participant and the group-fast participant, respectively, offer advice and a checklist on how to make the most of the fasting experience. A list of resources, subject index, and background about the author follow.

PART I

TAKING A PERSONAL MEDIA FAST OR DIET

CHAPTER ONE

WHY AND WHAT

*The Benefits, Purpose, Background and
Guidelines of a Media Fast or Diet*

The film *The Impact of Television* begins with the interview of a young American boy. When he is asked if he'd rather give up talking to his dad forever or his TV, he only has to think briefly before he answers, "Talking to my dad." Given *my* choice between *being* a father—both to my young daughter and to this book—and *my* television set, I chose to unplug the TV.

I also chose to unplug the radio, cassette player, computer, DVD, VCR, CD, and to ignore films, newspapers, books and magazines during the entire month of July. By the end of July, I was so rewarded by the experience that I decided to also abstain from speaking and eating. Thus I stared three of my mindless habits—food intake, run-on talking and media consumption—right in the eye. This first triple fast concluded in August 1989, but it was the first of many fasts I have since facilitated for thousands of students and other friends for over two decades.

There was a definite relationship between my action and the interview with the little boy. I had read that the *majority* of boys so interviewed had chosen to abandon their fathers, rather than their televisions. I was also familiar with the German research, in which some German families were paid to give up television for weeks. While some of the families survived and others enjoyed the experiment, many suffered "withdrawal" symptoms and asked to pay to have their TV sets returned. Similar disruptions occurred recently (2010) in Korea, when the BBC asked families to part with their computers. Although a growing literature about this and related research (media deprivation, sensory deprivation, etc.) existed, I knew I needed to look no further than my own child, and those I have met, who usually try to turn the TV back on immediately after "Daddy" or "Mommy" turn it off.

AND YOU?

What about you? Have you ever wanted to "get away from it all"? Have you ever felt "fast media"—desktops, laptops, iPhones, DVDs, voice mail, e-mail, junk mail, snail mail, gadgets, upgrades, listservs, chat rooms, agents, the Internet, iPads, 1000-channel cable and satellite TV, BlackBerries—are changing too quickly to be digested? Has it ever seemed that *your* children, parents, partner or friends preferred *their* TV, computer, CDs, palm device or video games to you? Or vice versa?

In an age of fast media, thousands of almost invisible people have abandoned media for a simpler lifestyle (see *The New York Times*, Chapter Seven). Although I am not advocating that you necessarily join them permanently, I am inviting you to change gears for a week or a month, whatever works best for you. *If* you feel inundated by paper or machines, and *if* you wish to hear yourself think again, my invitation is for you to choose your own media or media-free path before the couch-potato farmers harvest us all. For many of us, it is time to take a *media fast* from *fast media*.

BENEFITS

Why should anyone wish to abstain from the allure of media glamour and sensation? Clearly, not all of us will wish to do so—media fasting is not for everyone. But if you do wish to sustain a planned fast, some of the many reported benefits for others have included:

1. Regaining control of one's life

2. Saving time—many people report regaining several *hours* in their day for play, work, sleep, catch-up, family, hobbies,

community, travel, service, spirituality, personal reflection, friends, creativity, etc.

3. Thinking for yourself, rather than recycling slogans, jingles and clichés

4. Sharpening your senses, memory, perception and thinking

5. Saving money—add up your monthly cable, Internet, video rental, subscription, movie, CD/video/audio purchase, and equipment bills; then multiply

6. Creating music, poetry, art, fiction, drama, dance, crafts, etc., or your own media, rather than over-consuming

7. Freeing yourself from enslaving habits, schedules, mindsets, etc.

8. Turning off the "speed-up" world long enough to slow down and take personal inventory

9. Changing one's long-term relationship with media by becoming more selective, critical or empowered upon social reentry

10. Making important life choices about purpose, future, career, relationships, direction in an uncluttered atmosphere

11. Rediscovering nature, culture, community and other aspects of a balanced life

12. Finding and developing hidden or neglected talents (so as not to "die with your music still in you")

13. Saving vital natural resources (such as the 70% of metro newspapers that are unread, contributing to wasted forests and oxygen depletion)

14. Being of service to others—family, orphans, charities,

friends, the terminally ill, the abused, victims, homeless, etc.; many seek understanding and companionship

15. "Getting one's act together," feeling organized and on top of one's work, catching up

16. Bringing the family or group (back) together around common activities or discussion

17. (For classes and groups) Educating numbers of people about the perceived effects of media upon our attitudes, actions and thoughts in each of our individual worlds

18. Exercising, losing weight, enjoying outdoor living—many (re)discover their bodies, the great outdoors, sports, games, etc.

19. Awakening yourself to other, or higher, dimensions of seeing or being, including (re)discovering aesthetics, learning, spirituality, growth, altruism, public service, and even "enlightenment"

20. Restoring health and happiness by reversing burnout, stress, and by regaining meaning and fulfillment

21. Building relationships—often spouses, parents, partners, etc., feel they have been replaced by a TV, text messenger or computer; a fast provides the creative atmosphere in which to reverse that process

These are only some of the benefits that some participants in media fasts have discovered. Benefits are relative to each reader's values and needs; so, prior to fasting, you might wish to ask: "Given my personal life purpose and temperament, how may I customize my experiment for maximum effectiveness?"

CHOICES

Typically, people who wish to fast choose one of three approaches:

1. *Media blackout*—attempting to remove all media from your life, such as by living alone in the woods, your (unplugged) apartment, or seacoast.

2. *Practical fast*—eliminating all media except those crucial to survival. Weather reports on approaching hurricanes, Web sites all employees are mandated to read at work, and textbooks a student must read to pass a course should not be eliminated. There are many other exceptions.

3. *Media diet*—carefully selecting which media you will eliminate or otherwise modify. When one diets from food, a "high protein" or "low cholesterol" or "no sugar" diet changes not only the quantity but also the substance and ratio (of food groups) of intake. Similarly, in media dieting people may wish to change their ratio of tabloid news to gourmet news Web sites or PBS. They may wish to eliminate an addiction, such as to MTV, pornography or radio. They may prefer an "upgrade," such as reading the unabridged novel vs. seeing the made-for-TV movie or comic-book version, etc.

To make intelligent choices about which experimental approach is appropriate for you, please read on about deciding your purpose. Your purpose is tied in closely with your choice, as is your selection of location and timing.

A WORD ABOUT METHOD

Most people find it helpful to keep a diary about their fast. You can make entries chronologically about your feelings ("I want my MTV") and thoughts ("Hmmm…maybe I am addicted to news, after all!"). I usually ask classes to not only write down all observations and breakthroughs that enter their heads but to also pause after two or three days and reread all their entries.

Usually, during this process students spot patterns: "Seven times I was feeling something like withdrawal symptoms for my CDs…" or

"Wow! I wrote down three times that I feel great by taking up cycling again, instead of watching the soaps." I ask them to reflect upon these patterns to find deeper truths about themselves and society. They are asked to write these down as *reflections*. At the end of each week I ask them to also reread their reflections and, based upon going deeper still, to write down *super-reflections*, or penetrating insights into their aggregate pattern recognition and about the entire experiment.

How far you might wish to go with your diary (or portable mini-cassette recorder), whether you make daily or constant entries, whether you write super-reflections or just meditations, is up to you. What is important is that each entry gives you a basis for more accurate memory, which will become important when you finally take stock to overview all you have learned.

In Chapter Two I will say much more about what you might do before, during and after your fast, but for the moment you might just look around the house for a notebook that could serve as a valuable companion throughout your experience. Keep in mind that a *personal* fast is much less structured than a group fast and need not pretend to be scientific method, although you are certainly encouraged to organize or quantify any aspect of your experience which helps you discover patterns of hidden truth.

A key theme of media fasting is that learning can be experiential and reflective. Although there are many helpful books and studies on how media influence our lives (see "For Further Reading" at back of book), fasting is by nature an *alternative* to learning from mass reproduced texts and studies, which often present prepackaged notions of truth to large groups of people. Such mass mediated messages can assist in creating *homogenized* thought. If you find this hard to believe, ask a group of people what they think of a former world leader, such as Saddam Hussein or George Bush. Then ask them how many of them personally *knew* those leaders. Usually, what they think they know is a result of the media packaging they have received, which produces relatively uniform thoughts about, for example, Saddam Hussein and George Bush.

Media fasting invites us to learn more by experience than by secondhand acceptance of artificial sounds, images, words and signals.

In that sense, this book is not research on a grand scale written while I, hidden within my laboratory, inspected several German families who were paid to give up their TV sets. In fact, I deliberately abstained from researching via books, journals and strict scientific method during the fast (when some of this text was written). So, for the first time in over twenty years I have presented a manuscript without indented quotes and footnotes. I allude to research and authors from memory.

This writing is meant to be of interest to the general public. I momentarily discard much of the jargon, referencing and stuffiness of academic writing. This *informal* research is more in the mode of Thoreau at Walden Pond, Byrd at the North Pole, and Glenn in outer space: by abandoning one's familiar surroundings and habits, a fresh and revealing perspective may be discovered. In this case, the familiar surrounding is mediated communication. You, too, can become an environmental explorer, choosing your own territory.

PURPOSE

Communication media may be our most pervasive surrounding of the twenty-first century. Given the current patterns, media—not drugs or alcohol—will be the leading addiction of this millennium. Thus, to abstain from media injection is to call attention to this consumer/media imbalance. It is also to infer questions about our relationship with communication and its effects on our consciousness and lives.

With all this in mind, it is useful to ask what purpose *your* media fast might take. Before beginning my first fast, I actually made a list of purposes I hoped to at least undertake, if not fully accomplish. Some of these overlap with the amalgamated list of benefits from other fast participants I listed earlier in this chapter. Here is my first list of intended purposes:

1. To *deliberately focus* my consciousness, which is somewhat scattered and dizzy from programming overload and information excess.

2. To *regain control* over my personal choice and self-discipline. If the media (or any other external stimuli) do seem to

control my thoughts and habits, who is responsible for making a change, if not me?

3. To take *personal inventory* of deeper identity, thoughts and feelings. Who am I, under my media programming? What is *present* when secondhand learning is *absent*?

4. To *save the environment, money, space and time* on a planet with several terminal diseases, due to diminishing vital natural resources.

5. To *bring greater balance*, if not *healing*, to my tired *senses*, particularly to the eyes, ears and brain. Days of relative silence and observation by sunlight seem to first soothe, then sharpen instruments of perception.

6. To informally *intercede* or *represent* millions of others who feel some change in their relationship with media is necessary. Many of these may have given up on such change or become frustrated with the seeming limited alternatives (see "Silent Minority and Silent Majority" in the Introduction). However, "the journey of many miles begins with but a single step"...or person.

7. To remember once again that it is our consciousness and actions that created media and its content in the first place. We *can* ignore, *change*, enhance, edit, abandon and *create* media and its programming. My behavior need not be determined by the media environment.

8. To allow myself to become *more natural* and genuine. Except human beings, all species seem content with their natural environment, instinctual rhythms and movements. When the artificial-media environment and its illusory stereotypes and scenarios recede, what more natural rhythms and interactions with others will occur, if any?

9. To briefly *pose* "the *major questions*" of philosophy, psychology, religion and existence in a different way. "Who

am I?" "What is my purpose?" "Why do I communicate?" "What is worth communicating?" "Does communication have purpose(s)?" "Does *human* communication have purpose(s)?" "If so, what?" "Does *human mediated* communication have value?" "If so, what value?"

Thus, one of the deeper purposes of the examination was to inspect *purpose* itself—my purpose, human purpose, communication's purpose, mass communication's purpose, each medium's purpose, etc. It was amazing to me that of all the research about both human and technological communication, very little writing dealt with *why*, rather than *how*. If there is a constant ballyhoo about the problems and effects of technological communication, should not fundamental questions be examined, such as "Why have it in the first place?" Should not each medium be thus examined? Does it have a useful *purpose*?

THINKING

Important German philosopher Martin Heidegger, in his book *What Is Called Thinking*, wrote that "thinking" is that which is receding from us. There are several ways one may interpret what he meant, but a new translation of his insight is possible every time another medium becomes widespread within society. The more programming we ingest from artificial sources, the more our own personal thinking recedes from us and the more likely we become to parrot "knowledge" which is prepackaged, assimilated, and echoed by others.

So one important purpose for me in my fasting was to *think about media*, rather than let it continue to do my thinking for me. Since this was part of my purpose, I would like to share some of my lines of thought with you as they underscore the importance of fasting. Here are four areas of thought that seemed important to me (and perhaps others) if one is to pursue the deeper reasons for fasting.

1) **UNDERSTANDING MEDIA IMPACT:** In the United States the government attempts to test each food and drug before it is purchased by an innocent public. In *Food for Naught*, Ross Hume Hall notes that food testing is vital. Often chemicals added to food seem harmless in isolation but combine to form lethal compounds. Yet no extensive testing of each

new *medium's* potential side effects, hidden effects and long-term effects is implemented by the U.S., or any other government. Within virtually all countries, the primary questions asked about each new communication technology relate only to its potential political or economic profitability and its practicality as a labor-saving or information-extending device, depending upon the type of social system it serves. Who is asking about potential future media effects?

For example, many of us have now stared at cathode ray tubes (TVs) and computer monitors for decades. Would we stare that long at light bulbs? at the sun? Are there subtle residual effects on our eyes? optic nerves? brains? entire nervous systems? Another example—some research strongly suggests that pregnant women who frequently sit close to computer terminals or television sets place their unborn children at risk.

Apparently the radiation from such screens can have negative effects upon the health of embryos. If the research proves valid, is the radiation inconsequential to adults? What are the effects of listening to loud radios? stereos? CDs? headsets? Of repetitively reading parallel lines of meaningless symbols, *such as these "words"*? What are the effects of this same "reading" under *fluorescent* lighting, which, in Mott's research using children, correlates with greater hyperactivity and irritability?

2) **DIMINISHING IGNORANCE**: Communication may be one of the great unknowns in society. We seldom ask "Why?" We more frequently ask, "What will it do *for* us?" than "What will it do *to* us?" before we implement a new medium. Whether as individuals or as a society, we rarely ask, "What is the *purpose* of a new medium?" before we introduce it into our lives. Like purchasing a cute bear cub, we obtain a new "pet," which soon grows to overpower us. More long-range vision seems essential.

Fasting or abstaining from an unknown is no guarantee that it will become known. However, Marshall McLuhan was astute in observing that if you unplug any medium from any society, you quickly begin to observe what real functions that medium serves. For example, a sustained power failure in a major city (i.e., temporary removal of the medium of electricity) immediately reveals various uses of electricity—lighting, air conditioning or heating, machinery, appliances, timekeeping, clerical work (e.g., I am currently "typing" on a computer which would become inoperative), mass media, stock exchanges, refrigeration, etc. All these would be crippled and some would be terminated without electricity.

A "fast" works on the same principal but reverses the process. If one *unplugs oneself* from some sector of society or personal experience, one may potentially begin to discover what functions that sector fulfilled in one's life. For example, after a lengthy food fast, I feel weak, lighter and more "pure." Thus, one common-sense hypothesis to test is that food (at least the types and amounts of food I usually eat) may well provide my body with strength, weight and contamination. Similarly what, if anything, does "the media" give my body? my mind? my spirit? A media fast, depending upon its length, setting, conditions, consistency, and other variables, is one way of approaching these questions.

3) **MEDIA ENHANCEMENT**: A converse question is "What do *I* give to mass media?" For example, if I (or all human beings) am healthier, wiser, stronger and more mature, will I not tend to create communication that reflects such a condition? A common-sense illustration of this phenomenon is that I (and any other author I know) write with far greater clarity and skill when I am rested, exercised and relaxed than when I have not slept, eaten, moved or unwound in days. The last few poorly typed, disorganized, ungrammatical, coffee-stained pages of many student term papers, which were thrown together to meet a deadline, often illustrate to me the latter condition.

Can "fasting" from such imbalance increase the quality of my personal expression and creativity? In my case, usually it does. Hence, if I am writing a screenplay or newspaper article, it is much more likely to be clear and accurate if I am focused, energized and disciplined than if I am dissipated, scattered and "burned out." Hence I have *some* control over what I contribute to mass media—whether as a media producer or as a consumer—simply by being more alert, alive and aware.

4) **TWIN PURPOSES**: Thus, if approached with the right attitude and process, the fast can serve these twin reciprocal purposes:

    a. I can gain more detachment, and thus less subjective

perspective, on *what I leave behind* (and the related effects) when I fast.

b. I can increase clarity, focus, and freshness in *what I will bring back* through my own impact.

Of course this is just a short essay on the list of my *initial* purposes and objectives for such a fast. I later discovered far larger purposes than are immediately visible, which I will discuss in the final chapters. *Your* purposes may overlap with or be totally different from mine. You may wish to finally visit the Pyramids or write your novel or study martial arts. You may wish to fast with your partner to work out your relationship in a relatively quiet private atmosphere. Or you may wish to fast with the most open-minded purpose of all—simply to see what happens.

BACKGROUND

Historically, the fast was used for a variety of purposes. The usual and traditional food fast meant total abstinence from food over an abnormal period of time. However, there were many variations on fasting—some including light eating, some including specific liquids. Fasting was often a religious custom celebrated on a holy day or at another specified time. Depending upon culture and custom, fasting might demonstrate to the gods, God, or others the state of repentance, piety, atonement, sacrifice, sorrow, purification or communion.

In a more secular society, a variety of social causes have adopted the fast for political purposes: a *hunger strike* is the refusal of one or more political prisoners or leaders, etc., to eat until authorities grant specific demands. In the mediated age, such strikes may be staged as much for cameras and reporters as for authorities. News media immortalized Mohandas Gandhi during his fasts, which had as their purpose social and political reform.

More recently, international media also focused attention upon such movement leaders as California migrant spokesman, César Chávez, and Irish nationalist Bobby Sands. Sands, like many other political fasters worldwide, used the fast as a form of protest, pushed it to the ultimate extreme by refusing to break the fast, died, and thus achieved martyrdom and global recognition for his cause.

In the twenty-first century the motivation for fasting may be far more personal than political or religious, and thus fits in with dieting and fitness trends. Nor is it unrelated to the recent increase in *anorexia* and other weight-loss obsessions, in which primarily teenage girls use any means, including both sustained and erratic fasting and forced vomiting, to obtain the "thin look" modeled by media's glamour department.

Thus the histories and current motivations for fasting are neither as uniform nor divine as one imagines. Frequently, "breakfast" is now a mindless ("I don't know who I am before that first cup of coffee") ritual, whereas originally to "break one's fast" in the morning was a thoughtful and deliberate transition from one state of being to another.

In the age of *fast media*, what stands out about a *media fast* in mainstream Western society is that it is a deliberate, purposeful action in an age in which "the news," like the "breakfast" it accompanies, has become ritual and addiction. In Eastern societies, monasteries, and more traditional religions, however, it is the many types of fasting that are still ritual and custom.

MOTIVATIONS

In undertaking the fast, I wanted to look honestly at my own *motivations*. What did they owe to the religious, political and weight-watchers school of fasting? Was this merely a gimmick? Was it a casual and mindless escape from stress and the flood of paper in my mailbox? Was it to build my ego and make me rich and famous (sound like a TV program title?), just the opposite of the biblical dictum in Matthew: "But thou, when thou prayest, enter into thy closet"? In other words, was my motivation to make a big deal of a rather brief and remote individual experience? Or was there a point in using the fast toward other purposes, such as those listed above?

A strictly commercial motivation would lead me to the pitfall of thinking that one can market and sell the "media fast" as if it were an arbitrary technique, rather than a unique and personal experience. Such a motivation seemed contradictory to the entire tone of the experiment. Fortunately, I emerged from questioning my own motivations, knowing that I was somewhat compelled by personally valid reasons—to restore balance, inner peace and quiet, space to hear myself think original thoughts (if such exist), care for my family and to lose unnecessary mental weight. But there were deeper and more penetrating motivations—to provoke thought in myself and others; to encounter my world from afar and afresh; to take deeper and fuller responsibility in my sphere of professional activity—communication; to have impact, however small, as a world citizen on the state of the planet, our media, and our understanding of both.

In a world of *fast media* where *new* technologies, programs, software and publications come at you *faster* than you can digest the *old*, I sought to *slow down* to the speed of comprehension and overview—a speed where Thoreau and Emerson, among others, found transcendence. Moreover, my motivation was *not* against mass media or their messages, but rather I sought to see how and if each medium should be ingested or could be creatively employed.

The personal motivations for taking the fast were not necessarily selfish. After a dozen years of grading hundreds of papers, reading hundreds of books and journal articles, analyzing thousands of films and programs, and undertaking the other usual assignments of a professor of communication (committee paperwork, numerous subscriptions, days and nights of screening as a judge of student and professional work, producing media programs, collating research by day and night, seeing the same videos and films dozens of times—often at slower speeds or with frame-by-frame analysis) with little relief, I wondered if my brain was, like Paul Revere's horse, driven close to death by deadlines. How effective could I be in further assisting students, colleagues, family, professionals and public without giving my own personal tape heads a good cleaning and my lenses a thorough wiping?

When I observed that McLuhan, who was always reading and

writing several books simultaneously—and many other overworked "brains"—suffered strokes, brain tumors, nervous breakdowns, exhaustion or related stressful conditions, I wondered if the human brain, like any other delicate motor or organism, did not require proper care, rest and balanced use. What had the endless consumption of mass media—both academic and commercial—done to *my* mind? to society's collective consciousness? What is the proper use of the mental machine for maximum efficiency, quality performance and mileage? To serve society and communication, must I not first bring myself back up to speed? or to stillness?

You know your own condition better than anyone else. Does your brain need an oil change? Does your body need a rear-end alignment? Does your life need a tune-up? If so, take off that digital watch, put down that Day-Timer and e-schedule, and read on.

GROUND RULES

A workable media fast is best safeguarded by *ground rules*; that is, rules not to be broken for any reason. I established only *one* ground rule, and that is that I would fast from media whenever *practical* and *not antisocial*. If I fasted with the motivation of ultimately serving a larger purpose, including other people, of what benefit would a fast be if it alienated other people?

For example, imagine trying to unplug *all* the media in your environment—asking your shuttle driver to turn off her radio; telling the teenager on your subway to shut off his iPod; tearing down all the ads in the airport; not looking at the cover of a magazine that is hidden in your daily mail; wearing extra-strength earplugs, so as to shut out the Muzak (and conversation) when shopping and in elevators. This approach, devoid of my practical ground rule, seemed to me totally unrealistic and antisocial.

The same *ground rule* governed my speech fast. I spoke when spoken to, answered the phone, and shouted "*No*" to my two-year-old when she started to run near a moving car. Imagine what would have happened if I established ground rules that prevented me from saving my child's life and assisting others.

17

I can remember my first speech fast as a child, when I carried around a flash card that said, "Sorry, I'm on a silence fast," which I whipped out of my pocket whenever anyone spoke to me. At the time I did not realize that technically I was not on a *silence* fast (fasting *from* silence would be quite a trick!). More importantly, that whole approach seemed unnatural and attention-getting. Everyone one meets does not need to know that a media fast or speech fast is occurring. Indeed, some people feel awkward and wonder how to respond. Unless one escapes to a cabin in the woods (not my approach this time), fasts need to be *inclusive* and low-key. My flashcard ground rule was far less successful than simply being pro-social.

The one *ground rule* I set was easy to apply in virtually every situation. Could I fix the fuzzy pictures on *Sesame Street* for my daughter? Definitely, as long as I did not linger or become involved in what was being said or shown. Could I watch a safety videotape played on an airplane to tell passengers how to use oxygen masks and find exits? Yes, briefly, since it covered potentially a life-and-death matter. Could I mail a magazine article I had *already* read to a friend to whom I had promised the article? Why not, if I did not begin rereading it? Could I tolerate background music on a telephone answering machine before leaving a recorded message? Certainly, if I really needed to make the call and did not become seduced by the music.

What I could not do was watch, read or listen to media for entertainment, education, therapy, habit, updates, or all the usual reasons. Hence, about ninety-eight percent of my consumption was cut down. The remaining two percent exposure to mass media came at those times when it was essential to briefly listen, read or look, so as not to disservice, alienate or endanger someone. This 49 to 1 (i.e., ninety-eight percent to two percent) ratio is of itself revealing. In the meantime, I learned how to avoid "ambush" media before I walked into a questionable environment.

GUIDELINES

It was also important to establish *guidelines*. Unlike ground rules, which are hard and fast, guidelines are more like suggestions or intentions, and therefore somewhat flexible.

As a general guideline, I considered that my *mass media cut-off point* would constitute any form of communication created for or distributed to an audience of over five hundred. This number easily eliminated network and cable TV, popular Web sites, all radio signals *we* could pick up without ham sets, distributed videotapes, books, national and urban magazines, etc.

However, I had to make momentary "judgment calls" from time to time in applying the guideline—did a newsletter that came in the mail have a circulation of over five hundred? If I had set a ground rule, I would have had to locate and phone the editor to find out the exact circulation. However, since this was merely a guideline, I simply discerned if there might be any practical reason to read the newsletter if it *looked like* it might have a mass (vs. community) circulation.

For the most part, when in doubt, I ignored these borderline cases. For example, there was no reason I should avoid transcripts of speeches or audiotapes of lectures, etc. Also e-mail and phone calls were not from or to "mass" audiences, so they were perfectly acceptable. Still, I kept all this to a minimum, so as to focus on what is *present* in the *absence* of external manufactured stimuli. Nitpicking is not the point.

During the speech fast, the guideline was "speak only when spoken to." If the doorbell or phone rang, when necessary I answered it. If my wife or child called for help, they received it. If a neighbor said, "Hello," I did not ignore him. However, again I sought to minimize idle chatter and noted how easily a nod, gesture, or pat on the back (to a child, for example) might easily substitute for lengthy conversation without anyone knowing I was fasting.

Fortunately, during my fast I was not placed in the difficult situation of having to read a specific book or screen a specific film for my job. I had deliberately chosen July vacation and sabbatical leaves for that very reason. September through May is prime time for job-related reading, listening and screening.

So, one guideline I had set for myself was that such fasts, when brief, be conducted during the summer. Television is airing reruns, and many media outlets know they have lost partial audiences to the beach, travel and the wilderness, and thus hold their best and new material for fall and winter. So, if one *must* catch up, due to a media-related career, not nearly as much is missed in midsummer. For example, most major staged and telecast world events—the Olympics, regular elections, sports playoffs (except Wimbledon), conferences, political sessions, etc.—avoid the extreme heat of July. And although favorite Web sites, DVDs and CDs might be missed, they would still be waiting for me in August.

Summarily, it became obvious to me that my various fasts needed to be practical, pro-social, timed (one month, in the case of summer) and during the nadir of media activity. It also became apparent that one *ground rule* (which basically stated that I should follow the pro-social spirit, not the letter, when complications arose) gave birth to several *guidelines*.

These guidelines determined the scope of the media from which I would abstain, the timing of the fast, the length and intensity, locations (which I decided should be the same locations I would be if *not* fasting), and my diary methods. The latter, I decided, should simply be to jot down observations and thoughts in the diary as they came to me, rather than at arbitrary times, such as hourly or daily. Many of one's best observations are forgotten or mutated if not recorded immediately.

Should you undertake such a fast, obviously you are at liberty to choose any method you wish. However, the following recommendations may prove practical. If your purpose and motivations are clearly established and stated at the outset, ground rules easily follow. If ground rules are kept realistic and minimal, then workable guidelines are easily established. To the extent such guidelines are malleable, clear and consistent with your purpose, the experiment should prove relatively simple, effective and rewarding.

Attempting to establish the form or the structure of the fast first, before you determine the purpose, usually produces some element of artificiality, inconsistency or unnecessary difficulty in following through. Preparation for a fast cannot be underestimated. Establishing the purpose, motivation, ground rules and guidelines, in one sense, is more valuable than the fast itself, since the latter will simply follow the course already charted.

When fasting from food, deliberate steps are usually taken to gradually lessen the intake of food, prepare the body and establish the appropriate atmosphere and attitude. How important this is for *any* fast from primary stimuli. As the master archer put it, "When the bow is aimed and taut, *then* let the arrow fly."

As a reminder of this preparation, you might wish to write your purposes, motivations, ground rules and guidelines respectfully on the first four pages of your diary. That way you can refer back to them as needed, especially immediately following the experience, to see if you accomplished your mission.

Remember that you will feel obligated to enforce your ground rules, so do not set any that might pose impossible logistical, legal or interpersonal problems. And remember that if any of this seems too structured or complex, you can keep the fast informal and see what you learn as you try out your own process. Above all, remember to explore and have fun.

By now you may be aware that there may be many creative "things to try" during a fast. There are also other creative logistical steps to take before and after the fast. How to maximize the potential of these three simple stages—before, during and after—is the meat of Chapter Two.

CHAPTER TWO

How to Fast or Diet

The Experience—Before, During and After

This chapter is divided into two parts: 1) tips on how to conduct *your* media fast or diet—before, during and after; 2) how I conducted *my first* media fast—before, during and after. Part One allows you to think about options and ideas if you choose to take a fast, while Part Two gives you a case study, or possible road map, to consider.

PART ONE: YOUR FAST—BEFORE

If you decide to fast, in addition to preparing a diary, purpose, ground rules and guidelines, you might wish to consider other forms of preparation. On the other hand, you may wish to conduct a more spontaneous, unstructured fast, or try both approaches at different times. If you do decide to prepare in a systematic way, you will have a totally different type of adventure and learning. If you elect that more structured approach, here is a wise way to proceed.

YOUR PLAN—BEFORE

Devising a specific plan can be most useful. If you usually absorb media for one, two or several hours per day, how will you use that time? Do you need to tape reminder notes on your thin (handheld) devices, computers, TVs, radios, etc., or will you simply unplug them? Are there books, magazines, CDs, DVDs, to put in the closet or other ways to create a media-free zone around you? Are there logistical necessities, such as planning travel, having your cable TV shut off, buying theater tickets, canceling a newspaper subscription, or similar?

There is also thought to be given to your big picture, or overall adventure. How much time will be organized and how much left to chance? Is this a major opportunity for you to make important choices about life, career, relationships and priorities? Will you take personal inventory or primarily contemplate how media influence you?

It is up to you to determine how much specificity and scope you will build into your plan. To the extent we know ourselves, each of us can predict how much structure and spontaneity we enjoy in our lives. My own personal preference is a balanced approach—equal amounts of planned and open time allow the fast to create two types of learning. So when I fast, I usually plan to participate in interesting events *and* to leave lots of open space to digest and write about each experience.

YOUR COMMUNICATION—BEFORE

It is smart to inform key people in your life about the fast before it begins. Your partner, family, roommates, date, neighbors and friends may wish to be notified if they might be placed in awkward situations. Certainly you need to think through if you need to alert your boss, parents, teachers or anyone else who has the power to say "no" to your media freedom. There is also the question of what you wish to communicate with your*self*, not only via your diary but also possibly via your Day-Timer, lists of experiments you wish to try, and even reminder notes that say "No Media" on your mirror and car radio/CD/Internet.

YOUR TRAVEL/LOCATIONS/ SCHEDULE—BEFORE

Part of your planning includes *where* you wish to fast. Traveling to a beach bungalow, mountain cabin, desert hogan or campground can give you a back-to-nature oasis closer to Thoreau's *Walden* experience. However, if you desire a valid before-and-after comparison, it is better to conduct a stay-home fast and otherwise live your life as usual.

Comparing a month at the beach to a month at home, staring at Web sites and TV, is like comparing candied apples and orange juice. On the other hand, comparing an *unplugged* month at your apartment, work and usual activities to a plugged-in month of the same helps you better evaluate the role media play in your normal life.

Sojourning to different countries and cultures while fasting can be rewarding. So, too, can alternating between natural and urban settings, between outdoor and indoor experiences, between different types of transportation, and similar contrasts. No matter what your itinerary, it is good to give thought to and, whenever possible, organize your logistics prior to the actual experiment.

If you live your life by a Day-Timer, planner or PC schedule, it is your choice about whether they, too, need to be unplugged or whether you will arrange your day as usual. Part of the fast experience involves opening yourself to novel breakthroughs in consciousness and experience. Those of course cannot be scheduled.

YOUR EXPERIENCES AND EXPERIMENTS—BEFORE

One of my students realized that because he listened to the radio while showering he had never fully experienced the drops of water hitting his skin until he unplugged the radio. Another student said she was online, building Web sites, so much that she had forgotten what it was like to breathe fresh air and soak in sunshine. A third student realized that because he rushed to the TV set to see the ballgame after work, he seldom fully chewed or tasted his dinner.

These three experiences suggest there are untold micro-experiences awaiting the student of life. At the micro- or moment-to-moment level of existence, you can more deeply feel what it is like to breathe, shower, taste, rest, see and smell—all of which are taken for granted—in a more conscious way. At the "macro," or overarching level, there may be far larger experiences awaiting you—helping the homeless, sampling new philosophies or religions, or coloring in your experiential rainbow by skydiving, taking kids to the circus, and attending your first bullfight all in one weekend.

Could this experiment be the opportunity to explore what you always wanted to do—painting, gourmet cooking, acupuncture, sightseeing, bungee jumping, line dancing, creative writing, league softball, stamp collecting, civic activism or Tai Chi?

You may also wish to conduct small informal experiments. If you typically watch hockey, orchestras, football or rock concerts on TV, how is it different to attend each of them in person? If you jog through the neighborhood wearing headphones, what is it like to jog without them? Do you see, hear or think differently? How long can you walk through the city without encountering distracting media sounds or images? There are as many informal experiments to conduct as there are hours to fill.

YOUR THINKING—BEFORE

Part of the value of a diary is to push your thought beyond a journalistic record of routine chronology, to more penetrating reflections. As you think and write, can you detect patterns that guide your and others' lives? So often our minds seem programmed with commercials, news and pop songs, that I wonder if independent thinking is still possible. What lines of thinking—perhaps new to you, will you contemplate? Since media do much of our thinking for us, it is no wonder that we hear that "thinking is a lost art." Do you wish to increase the joy of creative thinking? Chapters Three, Four, Five, Nine and Ten are intended to provide much food for independent thought.

YOUR RELATIONSHIPS—BEFORE

In the current millennium, some people voice that human interaction is a lower priority than Mommy's laptop, Pat's video games, Daddy's TV or Fran's headphones. Are there relationships in your life you wish to deepen, explore, clarify or initiate? Is fasting an opportunity to become a better parent, partner or friend? Are there people in your life requesting or requiring more time, depth or attention? How is morale in the office and at home? Can the unplugged life allow you to study or change interpersonal tension and fusion? Some people use a *tandem* media fast to deliberately build quality time into their relationships. Others find that human interaction with many people increases organically without the need for deliberate interpersonal processes. Whatever your approach, if you have more free time each day, there are many possibilities for serving, understanding, enjoying, catching up with, assisting or meeting others.

YOUR PHASE-OUT

Food fasts often require you to phase out eating gradually, so as not to shock your body. Heavy media users may wish to take the same approach by beginning to reduce intake a few days before the experiment. As you slow down consumption, you may find that the adjustment between two worlds is much easier. You may also find yourself thinking more realistically about what the fast will be like, so as to better prepare.

YOUR FAST—DURING: IMPLEMENTING THE PLAN

Some people emerge rapidly into their full fast by taking copious notes immediately and trying many new or natural experiences. Others continue about their normal lives and slowly observe themselves in the non-mediated mirror. In general, it is a good idea to pace your fasting events—whether a night at the opera, a day at the races or a weekend of resort romance—such that you can reflect upon, and possibly write about, each experience.

It is wise to begin habits, such as writing diary notes, immediately if you wish to avoid foggy memory, leading to spotty entries. You may wish to post your guidelines, ground rules and purpose on your refrigerator door or bulletin board. Jotting down fresh ideas for new adventures, preliminary thoughts about possible "before-after" experiments, and similar thoughts, prevents them from slipping away.

ADVISORS—DURING YOUR FAST

You will probably *not* throw a tantrum when you miss your favorite soap opera or *Dancing With the Stars* for the third straight week, but a few people have. Most withdrawal symptoms, if any, are easily sublimated by finding a creative alternative activity or writing about these feelings in your diary. However, to be on the safe side, I always asked a wise friend or two if I might call them, should I hit a ceiling along the way. The fast advisor (or companion) not only provides a safety net for unusual feelings but is also someone to share richer breakthroughs and insights with as well.

Such people may also serve as contact points with the outside world, just in case you do need to hear vital information. For example, asking your advisor when the approaching hurricane might arrive or when to turn back your clocks one hour is *not* considered cheating.

COURTING THE MUSE

Most of us do not consider ourselves creative geniuses. Given a little time on our hands, however, we quickly remember that it is fun to create, whether a love letter for someone special or a garden for our family. Building a toy for a child or baking/cooking for an orphanage have a creative side and paint a smile on the hearts of all concerned. Even if you are not itching to create paintings, are there other artists you wish to enjoy by visiting a museum, gallery or concert hall? Even writing in the diary can become an art form—every insight can be written with a little more polish, wit or thought.

THE REAL INNER CHILD

My good friend Fred Donaldson used to give workshops on the art of play. He found that adults had forgotten the joys of unplanned frivolity. Are there games, sports or unplanned romps you wish to enjoy? What can you learn from your children? Actually, we can play most anything when we stop taking ourselves seriously. Although the entertainment value of media itself intends to be playful, one becomes sedentary or trapped indoors, watching *others* play game shows and sports.

Participating firsthand lightens your load, increases friendships, relieves stress, balances other activities and creates inner freedom.

KNOW YOURSELF

Some fast participants go whole hog by using the fast as a personal or professional retreat. Without distractions, prioritizing your career goals or evaluating your life purpose is much easier. Sometimes such contemplation is saved until thinking about the effects of media withdrawal and after some fresh experiences. Sometimes insights about self seem shallow or gradual, then build into important breakthroughs. No matter what the degree of personal penetration, if you keep rereading and enlarging your diary, and if you do not stop thinking, eventually an inner voice begins to speak up, where previously only media voices spoke as memories.

MONITORING CONSCIOUSNESS

It is important to flag fleeting thoughts and pen them quickly. Sometimes a meaningless phrase like "I'm a material girl" or "You deserve a break today" or "It's the real thing" is spinning in the mind, seemingly from nowhere. Upon close inspection, the first phrase is from a pop song over twenty years old and the second is from a commercial considerably older. By observing our thoughts, we begin to recover their origins and ask if they are information we would truly wish to implant in our permanent consciousness. Some people keep their diaries by their beds or carry portable tape recorders so that fresh thoughts are quickly captured, even during twilight time. Seemingly trivial phrases or idea snippets in consciousness sometimes turn out to be more revealing than at first glance. Even thinking about thinking can be rewarding.

BEFORE–AFTER SETUP

Some informal experiments involve trying the same experience two or three times, with slightly different conditions. For example, I once watched a basketball game on TV (before the fast), then saw a live basketball game between the same teams (during), and finally took a small portable TV to the live basketball game to compare the two simultaneously (after). The experiment was fascinating.

If you wish to set up a "before-after" experiment, such as seeing a Shakespearean play (during) and watching the movie version of the play (after), it is wise to pin down the logistics in time to ensure both halves can be completed. If they are spaced too far apart, you may forget key parts of the initial experience. For example, you might wish to see some TV police dramas just before your fast, then interview some real police about their actual lives shortly after the fast begins.

FULL-SPECTRUM EXPERIENCE

In a world of speed-up, we often rush through important events without looking family members in the eye or relishing the ice cream. Fasting provides an opportunity to slow down and enjoy the "little things," or the hidden pleasures of life. Thinking, feeling, growing, savoring, and just being may be taken to new heights.

Only you know what you are missing in your life—here is an opportunity to fill it in. I recommend diversity in your experience—if you travel, try some tempting detours, not just tourist stops. If you take a bath, don't just clean—savor the ease and comfort, the sensations, sounds and silences of bathing. If you take up a discipline or hobby, see what it is like to stay with it. As a martial arts black belt, little of my travel made sense at the beginning, when I was a white belt. Later, after much discipline and change, I began to think, feel and see in totally new ways. If you do not take up a discipline, enjoy the pleasure of your own company. "Getting to know you" and all the facets of your existence—relaxed breathing, a great night's sleep, smelling the coffee, going deeper into a conversation, relishing the breeze, praying or giving from the heart, writing a thank-you letter, walking an extra half mile to the waterfall—can change your whole day, week or life.

It is important to reserve the final day or two of your fast to make sure you have accomplished all to which you realistically aspire. Thinking deeply about all of your most important journal entries and memories can trigger perceptive overview thinking and writing. It is *your* fast: no one will benefit as much from this experience as you. So it is crucial to reserve time just before and after the final day of the fast for summary thinking and writing about whether you fulfilled your purpose, what you learned, what you might do differently next time, and how your life might change.

AFTER YOUR FAST—CHANGES

Just as astronauts experience a re-entry adjustment after weightlessness in space, you will need to make an adjustment back into the mediated atmosphere. Questions that you will immediately face are: "Will I consume the same media I did before the fast?" "If not, what will I change?" "Will I make changes in other aspects of my life and thinking?" Most people find that they become more selective and balanced in their media intake. It is wise to be conscious of deliberate changes being made upon re-entry. Writing down those new commitments can form a powerful conclusion to your diary.

AFTER YOUR FAST—WRITE-UP

Some of my colleagues and students have found that they can publish a newspaper or magazine article about their experience. A summary write-up could extend anywhere from three to twenty pages, depending upon the publication. An article is more likely to be published if interesting action photos are included. Naturally, such a write-up is not for everyone but, because it is an unusual topic, the odds of publication are greater in local publications. So if you are even thinking about it, why not give it a try?

Needless to say, it is important to also write up a summary page for yourself. If you lead a group on a fast, or lecture about your experience later, then you can quickly access a concise memory catalyst. A good summary need not exhaust *all* your best insights—you can always highlight those with a magic marker in the diary if needed later. Instead, a good summary might contain representative essences of your top half dozen or so breakthroughs, and thus entice audiences to want more.

AFTER YOUR FAST—PEOPLE

Checking in one final time with your advisor is important. Similarly, touching base with your boss, close friends or others to inform them of your "return" can be wise. If you have deepened or clarified relationships, it is also useful to discuss with each person how you intend to follow up and maintain or deepen the relationship.

AFTER THE FAST—SHARING THE EXPERIENCE

There may be people in your world who would be fascinated to hear about your experience—the Rotary Club, your class, E-Pals, civic groups, even the local lecture circuit. Friends at a dinner party, a Sunday school class or temple group, even the media itself, want to hear about novel adventures. Ironically, I've been on many television and radio talk shows talking about *not* using television and radio.

AFTER YOUR FAST—FOLLOW-UP

Many people choose to take a longer or deeper follow-up fast. Others wish to bring their entire class or group along with them the next time (see Chapter Six). You may wish to give some thought to what your next step would be. If the fast primarily cleared your cobwebs, you may wish to take another one every year or two. If it seemed enticing but incomplete, you might prefer to take a complementary fast (i.e., if you took an urban fast, you might try a nature fast; if you fasted from print, try electricity the next time and compare). If the experience seemed like it was truly your cup of tea, you might wish to visit a media-free zone. Some people are so enamored of their fasting experience, they seek to move to or establish a "no media" or "low media" community. Again, I am not recommending such total abstinence but I do provide information about peoples who make such recommendations, in Chapters Seven and Eight.

PART TWO: A CASE STUDY—MY FIRST FAST

Since no two fasts are alike, I thought you might like to see my write-up after my first fast. There is no reason why you should feel compelled to copy any aspect of my experience. This record is only one of literally hundreds of different approaches someone might pursue. If there are ideas that might guide you, please borrow them. If not, please enjoy them.

Included within my experience are various lines of thought, inspired by my diary. Chapters Three, Four, Five, Nine and Ten develop some of these lines of thought into deeper meditations upon our media and our lives.

MY FIRST FAST—BEFORE

Much of my preparation for the fast was internal inventory. What expectations did I have that might prejudice my findings? Could I honestly stay neutral and open to the prospects that I might discover *nothing* of significance? That I would discover much of significance, but of a totally *foreign* nature? Were there elements of prejudice (cf. pre-*judgments*) which might filter out some experiences in favor of others for my notebook?

Also, from a semi-scientific standpoint, was I setting myself up to jump to false conclusions? For example, the fast was a significant change in lifestyle (I had previously ingested over two hours of broadcast TV, one hour of videotape, one hour of radio, one hour of audiotapes and three hours of print per day, and one movie per week). Thus *half* my day was liberated for other activities. If I liberated half my day by not working (grading papers, teaching, sitting on committees), would I have an identical feeling of liberation? Was it simply that the change in lifestyle, the feeling of freedom to create *new* or *no* activities in half of each day, was what was being tested?

Would the results of the fast make comments about media or about *me*? In other words, was the fast a mere placebo? Was *one* important variable my new freedom to spend more time outside? with friends? in silence? creating a novel experience, no matter what its nature? thinking more original thoughts?

Undergoing this thought process was important, so that I did not enter the experience rigidly or blindly. In that spirit, I did not wish to be ignorant about the scientific research already conducted, nor narrowly controlled by its findings. However, leading research encyclopedists, such as George Gerbner and Don Fry, commented that they were unaware of any truly substantial research in the field. Computer search-master Robert Sullivan only found three related citations. My own combing through thousands of references I had compiled for bibliographies in adjacent fields revealed only twelve notable citations.

Moreover, when most of the research was examined it proved to be testing different questions than mine. In virtually all tests conducted to date, subjects were *asked*, *motivated*, *forced* or *enticed* to give up one or more mass medium. For example, the Swedish teenagers deprived of television in 1980 and examined by Windahl, Hojerback and Hedinsson (*Journal of Broadcasting & Electronic Media*, Winter 1986) unavoidably lost TV exposure due to a television *strike*. Similarly, a newspaper *strike* in New York had been studied. Lindlof's deprivation and incentives study (*Journal of Broadcasting & Electronic Media*) used subjects who were prison *inmates*. Similarly, the research literature on hunger strikes and activist fasts was devoid of studies about *voluntary media* fasts.

Thus, one discovery I made *prior* to the fast revealed a dramatic ratio. In the current literature about social communication, there are over one thousand times more titles and programs about *users* of mass media and about media than about non-users. This ratio might be viewed as a means by which media reinforces itself; that is, reinforces the assumption that media are an unquestioned given, which necessarily pervade all humanity.

Before the fast I also interviewed or read the writing of most of the people I knew who had conducted *firsthand* research; that is, who had conducted some type of deliberate abstention themselves. Many of these had simply given up on or escaped media. Others wanted a change of pace. Still others, like Ken Carey, desired to build a new and more natural society. Ken had pioneered Terry Turowski's community (see Introduction) within remote woods in Missouri. In *Return of the Bird Tribes*, Carey wrote in 1991 of his seven-year media fast as a time for changing awareness. He discovered that his body, once it was more in step with nature, was a type of "biological radio that could be adjusted to receive different informational frequencies." This shift from "outer" to "inner" media also retrieved an earlier vision of *news*: "The news we received came from the earth, from the gentle passage of her seasons, and from the people around us."

Such informal yet rare reinterpretation of mass media (in which *mass* becomes the *mass*ive earth and its *mass*ive populations of species who are sending messages) "research" was as useful as the more clinical studies. After all, how many laboratory experiments in sociology can be funded and consistently executed for seven years?

Thus, one type of preparation before the fast was acquainting myself with research and experience already extant. Another was trying out the fasting idea on friends and colleagues to obtain their input. I did not wish to reinvent the wheel or overlook the obvious by foolishly working in isolation. However, most, instead of offering insight, seemed fascinated or engaged by the idea.

The only consistent objection a few colleagues had was "What if you miss something?" or "You'll fall behind." With full respect for their input, I was more intrigued by Turowski's answer to such questions (see Introduction): "I missed nothing of any true significance or value in seven years," and similar statements by other media dropouts. Besides, my wife Nancy, other close friends and my advisors would let me know if any earthshaking changes in human affairs were announced by mass media. From a more transcendent view, I was uncertain if contemporary human cultures *could* create unpredictable, and thus so-called newsworthy, events—murders, fires, coups, births, deaths, sports and elections seem perpetual, not novel. From this philosophical standpoint, what could I miss?

I found it necessary to consciously think through what activities I would undertake and in what locations. Variety and naturalness seemed appropriate. I would follow the activities already scheduled in my calendar but make sure that, if there were open times during the fast, I would provide a mixture of other customary experiences, including rest from activity. I knew the experience could not be very representative if conducted entirely in a cave, cabin or monastery, despite stereotypes that fasts often take place in such isolated locations.

Fortunately, many different types of activities were already scheduled for July, which balanced indoor with outdoor events, sedentary with athletic behavior, work with play, family time with travel alone, repetitive with improvisational activities, and professional with personal responsibilities. Included in the activities were the Summer Concordia Institute at Colorado State University (I was part of the faculty), a trip to Chautauqua in New York and a wedding in Toronto, which included brief visits with friends near Buffalo and Toronto, brief sojourns to spiritual communities in Colorado (Sunrise Ranch), New Hampshire (Green Pastures Estate), and Ontario (King View Farm), paperwork at Emerson College and my home in Massachusetts, time alone with nature, home repairs, visits to local colleges, family play, a media appearance (I had to think about whether this violated the fast or contributed to it, since I would be transmitting, not consuming), preparation for conferences and fall courses, supervising graduate students, a yard sale, a visit by relatives, caring for my two-year-old daughter, and daily exercise—basketball, swimming, tennis or a family walk.

It seemed wise to try as many different types of activities as practical, so that each could be contrasted. After all, I had to check whether changes in my perception, if any, came from the activity or the fast. So it was useful to engage primarily in familiar activities. It also seemed wise to have one five-day (Monday-Friday) period in which I performed repetitive, tedious work, since such periods are characteristic of many lives.

Although it would have been fascinating to fly to Moscow or London to test my firsthand perceptions against the image of such cities reported by the news and entertainment industries, such artificial contrivance seemed unnecessary, particularly as I had already made such trips and comparisons in years gone by. However, I did select experiences that I could contrast with mediated coverage of the same events, such as attending a televised baseball game, hearing a major televised speech live, and listening to a broadcast symphonic concert in person.

In short, much of the "before" preparation for the fast centered around considering the optimum, practical and natural use of my month. I thought through what would make the fast activities somewhat typical, rather than overly eccentric; what would ground the month in somewhat normal, often repetitive events; and thus make it somewhat representative and available to larger groups of people. Flying to some remote island would have eliminated many such people and greatly changed the message I wished to communicate. Moreover, I considered what was natural to me, given my ongoing responsibilities and relationships.

Three close friends agreed to be "advisors" to the project, if and when I needed them—Alan Hammond when I was in Colorado, Gary Diggins when I was in Ontario, and David Pasikov in New England, each of whom were familiar with various forms of fasting and communication. I touched base with each occasionally during the month to avoid insularity and check my perspective against an experienced and trusted one.

Finally, I checked my overall condition. Although my vision was 20/20 and my health *ostensibly* fine, I was aware of brain fatigue from years of incessant reading of abstract theory and image consumption. I had lost the clarity and rapidity of thought of my best graduate work, by at least "ten miles per hour." My senses frequently seemed groggy and eyesight would occasionally become fuzzy, particularly at the end of each semester; and my brain recycled endless fragments of media programming, from top-forty music and TV ads, to images from the classics (*Citizen Kane*, *Potemkin*, *War of the Worlds*—Mercury theater radio version). Excerpts I had shown in classes dozens of times popped up like toast—"distant replay" as opposed to "instant replay"—from memory. I had heard colleagues describe similar sensations and was aware that information overload, workaholism, media gluttony, and the white-collar society were producing similar symptoms in most urban settings worldwide.

It seemed important to "weigh in" *before* in this way and take stock of my condition, so that any changes *after* the fast could be accurately noted. During the last week of June, I began to slowly phase out media intake and give more thought to my state of mind. When I seemed to be in a neutral state, in which I would be receptive to noting the full range of experience, devoid of expectations and internal censorship, I began.

DURING MY FIRST FAST

Years before, I had been impressed by my friend Stan Brakhage's answer to the Beatles lyric "What do you see when you turn out the light?" Many of his films had dealt with the images one sees at such times, or when one closes one's eyes, such as afterimages and what Stan called "image-ination," Even phosphenes, the bright images one sees on one's retina when pressure is placed on the eyeballs, had not escaped his attention.

Similarly, my first sensations during the fast were of *media afterimages* and *sound echoes*, which stayed with me during early July. There should be nothing surprising about this phenomenon: we say "my ears are still ringing" long after an intense sound ceases. We see the residue of a light bulb's retinal impression long after we stare at it. Not all media afterimages have sustained carryover of exactly this nature. Indeed many are memories recorded years and decades ago, which surface when triggered, seemingly at random.

When I trained myself to look for these images and sounds, I could spot the most frequent ones more readily. Images that I knew from endless repetition—the face of Oprah Winfrey or Regis Philbin, or sounds that were replayed daily if not hourly, successful ad jingles and program themes—surfaced and superimposed themselves upon present experience.

"Barbed arrows" had their usual rate of emergence. These are the stunning images tied to deep emotions—a monk burning himself to death, a Vietnamese prisoner being shot point-blank, realistic guillotine sequences from movies, inescapable monsters finally cornering us via the camera—which surprise us repetitively over decades. I have chosen the term *barbed arrows* because, like those ancient weapons, once shot into the subconscious such images are extremely difficult to remove. During the fast, these arrows resurfaced at the usual intervals but seemed more isolated and vivid, perhaps because there was no further artificial backdrop upon which they might be projected.

I was tempted to ponder how much "media residue" we carry with us perpetually. It seemed to be the "hazardous waste" of memory. Then I caught myself interpreting these experiences prematurely and returned to firsthand observation. Although the residue thinned throughout the final weeks, I was aware of the high number of totally unpredictable memory replays I received. Those I had grown to anticipate were less frequent. Like Hal the computer in *2001: A Space Odyssey* (and the sequel, *2010*) we have vast interior programming which, when "uncorked," contains a huge number of seemingly unconnected "bytes."

The ubiquity of mass media is never driven home so much as when one abstains from it. Although I was not seeking media out, it frequently found me. While waiting on "hold" by telephone to speak with a company representative or customer service, canned muzak purred. While waiting to speak with a radio station manager by phone, his programming was piped online. Elevators, restaurants, answering machines, lobbies, public settings—all seemed preset with hidden tapes or broadcasts. Possibly transportation centers proved the most saturated—airports, bus and train stations are stuffed full of billboards, magazine and newspaper stores, bars with widescreen TV, seats with attached mini-TVs, radios blaring from stores, newspaper machines, video games and occasional hawkers.

However, I could usually find a place of silence in myself if not in the setting.

It was also easy to think about my attitude toward this wraparound media world, rather than become seduced by the stimuli. Nevertheless, these stimuli seemed the more provocative—each competing for my attention from the newsstand. I noted more than ever before how much corporate energy is given to "capturing" an audience—through slick cover photographs on topical and sexy subjects, through rapid-fire images in TV ads, through easy-to-find centerfolds, through "top ten" hit countdowns, through up-to-the-minute sports scores, weather and news, through two-inch-high headlines, through prize giveaways for listeners, through serialized stories that keep us dangling, through...

What about these serialized stories? We are aware of flagrant examples, such as soap operas that leave us hanging and news stories that end with "We'll have more at eleven." But part of what I noted during the fast was that virtually all media are serialized. Most TV programs are called "episodes" within a "series"; sports events are almost always part of a "season" or series of games which accrues excitement as the series builds toward a super-series (or World Series or play-off); a leading news story is seldom isolated from a series of related stories.

In my case, the serialized expectation had been built around the Wimbledon annual tennis tournament. Media conditioning had planted in me the expectation that each day I would come closer to a sports climax. After a *series* of days in which news of who was eliminated and who survived Wimbledon created "not-to-be-missed" tennis matchups for tomorrow's broadcast, viewer interest increased toward the quarterfinals, the semifinals, and finally the grand buildup: Wimbledon finals. Such buildup is doubled, since the serialization occurs in both the men's and women's events.

It had never occurred to me that, since I follow the major *team* sports—baseball, football, soccer, hockey and basketball—much more than individual sports, I was "hooked" on media subplots as well. However, when friends started discussing Wimbledon each day, I caught myself hoping, much to my surprise, for an update. The media technique of "the sustained cliff-hanger" had invaded me unaware.

I was also necessarily humbled whenever my ears picked up as friends used these words about the weather. "Well, it's supposed to..." or "According to the report, it's gonna be..." or "They're predicting..." These indicators that a media forecast was about to follow were signals to stay neutral, and indeed properly skeptical, about the predictions. But again I discovered that the conditioning was deeply ingrained and I would take momentary interest at the prospect of a forecast, much like one of Pavlov's dogs.

Other habits that came out of hiding related to "timed actions," such as:

1. At 7:25 a.m., I usually turn on the local morning TV news, which is followed by the national news;

2.   When driving, as the minute hand points upward I program myself to turn on the hourly news exactly following the commercials that precede it;

3.   At fifteen or forty-five minutes following the hour, I am trained (by media programmers) to switch to an all-news radio station for sports and to remain on that station if commercials are still playing, thus delaying the sports update.

I had to reprogram myself to disregard my alter ego "appointment secretary" with electronic media.

My colleague Fran Berger, who managed radio station WERS in Boston, said she had the flip side of this experience. When she woke up in the morning, she could *tell the time* according to what was playing on the radio. If the news was on, or the weather or the traffic report, or the whatever, she knew exactly how much time she had to prepare for work or breakfast.

In either case, technologies like the clock, radio and television have become incestuously intertwined. I had to deprogram myself from thinking "It's time for..." Perhaps the most extreme example of such conditioning was depicted by mass media itself in the major cinema hit *Rain Man*. The autistic savant Charlie Babbitt (Dustin Hoffman) became deeply emotionally disturbed when the clock indicated it was time for his favorite game show, no matter which *time zone* he was in. Was this a metaphor for society's twin dependency upon a clock-ordered, media-diverted sense of security?

How would a "Martian with X-ray long-distance vision" interpret the millions of earthlings all interrupting their lives to sit and stare at *Wheel of Fortune* for thirty minutes? A giant time-lapse camera with a zoom lens on individuals could reveal large patterns of human movement orchestrated by media programmers. Like dancers at a disco, we move to the rhythms of unseen musicians.

The broadcasting "tease"—the ad, the promo, the preview, the *TV Guide* listing, or similar—serves as the *bait* before some combination of our needs and the program's or medium's allure *hooks* us into predictable audience habits. Formulaic suspense, dramatic dynamics, and "the strip-tease" effect (teasing us with adumbration about what is revealed at the end—"Tonight's guests are _____, _____, and those topless waitresses you've heard so much about"—hold us *on the fishing line* until we are fried in the skillet of addiction.

Beyond becoming more deeply aware of media residue, serialization habits, broadcast "clock control" and "audience fishing," I was also feeling changes in my senses and perception. As in a sustained food fast, parts of the body which were previously taxed with heavy workloads were becoming rested and then energized. The brain, nervous system, senses and heart (or emotions) all seemed to be "on R & R," the military term for "rest and relaxation" applied to soldiers who temporarily leave a combat zone.

Thus my ears actually seemed to be gradually healing. They more easily detected and enjoyed the natural surround—birds, running water, whispering leaves—which was deafened in urban, media and academic environments. Eventually, as with Zuccharelli's research, the ears also seemed to actually be "extending listening" as well. As with a handshake, my hearing reached out to welcome and encompass the soundscape, rather than lazily drink in random parts of it.

Although nothing quite so dramatic occurred with the eyes, a similar, yet more subdued change seemed to be occurring. The subtle, but almost permanent, bloodshot nature of eyes that read and grade thousands of pages per week—often with little sleep, particularly during grading periods—began to clear. Slowly, light and colors became more vivid. Instead of once again analyzing Antonioni's remarkable strategy for using cinematic color, I was relaxing into wonder at the shades of blue in the sky, green in the grass, and orange in the sunset.

The brain increasingly felt re-oxygenated, as the body feels after a tropical vacation. A steady stream of pleasant and surprising insights became superimposed upon the popping popcorn of fragmented media memory. As the latter receded, I seemed to have a consistent "fountain" of thought flowing effortlessly from subject to subject, as conversation or meditation dictated.

My head felt more and more at ease. Instead of being overloaded with materials coming in to be digested and properly stored, I had time to choose thoughts, select experiences, and focus upon activities at hand. For example, trimming my beard and brushing my teeth became *foreground* rather than accompaniment to the news. Consequently, I took more care with such details and raised the quality of my workmanship, even in combing my hair!

Such an expanse of time created the sense of eternity. Something both greater and other than sixty "seconds" filled each moment. Rather than feeling fixated upon the clock to slavishly find programs, I took my watch off and found it made absolutely no difference. Appointments could be kept intuitively (I was only late once); I noted the sun's movements more closely as my approximate timekeeper (apparently, indigenous peoples could use the skies for precise timekeeping); the present tense swelled to dwarf the "past" and "future." More importantly, certain robot-like fixations of the brain—"What time is it?" "Am I late for...?"—began to fade into a glasnost of fresh possibilities.

It occurred to me that whatever is meant by "time" could be used, rather than followed. For example, at the beginning and ending of the day I could focus upon what lay ahead or what had occurred. This was a conscious choice to briefly consider the "past" or "future," rather than accidental lapses in memory or fantasy which characterize all of us but are particularly caricatured in the stereotype of the "absentminded professor." Once the mind was no longer "absent" (fixated upon media) but "present" (grounded in the physical world round about), I could consciously use it to focus upon the day behind or ahead without it using me. Questions like "What are my priorities?", "What needs to be thought about or prepared?", "What is my purpose in this activity?", "Am I relaxed about that last committee meeting or still replaying it?" could be easily paraded upon the stage of consciousness.

Feeling "clear" about what had happened during the day before going to bed tremendously improved the quality of sleep. This was quite a contrast to falling asleep at 1 a.m., with the TV set still on while the late movie fed my subconscious and subsequent dreams or nightmares. Similarly, awakening early, refreshed, and relaxed, with much time to consider my day and focus upon each detail of preparation, even brushing my teeth, increased my sense of ease and my overall assurance with new circumstances.

Even the emotions seemed to be purifying. The deep subconscious fear implanted by well-made horror movies; endless gruesome murders, rapes and similar shown on TV news and detective series; the false emotional highs of game-show victories, lovemaking climaxes, resolved romances, last-minute rescues and favorite pop songs; the sensational photos and headlines used to sell newspapers; and the tear-jerking ads and heart-jerking human-interest stories were no longer pouring into my (sub)consciousness. Due to some excellent training I had received, I could more easily monitor these emotions, rather than lock horns with, or feel controlled by, their content.

Here again, there was a sense of personal interior decorating that affected millions. Many of us claim to be unaffected by the many mood messages of mass media. But a quick flashlight upon our subconscious minds "doth make liars of us all." During the fast, deeper work could be done to spot the emotions attached to surfacing memories, including media memories, and to dissolve the similar emotional memories attached to people and places that reappeared through my inner windshield.

In cleaning this emotional windshield, I regained greater control over emotions, rather than them controlling me. This did not lead to an amputation of emotion and a zombielike state. Instead, emotion could be expressed more purely, genuinely and appropriately, and with less invisible prompting from stored media memories. Interviewing my heart and mind in late July was like interviewing an attic or garage after a yard sale. At last freed of constipating clutter, there was more space for free movement. Indeed other thoughts, feelings and people could be easily welcomed.

So far, this experience seemed to have a near Utopian ring to it. Was I merely insulating myself from the cruelties of the outside world for personal security? After all, millions of people continued to be starving, fighting, contemplating suicide and facing nuclear annihilation, despite my minuscule experiment. At any given moment, entire species faced extinction, brutal experiments, and slow, painful death. A thought of this nature leapt up as I passed a newspaper stand and sensed the many horror stories told on the tabloid pages.

But my fast was not quixotic. Like everyone else in Boston, Buffalo, Toronto, Chicago and Denver, I saw violence and poverty firsthand. The homeless and panhandlers approached me. Both in Lawrence and in downtown Boston, my wife and I were ten feet from bloody street fights that erupted between two teen-age gangs at crowded urban events. The difference between the fast and media was not that we were shielded from poverty and violence, but rather that, in our firsthand experience, the blood was *real.* What we felt arose without the manipulated editing and soundtracks of intervening parties, and in one case we were able to assist one man (usually described by the local media as a stereotypical "youth") who was hurt. My wife helped arrest both his bleeding and his shock, while I located medical help.

This experience stood out in marked contrast to the feelings of helplessness, grief or fear, on the one hand, or callused protection of the emotions on the other, which most people experience in viewing media violence. There are also increasing questions arising about those who copy, feast upon and crave even more sensational media violence.

Summarily, the thirty-one days were not "all roses." But I *did* take time to smell the roses. In fact I could smell *both* the roses and their lethal fertilizer more vividly. I could hear the crisp sounds of insects buzzing around the roses with *my* own crisp antenna. Finally, I had slowed to the speed where I could also plant and grow flowers, or even food for the hungry. After all, who would weed my garden, if not me? Probably not those consuming eight hours of TV/DVD, seven hours of office computers, four hours of radio, three hours of recorded music, and two hours of print each day.

AFTER MY FIRST FAST

Following substantial *food* fasts, many say they experience a significant change in attitude. Instead of "living to eat," one "eats to live." Smaller portions, fewer snacks, livelier taste buds, more time, greater energy and increased self-control characterize the typically successful experience.

The media fast had many parallels. All of the senses seemed enlivened—not just the eyes and ears. This enhancement did not seem surprising, given the notion of synesthesia, which suggests that all of our senses are connected. A more rested and relaxed brain provided me with crisper, clearer speech patterns, sharper memory, and quicker access to difficult reading.

As with "re-entry" during food fasting, "less was more." Necessary news, consciously and carefully selected, seemed sufficient. Entertainment in balance, rotated into the lineup—in due proportion to sleep, work, meals, family care—seemed far healthier and more appealing than renting five videos at once, just to keep up my pre-fast habit. Just as each bite of food seemed fuller and more multi-flavored (many ingredients stand out in a casserole or salad, instead of tasting like mush), each sight and sound seemed more distinct and individually contoured, more fresh and animated.

Furthermore, there was the sense of self-control. If fasting in one area could be undisturbed by "temptation," why not fast from all external controls? I elected to extend this momentary dominion over media into as many areas as seemed fertile. So I added a one-week speech fast and food fast onto the end of the media fast. Although the speech fast proved impractical, and my first day of food fasting caved in with a snack after ten hours, the latter then went smoothly as an "intestinal cleanse" (a one-week juice fast with a cleansing of the digestive tract). The former became a "practical speech fast"; that is, a fast from unnecessary chatter but not from practical replies to other people's questions, etc. The phone and doorbell were too active for me to remain totally silent.

The combined effect of all three levels of abstinence produced far greater focus and effectiveness in my work and relationships. There was new meaning to the Eastern wisdom "unmoved by worldly appetites" or Uranda's similar dictum: "None of these things move me." Martin Exeter had frequently used the phrase "not controlled by externals," and other philosophers and leaders had laid similar emphasis on transcendence. In one sense, this return to equilibrium was one point of *any* meaningful fast, and I was grateful to see that the same stance could be taken vis-à-vis mass communication.

Thus, in returning to media, I did not find them irrelevant or trivial. Rather, they were reduced to one color on my easel, with which I might mix and paint at will. The same became true with food and speech when they were truly necessary, rather than mere habit, diversion or cover-up of some deeper psychological condition.

One danger of some form of fasting is that one is accustomed to isolation and becomes antisocial. After the fast, my experience was quite the opposite. People seemed friendlier, closer, and far more vibrant than before. Two-dimensional pages and screens paled in comparison. I pondered how much I had substituted *machines* and *pulp* for *people* in my mediated career?

Given the statistics about our use of media, I wondered if a visiting alien would think we relate primarily to machines (particularly TVs, laptops, headsets, DVRs, iPads, and radios) and paper products, rather than to others of our species. Had "the media" become our primary and substitute relationship, a trend made all the more obvious by dial-900 sex services, talking computers, teen conference calls, and videos designed as masturbatory aids?

To offset this tendency, I deliberately became not only more available to my wife and daughter but more fully *present* and focused when I was available. I developed the same attitude toward students, colleagues, media professionals, neighbors and unexpected callers I encountered. I also became more appreciative of the human capacity to create and modify these media machines, rather than marveling at the machines' new bells and whistles. People became much more important.

Naturally, the increased sharpness also increased my professional and personal effectiveness. During a second film screening it was much easier to spot more subtle director and cinematographer strategies than before. I had gained at least three uninterrupted working hours back in my day. I was composing music again, writing more creatively and, at thirteen pounds lighter, making more shots and rebounds in basketball. There were more quiet times for meditation, perspective and attunement.

Much more aware of what I paid attention to, I more carefully edited my gaze. This permitted me to be amused at our stance of trying to change the media through politics and citizen's groups. If no one paid attention to *The National Enquirer*, it would quickly fade away—a much simpler and less-draining process for "reform" than attack and counterattack. I could be my own FCC and legislate what *I* licensed and censored. In this stance there was increasing power.

Returning to occasional observation of mass media was fascinating. The screen seemed so shrunken and flat. Music and drama were still moving, but not as puppet-like as before. The cosmetic sculpting of backgrounds, made-for-TV colors, and the hyped voices of disc jockeys stood out like bagpipes in a symphony. Newspapers never seemed so much like uprooted trees and synthetic chemicals stolen from nature. I was strongly reminded of the classroom remarks of my old friend and teacher, Canadian novelist Robertson Davies, who called television "such a diminishing medium—everything of depth, scope, and grandeur recedes within it."

Indeed, media no longer seemed secondhand, but rather third or fourth. For example, the day I returned to television, the striking videotape of a U.S. Marine Commandant, Colonel Higgins, assumed to have been hung, was displayed. I was reminded that what I saw was not Higgins but the color broadcast of a black-and-white video. What I saw was *third hand*. However, those describing the tape as reporters and anchors had no immediate contact with even the makers of the video and thus were *fourth* hand. Finally, when my former colleague, Professor Sherman Teichman, was called in as an "expert" to discuss the matter on TV, I no longer saw even the video of the video, or the reporters covering the story. The commentary became educated speculation by an expert— *fifth* hand information. Any opinion I might offer about Higgins' death would similarly be many times removed from whatever happened. When the media later called me for comment about Teichman's views, they were actually asking me to offer *sixth* hand observations.

Relative to the slow pace of the sun across the sky and the gentle rustling of the wind against the trees, much of the media speed-up I returned to seemed like manipulated hocus-pocus. Ironically, only a few characters who I had dismissed as bland, such as Mr. Rogers and his "neighborhood," seemed to smack of natural rhythms and pacing. Ads seemed particularly bogus, if nevertheless slick, clever and glib.

This change in perspective did not make me condescending or critical of media. On the contrary, when an excellent program or article was spotted, it seemed to shine in contrast to a sea of mediocrity. I was keen to write the writer, director or producer a note of appreciation. In a similar way, outstanding acting or technical excellence stood forth as never before.

Indeed, nothing was taken for granted. I watched with greater care, deliberation, enjoyment and appreciation. I read with more retention, interest and respect. I was able to appreciate more "tracks" (e.g., sound, lighting, design, costumes, etc.) of the polyphonic media.

However, there were exceptional moments that reminded me of the penetrating power of mass-communicated messages. When I first heard of the Higgins hanging via radio, an element of mild shock crept into my nervous system. In viewing the broadcast video shortly thereafter, I felt pain for at least a few seconds. Upon hearing that the Chinese "hero" who had single-handedly stood in front of and stopped a line of tanks had "possibly been executed" during my fast, a note of deep sadness quickly came over me, although just as quickly I could monitor the feeling and let it recede. Fast or no fast, diminishing or not, mass media could still push emotional buttons, not merely in me but worldwide.

This syndrome was emphasized to me late one night when I was flicking through the cable channels. I became momentarily mesmerized by a movie about "the black Dahlia," an aspiring model/actress, Elizabeth Short, mysteriously murdered and vivisected in California in 1947. There was really no point in watching the program. I had discovered it in midstream and had no clue who was directing it, nor did I know half the plot. It was late and time for sleep, since I had an early morning meeting the next day.

However, fifteen minutes into trying to figure out who had killed this mysterious character, I knew I would soon be "hooked." Numerous rationalizations filled my brain about why I should see the show through—anything this galvanizing must be well made and worthy of discussion in class; falling behind on sleep could easily be counterbalanced the next night; perhaps it would soon be over; maybe I could catch the news replay at 1 a.m. during the commercials; etc. But underneath all these rationalizations, I knew a compelling seduction was taking place due to the style, music, atmosphere and mystery of the film. I watched for another half hour.

When he first saw people watching film, George Bernard Shaw noted that they were "fascinated as if by a serpent's eye." I was such a person. The contest for control had not ended. I knew I had lost forty-five minutes and that the mystery might not be solved soon.

I turned off the TV.

Part of me, however, still wonders, when given half a chance, "Who killed the black Dahlia...and why?" Such questions, in the eternal soap opera of mediated existence, are not entirely different from "Who will be the next American Idol" or "Is it supposed to rain tomorrow?" or "What's the final score on the Red Sox game?" or "Did they kill the hostage?" or "What are the lottery numbers?" Those who can answer such mysteries hold our unconscious attention and, whether we admit it or not, our collective respect.

My media consumption was probably reduced by seventy-five percent after the fast. It doubled again as I monitored the "new fall lineup" of programs and premieres. My students, employers and colleagues count on me to be up-to-date as a teacher. I must also selectively read books, magazines, newspapers and journals within and beyond my field.

But there is a difference now. *Nothing* I consume is taken for granted. *Any* book or program could be abandoned midstream if I heard the word "Daddy." I am reading and watching attentively for what feedback I may give the makers of mass media, rather than being habitually sucked in by their plots.

On the other hand, I may prescribe a video for myself on any given evening as a means of relaxation, usually with my wife or friends. Here again, I'm in control but, paradoxically, a different type of control in which I say to myself, "*Don't* be in control. Relax. Enjoy the experience.

It's just a movie. Have fun." Here the theme returns to personal responsibility. It is not enough to monitor the media but, rather, to monitor the way I behold it in any given situation.

Overall, the media fast and its twin spin-offs (more on the speech fast in Chapter Ten) were useful, educational, liberating and penetrating. I can highly recommend the experience.

However, honesty and modesty must also prevail. Lest I claim a *personal* victory in the experience, let me direct you to the Acknowledgments section of my Introduction, where much of the real credit belongs.

Lest I become too cocky about who is in control, I shall also properly remind myself that *The Black Dahlia* will no doubt replay in "reruns" at various times and on who-knows-how-many channels. Indeed, it was the basis of a Hollywood feature film just a few years ago. When *The Black Dahlia* plays again, no matter what the medium, millions of us, probably myself included, may wonder all over again who killed her...and burn our suppers waiting for an answer. And for those who cannot wait, Google may lead to dozens of theories and blogs about the gruesome homicide.

PART II

LEARNING FROM THE FAST

CHAPTER THREE

LESSONS FOR SELF

The Authority of Firsthand Living

In this chapter, like the two which follow, I wish to explore some of the deeper themes related to both the presence and absence of media in our lives. If you want to explore such themes, read on. If you are more interested in the practical aspects of fasting, such as taking your group on a media fast, you might prefer to skip over to Chapter Six.

WHICH REALITY?

Boorstin's *The Image* contains one of the most tragicomic revelations of the 1960s. Having just displayed her child, a mother reportedly says, "If you think he's cute, wait'll you see his *picture*." I know of other experiences to match it. One warm clear day in May, I was standing on a street corner discussing work with a colleague. When it was obvious we needed more in-depth discussion, I suggested "Why don't we walk to the park and discuss it?"

"Sounds good," he replied. "I'll just run in and check the weather first...it comes on in two minutes."

In both cases, firsthand reality was obviously not good enough. Neither the actual appearance of a child nor the direct experience of idyllic weather—without a cloud in the sky—could supplant the established authority of the photograph and the radio. My travel to remote towns in Europe as a teenager was similarly revealing: "Where's your cowboy hat?" I was asked. "Do you have an extra switchblade you could sell me?" "How many Negro servants does your family have?" "I'll pay you good money for a pack of Camels." "Why don't you go back to the States? We don't want your nuclear weapons." In all these cases, who I was—a curious, typically rebellious and questing adolescent— was blocked by media-created images of Americans. What could have quickly been discerned by others through direct observation was negated by programmed stereotypical responses.

Plato's warning that we would replace personal experience with substitute dependencies was prophetic. One of my childhood neighbors could tell me the batting average of every baseball player on TV when I visited, but could not tell anyone the exact height or eye color of his six children. His wife, conversely, could tell us the condition of every character on the daily soap operas but not exactly what her husband was wearing. During a recent fast I discovered that I had not noticed a spider's web in our attic for many weeks, although it had tripled in size and intricacy. But I could tell you more than you want to know about other webs—the World Wide Web or webs of intrigue around Monica Lewinsky, Bill Clinton, John Edwards and others. The media loves to spin other webs around someone new each month—Paris, Tiger, Lindsay, O.J., Spitzer, "W.", Britney, A-Rod. So deep is the media saturation that a single word identifies a web of scandal for most, if not all, of us.

Newsweek editor David Gergen commented that television increasingly gives the world "a common understanding," a "shared experience," and a "similar world view." At the rate such "omniculture" is growing, it will be possible for members of *virtually* all national neighborhoods to have similar *artificial* experiences of unity within the next century. Already, representatives from every continent have simultaneously viewed coronations, funerals, major sports events and the Academy Awards. Teleconferences, translated magazines, multinational corporations, ads and syndicated programs already give "world citizens" the sense of an increasingly shared culture. On the Internet, we can talk to cyberfriends halfway around the world as cheaply and frequently as neighbors.

FASTER AND NEWER MEDIA

The magician's craft depends not only upon diversion of an audience but frequently also upon cleverness and speed. The diversion and cleverness of media are evident to anyone who tours a special-effects studio, develops her own photographs or makes multilocational Web sites. But the *speed* of information travel—like the speed of cars and jets—is often underestimated, since these are objects to which we have become accustomed.

"*Fast media*" exceed the "speed limit" in many manners. They broadcast information to us faster than we can question or often digest it. *Fast media* makers must make hasty decisions, and thus have insufficient time for extremely thorough documentation, self-examination, deliberative reasoning, expert feedback and numerous rewritings. Indeed the *faster* the medium, usually the less time human beings allot for its "turnaround" process, for careful thought and cross-examination. It took scientists thousands of years to prove that the earth was not flat. Journalists, however, did not even deliberate thousands of minutes before reporting authoritatively that the earth was "pear-shaped" when tentative findings suggested that possibility. Media "facts" are confirmed in the *fast* lane. Indeed, no sooner are news Web sites updated on the Internet than they are obsolete. The rapid speed of change is even accelerating.

Syndicated columnist Georgie Anne Geyer wrote: "The stories coming out now are increasingly *fast* stories. " Microwave stories and processes have ushered in new technologies—electronic news-gathering tools, online newspapers, satellites, remote trucks and vans, helicopters, gourmet news Web sites, computer retrieval systems (making obsolete the news office "morgues")—which respond to increasing competition and an accelerating world pace.

McLuhan argued that when communication travels at the "speed of light," we too are transformed, as if disembodied spirits over telephone wires. What he failed to note was that speed-up also creates more stressful, rather than supernatural, effects. Many people tire of speed-up after its novelty recedes. Others wish to slow down to the speed of comprehension and digestion. Subconsciously, one appeal of books is that one can choose one's reading speed and quantity. Magazines, Web sites and newspapers also seem to suggest this same leisurely choice of pace. However, intrinsic to each is the notion that it will soon be outdated and that the reader should digest it prior to its sequel or update. As Harold Innis told his colleague Tom Easterbrook, "There is nothing so old as yesterday's paper."

A movie, CD, tape, DVD or broadcast sets its own pace, such that one's mind "turns" and one's foot taps, following its shifting metabolic rate. Going to see a movie and taking a roller-coaster ride differ only in degree, not in kind: the tempo and course of manipulation are predetermined and will be replayed endlessly for new audiences.

"Speed-up" can apply to every medium and every information industry. Brokers, computer experts, researchers, teachers, correspondents and librarians all talk about the "impossibility of keeping up" with their field. No wonder. The amount of stored knowledge has doubled within the past *two* decades but is expected to double again within the next *single* decade. For anyone seeking to "keep up" with the contours and content of new media, such geometric growth is extremely frustrating. Moreover, no single "map" or directory exists which comprehensively lists the outlines of current knowledge. Indeed much "knowledge" is being generated too quickly to chart. Furthermore, some information is considered "floating": spreading computer viruses and incessant global monetary transfers give some indication of the speed and distance data travels.

When there is a corresponding speed-up in human consciousness, and a parallel doubling and redoubling of the information stored and replaced in individual brains, a unique form of dizziness occurs. "My head is spinning," "My migraine is recurring at more frequent intervals," and "I can't hear myself think" are phrases frequently repeated in white-collar activity hubs. Individuals also become aware of an increasing rate of personal error and lost perspective in such environs.

To the extent we permit them, *fast* media, like the slower mechanical media before them, block the perception of more natural sights and sounds surrounding them. However, unlike *slow* media, fast media often control consumer speed and thus condition behavior patterns, such as the time and tempo of our media dosage. Even the birth of the (audio) tape recorder, the DVD, DVR and the VCR have not prevented the majority of media consumers from "eating" programs at the "feeding time" and chewing velocity of programmers. Rather than record programs, then play them back in slow motion, or choose sequences for replay and closer inspection (as the newer technologies permit), by and large we still follow the accustomed tempos and timetables of broadcasters.

Thus the time for interpretation or response to particular sequences and scenes, songs and sounds, remains preset. Ratios that I calculated indicate that we prefer *the metronome* of mediated experience *as scheduled* to the natural reports and rhythms of our senses. Although the Internet seems to be less scheduled, there is still pressure to keep up—if we don't read our E-mail, webisodes, or view hot new sites our friends tell us about now, there may be plenty more tomorrow.

FRAGMENTED MEDIA

By the nineteenth century, Karl Marx had argued that human beings were alienated in four ways—from nature, from what we produce, from our families and from ourselves. Instead of being self-reliant by growing food, making clothing, building homes and caring for our families, we have increasingly abandoned such "roots" for factories, businesses, institutions and suburbia. Our children are now cared for by babysitters, childcare, and frequently by *television* or computers. We no longer consume what we produce—and are thus isolated from the "fruits" of our work, which fruits we may never see, use or condone, fruits such as nuclear power and weapons, hazardous waste, and food preservatives.

As "partial people"—that is, people isolated from the "whole" of the natural ecological matrix—we live in a world of fragmentation. Working a field for months, year after year, may give one the feeling of "knowing" the entire field—every plant, bug and weed—or knowing every season, "knowing one's own strength" and knowing an ongoing process behind organic growth and climate. "Fragmented" man, conversely, is not only alienated from such experiences but increasingly consumes *fragments* isolated from their contexts. Foods are one example: a package's listed ingredients may reveal many synthetic substances extracted from living organisms mixed with inert chemicals.

Media fragmentation grossly extends such vivisection and extraction. Radio is a synthesis of sound imitations extracted from the sensorium, including vision, smell and taste. "News" is the juxtaposition of isolated stories segregated from their numerous—social, political, historical, anthropological, ethnic, natural, legal, psychological, global, etc.—contexts, often displayed side by side as random patchwork quilts. "Shots" or images are two-dimensional reductions of amputated, frozen time and space. "Xerox copies" or printing are unoriginal replicas of isolated symbols. "Bits" and "bytes," as their names imply, are segmented units of information. We conceptualize them as solids, rather than part of the fluid interchange between energy and matter, as Einstein described.

Whatever the true state of communication, we have come to both see it, and consume it, as a mosaic of "bytes" (including sound bites), shots, notes, letters, and other modules of information. One eight-minute scene from a rented James Bond video movie might include, for example, ninety-four sounds from four geographical locations, two recording studios and two *re*-recording studios, and eighty-six images including sixty visual fragments from one U.S. location, and seven and nine respectively from locations in Ecuador and Japan. We cement these fragments into a "whole movie," just as we synthesize the dots on a TV screen or in a newspaper photograph into complete pictures. The World Wide Web is even more scrambled—one can hop from continent to continent quickly, without even knowing it, or be in the midst of hoaxes, pseudo-identities, and fake sites, without a clue.

Fragmentation was arresting to those who first saw the tricks of image-making. When reacting to some of the first "medium shots" and "close-ups" he saw in early film-making, George Bernard Shaw reputedly commented, "They'll never pay to see just half an actor." Some indigenous peoples tried to follow the actress off screen. Others went behind the screen in search of the missing context into which the actor had disappeared. But we, in our sophistication, accept the visual parts as representing complete entities, and thus drink a steady diet of alphabet soup. We make words of this alphabet and then assume such words correspond in some way to our memories of firsthand experience.

Summarily, the fast stream of fragments we consume deemphasize context and contemplation. To the extent we swallow such a menu lump sum, our subconscious inventory is a scrambled, bloated conglomeration of shared shrapnel, fully alienated from any natural continuum in consciousness. Memory of firsthand experience is punctuated with unrelated "mix-ins"—homeless images, severed jingles and truncated phrases—which suddenly resurface, like overflow from a garbage disposal.

It is not surprising, therefore, that all of us have difficulty separating the real from the recorded. "Did that really happen or did I see it in a movie?" "Was that on the news or in a show?" "Was I dreaming or did that really transpire?" The most extreme case studies of such confusion frequently involve mental institutions and prisons. John Hinckley supposedly was motivated by a media-governed fantasy (in which he played the leading man opposite Jodie Foster) during his assassination attempt on Ronald Reagan. Voters in turn were supposedly influenced by another media-created fantasy—the same Ronald Reagan, whom many older voters associated with his heroic all-American acting roles. "Copycat" killers and thieves, who imitated TV crimes, have admitted thinking they were "on camera" or wanting to be.

Teenage murderer Ronnie Zamora pleaded "not guilty" in a Florida trial as his lawyer built an incredible *credible* defense: since Zamora had been "raised by a television set," not by parents, babysitters, religion or education, it was *natural* for him to live life as it is lived on television and not to recognize the "real" world as a separate environment with its own rules. In essence, TV was on trial for murder. Zamora pleaded "not guilty" to murdering his neighbor, since it was television that had taught him how to kill.

SUBSTITUTE RELATIONSHIPS

In some countries *many* human beings now spend more time with communication implements than with other human beings. Some informal votes I have taken in classrooms showed that roughly one-third of the students spend more time with their handheld media, PC, CD, VCR and TV than with any one individual or with textbooks. Another third said they spend "about the same amount of time" with electronic media as with people. Comedians joke that they prefer TV to their wives because the TV "is already paid for" or "makes better conversation," while comediennes joke that they prefer TV to their husbands, since the former are "more intelligent, sexier and better programmed." Academics, writers, scientists, journalists, executives and others often half joke about being married to their computers, rather than their mates. Freud and Meredith, among others, assumed that at least some truth lurks behind all forms of humor.

If, on the basis of observation, aliens deduced that we are married to our TVs or computers, rather than other human beings, statistics might well bear them out. Morris Shepard, head of the Public Policy Division at Northeastern University, cited a return to people and relationships as one reason for his own television fast. So did eight others I interviewed who "missed" the warmth of human intimacy or interaction. The DAK electronics catalog now advertises a "Marriage Saver" TV set; that is, one that comes with a headset so that neither spouse's TV obsession will disturb the other.

The "substitute relationship" syndrome is not merely one of replacing one's associates with print or machines. Media relationships can change, rather than supplant, human ones. Recently, two psychologists noted that individuals steeped in *Playboy* or *Playgirl* Web sites and centerfolds, movie stars, magazine models and TV "hunks" often consider their own mates less attractive by comparison. Secondhand masturbation aids thus become more appealing than firsthand intercourse, since a spouse's demands, timing, emotional state, predictability, age or sameness may seem far less compelling. "Perfect" media software, cable and video mates performing a wide variety of fantasy scenarios can be controlled, replayed and varied at will. Seeming "impotency" or indifference, sometimes causing criticism, frustration or jealousy (of an imagined rival) by a romantic partner may result. A fixation upon idyllic imaginary romances, love/hate fantasies, or sexual relationships (such as John Hinckley's with Jodie Foster or Charlie Manson's with Sharon Tate) may also create problems for the beholder and the beheld. The popularity of "900" phone numbers suggests that even an electronic voice is often preferable to a human partner. The number of online "relationships" is staggering, including those in which one must pay incrementally at each stage of greater and greater forms of intimacy.

Other media "mates"—novel software, Nintendo, a satellite dish, a remote clicker or a subscription to *The New York Times*—seem of themselves harmless. However, once a fixation begins, time spent on the obsession is stolen from other relationships—with the children, friends, service organizations, students, spouse, relatives, colleagues or whatever—and this overall shift of interest has impact on the quality of our social fabric.

I do not hold the extreme position of those who blame media for every social problem—generation gaps, demise of the nuclear family, increased divorce rate and the reported sagging quality of human relationships. However, I can posit that reversing our media fixation back to firsthand experience and the discovery of individual purpose and identity would have a marked impact on human interaction.

PASCAL'S DICTUM

In effect, the French philosopher Blaise Pascal pinpointed an underlying cause for our persisting fixation with "externals," such as canned entertainment. He wrote "All men's miseries derive from not being able to sit in a quiet room alone." We seek distraction. Eastern philosophy does not differ considerably. At its root is a devotion to "being," to "accepting conditions as they are," to "going with the flow," or, in the terms of Islam, "to surrender." Both for Pascal and the Oriental sage, happiness comes from accepting the limitations of one's small room, from seeing within it all that is necessary for enjoyment and peace of mind.

However, media bespeak the human longing for "distraction" evident to Pascal. In embracing media so wholeheartedly, we seem to prefer the remote to the adjacent, the recycled thought of others to the freshness of our own, the infinite spaces of "twilight zones," "star treks," "space odysseys" and "the winds of war" to our bedroom walls, and the sensational to our own sensations. We point and click to everywhere but our own brains. The current eighty-five percent penetration of the remote channel clicker into American homes, and the concomitant habits of "zapping" (commercials), "zipping" (through the channels), and "hopping" (back and forth between or among preferred programs or stations) suggests that we are easily distracted, even from our distractions. For many, Russell Conwell's paraphrased insight will need to be amended. "All the world's in your own back yard" will need this marketing phrase at the end: "so long as you have cable and an iPad!"

Figures of speech, even clichés, have reflected our understanding of the "distraction syndrome" for centuries. "Greener grasses," "the pot of gold at the end of the rainbow," "questing for the Holy Grail," "quixotic seeker" and "pipe dreamer" all suggest our innate understanding that "over there" and "tomorrow" are better than here and now only in the romantic imagination. An entire travel channel and programs like *The Love Boat*, *Fantasy Island*, and *Lifestyles of the Rich and Famous* easily catalyze the "over there" mirage and remind us through their caricature that media, whatever other functions they serve, are inherently a "getaway" from responsibilities immediately before us.

Media may also become, like the dog, "man's best friend," given their consistent loyalty as domesticated and subservient companions. Indeed Max Beerbohm called radio "a friend in one's room" and Norman Vincent Peale praised the TV for its companionship to lonely shut-ins.

But what is it that these shut-ins learn from their new "friends?" Shut-ins learn to "shut out" or fear the remaining human beings on the outside who come to their door—the postman, strangers who claim their "car broke down," and neighbors collecting for charity. After watching hours of prime-time TV, in which endless crimes are committed against people who are alone, shut in, helpless or socially isolated, people living alone increasingly report that they are afraid to answer the door. Fear and distrust, no matter how subconscious, increase when media "friends" become constant companions to the companionless. When closely examined, "media relationships" are neither harmless placebos nor panaceas. For many, the honeymoon is over.

THE OTHER SIDE

To be sure, it will be argued that I have created a Berlin Wall between media and reality. Are not media part of reality? Can we not experience mass communication firsthand, just as we experience human beings, natural sounds and images? Why separate media from society, nature from culture, and consciousness from "externals" if all these are connected?

Such questions are important, since media do not have a life of their own and are in fact human inventions. The programming and content of media cannot be separated from human consciousness, any more than any object can be extracted from the universe. However, such awareness misses the point. Drugs are also inseparable from material reality. So, too, are food, oxygen and water. Their consumption, and the lack thereof, nevertheless has highly noticeable effects on the thought and actions of their consumers, *as if* these substances we ingest independently change us. Is it not so with mass communication?

Even if we grant that media *are* reality, that we experience them firsthand and that they are simply our mirrors, are their messages as direct as those of birds and bees? At a gathering of the Association for Education in Journalism and Mass Communication in Washington, D.C., Stanley Reardon of Kent State University noted that up to sixty-eight percent of the sources in news stories involving the military are "unnamed." The alarming rise of unnamed, anonymous and "confidential" sources quoted or inferred by mass media makes it impossible for the reader to directly encounter the news.

Furthermore, the amount of recycled archival footage, borrowed publicity stills and unconfirmed information render the consumer ignorant and deceived about what she is reading or receiving. Even media "reality," given its own status, is full of illusions, deception and substitutions. It is often impossible to tell which Internet images are photos and which are retouched, re-colored or generated online.

Advertising is frequently noted as most "dishonest" in its exaggerated representation of products. But all media are "distortions," in essence. Even the direct firsthand encounter with mass communication leads to the second-, third- or fourth hand encounter with what it is describing or depicting.

"What's wrong with that?" you counter. "I'd rather hear secondhand from the media that a hurricane is heading for my house the day *before* it hits than to hear firsthand the day it *arrives*." This line of thought seems reasonable. Communication tools have assisted in saving many lives, buildings and animals through warning and advance information.

However, once again there is a flip side to this "service." Many of the disasters forecast never arrive and several arrive only in a tiny fraction of the area receiving the warning. Every year heart attacks, panic, ulcers, massive evacuations and unnecessary worry are reported by people who responded to inaccurate media warnings. My wife and I sat surrounded by petrified people when a twelve-county "tornado warning" was issued in east Tennessee in 1988. Ultimately, the tornado only caused minor damage in one county.

Similarly, when relatives and friends of people living in a "disaster area" make telephone calls, they *usually* discover that their contacts were unaffected by the disaster. Of the nine times I have called friends or relatives living in the vicinity of an "earthquake," "flood," "fire," or "hurricane" reported by the news, each said, in effect, "Everything's fine. We're untouched. The media's just making a big deal out of it."

It is impossible to measure the unnecessary alarm, worry and shock caused (particularly to seniors, parents and children) by inaccurate or overblown news coverage. Ultimately, more good than harm occurs, and the saving of lives makes false alarms pale in comparison. However, Hadley Cantril's *The Invasion from Mars* that reported the effects of Orson Welles' Halloween radio re-creation of H. G. Wells' *The War of the Worlds*—which many people misinterpreted as an actual Martian invasion of New Jersey and New York—gives us some idea of how inaccurate or fake information creates unintended havoc.

THE AUTHORITY OF FIRSTHAND LIVING

For many, electronic communication has become a source of coitus interruptus in our communion with the earth. During a fast, one of my bus trips recaptured the feeling I had as a small boy—a feeling of an endless oneness with nature. As whole cities and small towns passed by quickly, I could easily become more philosophical about human existence. It became obvious to me that I could choose my own interpretation of the stream of images that passed. As with the first day of spring, the first night of summer, the first scent of autumn and the first snow of winter, my senses seemed both enlivened and relaxed. The endless streams of green—trees, shrubs, grass—in which the bus glided seemed as warm and natural as water to a fish.

I was reminded of what it was like to be "on the road." Kerouac had captured this feeling in book form, Kuralt on TV; Dennis Hopper and Peter Fonda in film; and Willie Nelson in music. But I was more interested in the *actual* feelings and thoughts that accompanied panoramic travel.

The memory of another trip hailed me: I had taken my summer Navy ROTC destroyer cruise from Long Beach to Portland, Honolulu and San Diego in July 1970. Although the journey had been interrupted with bouts of seasickness ("manning the rail," "feeding the fish," or "talking to Ralph," the colorful sailors called it), I had the opposite feeling one night when left alone on fantail (rear of the ship) duty. Overhead, seemingly thousands of stars illuminated the Pacific canopy. Round about, for as far as I could see through binoculars, lay a deep-blue sea of glass. An occasional distant ship or plane light added its momentary glistening to the tranquil magic.

Slowly I remembered that such starry nights were the natural panorama for pre-industrial people. As a cook heaved some garbage overboard and broke my romantic bubble, I nevertheless noticed how sharp my sense of smell was. Earlier that week the salt spray of breakers over our bow had also reminded me of another sense—the enlivening sense of adventure which close encounters with the elements quickly muster. Slowly, as I scanned the horizon to fulfill my night watch duties, I became aware that the destroyer could have easily been a whale or eagle, or even planet, soaring throughout the universe.

Later I would be equally impressed by the Soviet cosmonaut who commented, "Originally I looked for my country or city when I saw the earth. Later I thought more in terms of continents. Eventually all I saw with increasing awe was one earth." Somehow neither his nor my experience fully came through in newspapers or on television.

Following my sea voyage, another midshipman and I decided to travel back to Boston coast-to-coast, via jalopy. My colleague was eccentric enough as a traveling companion to delight Kerouac, Karakul, or even Chaucer. He reckoned it was better to buy an old, cheap jalopy to add even more adventure to the trip, save money, and possibly attract females.

I can remember most of the colorful accents, gas-station attendants, undomesticated animals, and landscapes we saw to this day. Even more extraordinary was sleeping near the edge of the Grand Canyon, with a vast aurora of stars overhead.

Most of all, I will remember the price we paid for buying a thirdhand jalopy. At "The Great Divide," the line of demarcation atop the Rocky Mountains, we inhaled extremely fresh air and a breathtaking view. What could possibly follow?

Halfway down the lengthy winding descent of The Great Divide, my traveling companion shouted, "Oh my God...the brakes! The brakes!"

After several dangerous moments, filled with emergency passing of slow-moving vehicles and drastic turns at up to seventy miles per hour, we managed to engage the emergency brake and somehow skid to safety. It was impossible to remove our hearts from our mouths. All the Hollywood chase scenes I have ever witnessed cannot total the experience I confronted in a five- to ten-minute stretch of zigzag highway.

Once the car was safely repaired and we were coasting across flat Kansas two days later, we swore there was *no substitute* for the adventures of *first hand* living...and no reason to buy third hand jalopies.

THE SMELL OF THE HOTDOGS— THE ROAR OF THE CROWD

During one fast, I ventured to a Boston Red Sox baseball game at Fenway Park for the first time in over a year. In the meantime, I had read many box scores in newspapers, "caught" parts of several games on the radio while commuting, visited the official Red Sox Web site, and seen two or three complete games on television. The first difference I noted, approaching Fenway Park, was the smell of hotdogs, and Italian and Polish sausages, each being grilled akimbo to sizzling onions and peppers. Next came the parade of anomalous hawkers, each displaying an obvious ethnic or community accent, near-Halloween costume and urban vocabulary.

Unlike my media experiences, carefully guided by commentators, I was guiding my own ambulatory experience through a cavalcade of sounds, smells and tastes. The smell of oiled leather prompted me to spot a glove, almost touching me, on the hand of a boy anxious to catch a foul ball. While the ballplayers were smaller than those on TV (only the electronic scoreboard provided occasional close-ups), the crowd was much closer, the blue sky overhead was endless, and the electric cheers following come-from-behind scoring in the late innings were galvanic.

As I stared at the players' uniforms, I was aware of a crispness of outline, as if I were no longer subtly straining to see through a gauze screen hidden on the TV tube. Colors were more precise, space was continuous—not dissected by editing, the outfield was truly pastoral and I felt the beaming sunshine. The only commercials posted on the scoreboard or nearby billboards could be easily ignored. Finally, my wife and I could talk to friends, cheer or laugh at any time without feeling we would be interrupting a continuous sound track. Relative to television, the grass *was* greener.

Following the game, I felt much more alive—quite the opposite of my post-TV game feelings of drowsiness and fuzzy thinking. Leaving Fenway Park, I couldn't help but wonder what the potential use of our senses is and which senses we never use. I also meditated on how much more awake and alive perception seems when it is *deliberately* employed. Finally, as the weather began to shift with the gentle wind, I amused myself with how much more enjoyable it was to experience weather changes than to hear them forecast.

A few days later, my wife and I joined a group of friends who had gathered to visit our friend Carol Proctor at her summer home, in Tanglewood, and to hear her play in the Boston Symphony Orchestra. Violinist Itzhak Perlman was the featured artist scheduled to perform a violin concerto by Tchaikovsky. Although Carol had encouraged us to bring our two-year-old daughter, Angelica, to the concert, I could not imagine that I would be able to hear the entire concert in peace. Trying to silence a two-year-old for two hours is a major challenge. Upon entering Tanglewood, I saw several other infants and toddlers.

"What gives?" I thought. How could an orchestra as venerated as the BSO allow babies and youngsters to disturb concerts dependent upon dramatic moments of silence, subtle changes in dynamics, and barely discernible counterpoint and "subplots" in the music?

As is often the case, I was mistaken. The Orchestra did *not* encourage the disruptions of crying infants. They simply pacified them with anesthetizing music. As the concert began, a hush fell over the *entire* audience. People of *all* ages seemed to breathe as one, as if conducted by the music. Infants simply "grokked" the sublime atmosphere and added their reverence to the "worship." The act of listening seemed to be a mere conduit for the transference of healing from the symphony to the audience. In one sense, the two could not be separated. Many of those listening on the lawn reclined on their blankets and seemed transported to Mecca. The only baby sounds that erupted were brief and blissful. A deeper invisible current, propelled by the carrier wave of music, seemed to melt the barriers of age, background and ticket brackets.

Nothing in my previous listening had prepared me for this experience. Although Angelica had been quiet for brief interludes during recorded music on the radio and cassette player, and although we had heard the BSO on television and FM radio earlier that year, "something had been lost in the translation" from live to recorded or broadcast performance. The mesmerized infants at Tanglewood seemed to be the first proof of this. Following the open-heart surgery Perlman had conducted, a standing ovation demonstrated that the adults were the second.

RESPONSE AND RADIANCE

In his *The Responsive Chord*, Tony Schwartz had indirectly proclaimed that Perlman's captivation of his audience was exactly the goal of mass media. Advertisers particularly, according to Schwartz, thrive upon (re)creating exactly the right vibration to silence an audience's intellect and cause the consumer to *respond*, as one tuning fork responds to the frequency of another.

There is nothing new to scientists about Schwartz's metaphor. Chladni, the founder of "acoustics," had demonstrated that a sensitively played violin, like Perlman's, could by means of its powerful resonance rearrange the pattern of sawdust on a floor several feet away. Such "resonance" seems also to rearrange the pattern of human emotion when played on heartstrings, also many feet away. Hans Jenny, the Swiss scientist who discovered "cymatics," posited that all matter is similarly resonating to the frequencies of an invisible world of oscillation. Such thinking, when pushed toward its limit, suggests that all of us are likewise held together, not by subatomic nuts and bolts but by the oceans of vibration surrounding and interpenetrating us. Scientists like Capra, Bohm, Plank and Chladni bear witness.

My first encounter with another fine violinist and thinker, Richard Heinberg, led me to read his scientific treatise *Resonance*. Inherent within Heinberg's premise was the view that sound, energy, music, math and physics express precise relationships with which we "resonate." Ultimately, the Boston Symphony Orchestra at Tanglewood had found "resonant" audiences that day by artfully and accurately sounding "the responsive chord." While a media fast does not guarantee that one's field of resonance and response will increase, the quality and intensity of vibrant interaction seems greatly enhanced when experience is pointblank, uninterrupted by a middleman.

Direct intercourse of this nature seems heightened, charged and sensitized. Despite all the improvements in audio equipment in recent years, many of us still prefer to hear Perlman, or Lady Gaga, Ricky Martin, Mariah Carey, Pavarotti, or the Rolling Stones for that matter, in person.

Another of Heinberg's books, *Memories and Visions of Paradise*, may take such consideration to a deeper level. Apparently, according to his research, all tribes and cultures trace their origins to overlapping Creation myths, stories of great floods, and similar parallel tales. The "paradise" myth—common to all extant peoples—tells of a time of greater resonance and deeper music. Like the carrier pigeon, Heinberg's work and lectures have a "homing instinct." Audience members claim to feel they are "returning" to a deeper sense of home, of an instinctive déjà vu, when hearing Richard lecture on this topic.

Ultimately, the longing for direct experience may relate more to Heinberg's (and Milton's) "paradise regained" than to a rebellion against information overload. This "heavenly" experience—often sought by a vacation to Hawaii or other tropical islands—is usually characterized with more "primitive" forms of communication than printing and broadcasting. The sounds of waterfalls, tropical birds, steel bands, the ukulele and lapping ocean waves accompany the more relaxed beating of one's heart.

Richard Heinberg, however, is quick to point out that paradise is much more a state of mind than a tropical environment. It is another name for Pascal's room, devoid of distraction, or my traveling companion's eye view from The Great Divide, whatever one's geographical altitude. It is not so much dependent upon the stimulus—such as Perlman at his best or a $2,500 bottle of vintage wine—as upon the consciousness of the beholder. That consciousness would quickly fade after twenty consecutive bottles of such wine.

No medium or its absence can guarantee this state. However, the authority of firsthand experience *can reduce* the confusion and illusions about the nature of paradise, and about its availability in paperback, cyber-programmed, packaged or transmitted form. That is one reason I had chosen a media fast from fast media.

CHAPTER FOUR

LESSONS FOR SOCIETY

Media Addiction and Freedom

Although most of us are both consumers and creators, social critics have lamented our collective shift toward gross "consumerism." Having graduated from high school in the "flowering" '60s, and from college in the "explosive" '70s, I seemed surrounded by a peer group of activists, initiators, authors, filmmakers, composers, artists and reformers. At various school reunions throughout North America, this same peer group sadly noted that most of these activists have become conformists, composers are now groupies, initiators are programmed, filmmakers are film addicts, and, in general, most of the creators are now consumers.

This observation reflects more than a concern about "selling out" values of social action to passive acceptance. It is likewise more than a comment about the cycle of change from the '60s and '70s to a more conservative era, which cycles seem historically ubiquitous. One concern of the Woodstock and Chicago Seven generation rests in the appearance of *lost motivation and energy.* The Gods of comfort and complacency seem to have replaced those of change and causes. Finally, the consumer seems to have triumphed over the creator.

Similarly, the Yuppie syndrome of the '70s and '80s seemed to deify acquisition and self-replication, rather than sharing and conservation. *Duplication*—through babies, products, ideas, goals and status—seems more attractive than *origination.* Indeed, I often ask my students if it is possible any longer to even want to originate. I ask them and I will ask you: "Have you ever had a truly original thought—one that cannot be traced to some form of media—TV, textbooks, the Internet, journals, newspapers?" Would you like to?

Martin Heidegger's *What Is Called Thinking?* suggests that *original* thinking is difficult, if not impossible. For him, true thinking is "that which recedes." The notion reminds me of a Eugene O'Neill character for whom "the curtain lifts, we catch a glimpse of something, and then the curtain falls again." Media, like orthodox religion and education, constantly promote the *duplication* of thought. What social mechanism encourages *truly original* thinking? Indeed, is any thought ever truly original?

If this question cannot be empirically answered, it inspires similar productive questions. For example, "If I cannot demonstrate that my thought is original, can I at least show that it seems original *to me*?" "Can my thinking counter stale media memories with *fresh, alive* thoughts *I* find original?" "Can I stretch and challenge my own mind to think in different and more productive ways?" "Can I *change gears* mentally in a *conscious* way, so as to monitor information going in?" "How *consciously* do I store mediated information with appropriate skepticism, selectivity and priority?" In short, "*Am I thinking or are externally generated thoughts thinking me?*"

Media is not *necessarily* antithetical to creative thinking. All media may be used to extend the creativity of individuals to others. The dangers of such extension, however, rest in the *duplicating* power and *authoritative* presence of media. When sizable audiences begin to memorize and store "new" or "creative" thinking from books or programs, such "original" thought can paradoxically *homogenize* the thought of an audience. Moreover, many audience members tend to accept such thought *unthinkingly.* Research about the effects of well-crafted propaganda, advertising, and dated or inaccurate textbooks confirm a relationship between media consumption and cloned thinking: much of what is consumed is unchallenged.

When many of the best studies are compiled, one finds that the aggregate media consumer tends to ingest and replay attitudes, trends, emotional associations and moods. The heavy consumer (heavy viewer, listener or bookworm) becomes subconsciously controlled by media events and their spin-offs. For example, imagine what Jung and other proponents of a shared "collective subconscious" would say happens during the broadcast of the Super Bowl? Or a widely viewed drama, such as *CSI* or *Lost*? Or the mass reading of *The Exorcist*? So-called "original" thinking melts into an ocean of groupthink and group feel after touchdowns, "bad calls" by the referees, nuclear holocaust scenes, the description of being possessed, and commercials.

Consider the possibility that such consumers are linked together, not only by similar programming but by a collective memory or shared subconscious. For example, Jung argues that we experience universal dreams of flying or falling, which are our shared race memory. If so, then every consumer who surrenders to media control extends a large ripple effect throughout society. Like pebbles being dropped into a pond, programs extend as far as sets are on and minds are "off."

Both the broadcasting waves and the connected subconscious minds of unthinking (cf. unconscious) viewers provide webs of control that increasingly link humanity. It was not simply Lee Harvey Oswald but the emotive broadcasts of the effects of "his" action that made a nation mourn. It was not the Beatles but the amplified carrier waves of their sounds that stirred teenagers into frenzy worldwide. The same is true about The Black Eyed Peas, Tiger Woods' love life, Eminem, the Columbine massacre, the Virginia Tech killing spree, Michael Moore's films, Puff Daddy's rap, the Spice Girls, Lady Diana's tragic death—each mediated phenomenon creates waves worldwide.

The passive consumer is perfectly positioned to be a naive "conductor" for such electrical current and its content. Such a perspective suggests severe warnings about the consequences of growing consumerism. For example, the German philosopher Immanuel Kant suggested that one might test one's actions by asking, "What would happen if *everyone* acted in the way I am about to act?" If everyone acted as a perpetual consumer, no work would be completed, no art of community would be *created* and, most importantly, everyone would become a naive carrier wave for *any* message or programming. Slothfulness, mediocrity and global brainwashing would replace creation, quality, and inventive, imaginative thought. There are those who argue that this condition is already upon us locally and nationally. *Global* lobotomy, uniformity and impotence cannot be far behind, they reason.

THE ROLE OF CHOICE

During my media fasts, I consciously chose to be a creator, not a consumer. I let my mind relax, find different routings and mix new ingredients. By returning to composing and playing instruments I had abandoned, I found a strong river of inner creativity that had been dammed. Although I am not condemning reading, I found that a temporary switch from reading books to *writing* one restored a full measure of initiative to my work.

This "single switch" in consciousness and in action might be described as living from the inside out, rather than from the outside in. It is characterized by rediscovery of the creative process, which many of us abandon—some forever—usually during childhood. Motivation sharply increases, so much so that virtually any procrastination from the creative process seems a total waste of time. As a child I can recall times when the games, tree houses, sports or skits we were creating became so all-consuming and enjoyable that we could not wait for the next day to begin.

The "adult" state does not seem universally characterized by such love for work and responsibility. "Creation" and creative experience often seem relegated to a few closely guarded hours or days—holidays, hobbies, playing with the children, continuing education courses— which are stuffed into the cracks of living. A deliberate "single switch" in attitude, and in electing to exercise *choice*, can reignite the inner fountain of creativity on a more full-time basis. The increase in energy known from this experience can redouble when one senses "If I can abstain from one type of overconsumption, I can abstain from any or all of them." As this balance (between what comes in and what goes out) is restored, a "blast-off" state, or energy boost, can be felt if the motivation for change remains pure and consistent.

The creator has a totally different mind-set than the consumer. Instead of being a pincushion of foreign influences, the creative individual is concerned about *her own* positive *influence* upon circumstances and people. Since teaching is by example, why not model *creative* rather than *destructive* or *vegetating* behavior? From Kant's standpoint, is it not more virtuous and enticing to envision a world of creators rather than parasites? of artists rather than audiences? of those who awaken and inspire rather than those who dream, then expire?

MEDIA AS FRIENDS, NOT VILLAINS

When the "single switch" is made from information gluttony to creative communication, one may return to media with new ears, eyes and thoughts. Instead of viewing media as mind pollution, each medium may be employed as a tool of creativity. When the mind and emotions begin to *originate* creative images and sounds, why not extend that creativity through books, radio, cyberspace, cassettes, or whatever is suitable? Media never have been enemies, in and of themselves. Rather, they simply amplify, disseminate and perpetuate the nature of human consciousness. To the extent the consciousness of the *creator* is inspiring and indigenous, his *consumer* may well be motivated to live more vividly and aesthetically. Indeed, if the creator is optimally successful, she may inspire other consumers to "wake up" and enjoy the creative process. To the extent one's work genuinely *originates* in the creative process, rather than *duplicates*, conventional programming, it will assist in the liberation rather than enslavement of audience members. The single switch is contagious.

HABITUATION VS. ADDICTION

Very few people will argue that media are not *habit forming*. However, scientific purists will often claim that no mass medium is strictly *addicting*. If addiction is held to a strict clinical definition, biological or physiological dependency is essential to distinguish the "addicted" patient from the merely "habituated" one. By such clinical definition, severe media dependency is, at worst, a borderline case of "addiction." Even those claiming to suffer "withdrawal symptoms" or "severe headaches," etc., when deprived of TV or rock music, etc., have not been verified in clinical experiments. Nor have the causes of such symptoms been shown to be media related.

However, if *addiction* is defined as *psychological* dependency (it is difficult to separate physiological and psychological mechanisms entirely, in any event), there can be little argument that media *addiction* is real. For our purposes, such a psychological dependency may be determined by the subject's answer to two questions about any medium in question:

1. Can I voluntarily take it or leave it in any given situation?
2. Is it essential to my survival?

If the subject truthfully answers "Yes" to either question and can back up the answer, no addiction is present. For example, air, water and sleep are essential to human survival and would receive a "Yes" answer to Question #2. These are required for the subject's normal living and thus are not classified as "addictive," despite the subject's dependency upon them. If, however, any non-survival substance—such as cocaine, alcohol, sugar, caffeine or fame—*seems* essential to the subject and cannot be ignored at will, a "Yes" answer to Question #1 would qualify the substance as *addictive*.

In this sense, media are not simply habit forming to many, nor *metaphorically* addictive. They are *literally* addictive. In Lani Silver's *TV Addicts* (National Public Radio, Washington, D.C.), several randomly selected North Americans made these statements: "I couldn't *live* without it...it keeps me from being bored." "I am very addicted to TV—I watch anything to keep my mind off my problems." "I feel like I should be doing other things but I can't." "I can't take my eyes off it." "You get glued to it." "I feel like I should be doing something more social and active." "I was never able to talk to my mother except during commercials." "I keep in my head—TV, TV, TV."

Nor is this a local phenomenon. While I am aware of an Internet Addiction Center within driving distance of where I am sitting, I have also recently read (ironically, over the Internet) of similar centers in Japan and Taiwan.

To social workers and psychiatrists accustomed to working with more traditional addictions, such phrases sound familiar. Other quotes confirm that often it is not the content but the process of mindless consumption that is addictive: "If someone asked me, I couldn't tell them what I watched." "My daughter just *stares* at the TV." "It's escapism." "I turn on TV automatically." "I used to watch anything and everything that came on...about seven hours a day."

Nevertheless, the "heavy user" or addict does seem at least somewhat influenced by the content. When research is synthesized, the aggregate "heavy user" seems more afraid that he will be a victim of violence; more likely to be violent himself (heated '70s research controversy to the contrary); less social, less attentive to maintaining family and friendship networks; more likely to transfer emotions away from life and toward media characters, actors and events; and more prone to form and accept stereotypes. Silver's *TV Addicts* also depicts how TV can drastically change a person's daily rhythms, have a hypnotic and tranquilizing effect, and alter personality over time.

Once again the parallels between TV, CDs, the Internet and other addictions are not surprising. The craving for the stimulus *may* be traced to its instant numbing or supplanting of real-world problems and its provision of emotional "highs," a sense of security, surrogate companionship, elation, therapy, tranquility, heightened sensuality, insularity, pain relief, freedom, bliss, or a variety of other sensations. Of course, MTV addicts may experience different hormonal sensations than PBS addicts, just as news addicts differ from entertainment addicts, cocaine addicts differ from heroin addicts, and alcoholics differ from chain-smokers. But the fundamental activity pattern and utilization of stimuli—particularly when the subject feels under pressure, whether for avoidance, sensation or security—seems central to the condition, whether the addition is meth or porn. Therefore it is not surprising to discover a group of people called "TV Addicts Anonymous" who, like "Alcoholics Anonymous" and the related "_____ Anonymous" groups, mandate that members 1) fully acknowledge their TV addiction; then 2) take action while surrounded by peer support.

COLLECTIVE ADDICTION

Society might be wise to acknowledge our *collective* addiction, and take action as well. We now have more magazines and journals in the world than ever before. The average high school student will have seen over twenty thousand televised murders prior to graduation. As Gerry Mander points out, television alone takes more of Americans' time than any other single experience and, for many, becomes one way you can spend your entire life. Social and political activists argue that TV and radio also serve as tranquilizers that, in affirming the status quo, inhibit individual action and social change.

Advertisers, programmers and circulation managers are not blind to this phenomenon. For the benefit of long-term ratings, sales and circulation, each would rather sell us a dependency rather than a product. An ad for potato chips says, "Bet you can't eat just one"; another for vodka is subtitled "Something you can *stay* with." "It's Miller *time*" infers that the consumer will drink Miller beer more than once—indeed at particular junctures, such as after a day's work or at any party or outing. The TV slogan "It's Howdy Doody time!", spoken by millions of children who watched "The Howdy Doody Show," taught the same lesson as early as the 1950s.

There is nothing new about this logic. Merchants have known for centuries that it is far better to have one lifelong "hooked" customer, who will guarantee continuing sales, than to have two occasional browsers, whose loyalty and consumption rate are unknown and unsteady. Thus the goals of advertising, media promoters and management become not to sell a single item but to sell a series or repeated purchasing habit. As one friend at NBC TV told me privately, "Sure it's sort of an addiction we're after...if they watch some special and don't change over to us, it's been a one-night stand—but if they like Leno or Brokaw or Couric, we've got 'em, day in and day out, five days a week, fifty-two weeks a year...advertisers love it when we can promise them long-term exposure and security."

The same mindset carries over to all media—newspapers would much rather sell a subscription than a paper; a recording company would much rather sign a contract with Stevie Wonder for multiple years than for just one of his songs; radio would much rather make it a requirement that you be listening to their station *when they call you* to win their jackpot contest.

Book- and record-of-the-month clubs, cheaper multi-year

subscription rates, etc., all tie in with the preference that audiences should become consumptive, rather than occasional or selective samplers. The ultimate subconscious goal is to sell consumerism and addiction, not programs and products.

Salespersons for mass media also use the term *selling audiences* or *delivering audiences* to advertisers. In such situations it is not thirty or sixty seconds of our time that is being sold, but "us," our purchasing power, our spending habits, our needs, wants and fantasies. Advertisers have already conducted research and tests about what will appeal to such needs and fantasies, depending upon our age, background, gender, income and values.

The hidden effects of media addiction vary from medium to medium and person to person. However, the transcripts and videotapes of many trials indicate a growing number of perceived patterns. For example, divorce, child custody, murder, theft, rape, assault and battery, drunken driving, reckless driving, and child abuse trials more frequently mention that the defendant has an "obsession" with television, X-rated Web sites, photographs, or printed pornography. Once again, that does not mean that media per se (so much as our use and programming of them) should be examined, or that the effects of one medium should be confused with the effects of others.

Long-term effects of addiction may often be far more subtle than patterns that surface in court cases. Staying up later each night, or changing one's job to see the soaps, hiding an earphone line up one's sleeve in class to hear the conclusion of baseball games, uninterrupted listening to music on the job to avoid boredom, missing appointments to see the next episode, wearing headsets while jogging to blot out the environment, reading a book through meals and events because "I couldn't put it down," and showing up late for meals whenever online are all examples of media hooking us and rescheduling our lives.

Perhaps one of the saddest cases I have encountered occurred when a failing student finally admitted the cause of his perpetual dozing: "The sexy scenes on HBO, Showtime and Cinemax aren't played until the early morning hours, so I have to sneak down the stairs past my parents' room to watch while they think I'm sleeping. Since you never know when the skin will come on, I watch for hours, waiting for the really hot scenes and then eventually sneak back upstairs into bed just before dawn."

"But, with all due respect, don't you see that you're failing my class?" I asked. "From what you tell me, you may fail other classes, as well, and lose your job—not to mention alienate your parents and friends—all because of this one habit. I am concerned about you."

"I know," he said.

"Then why not stop the early morning viewing?" I asked.

"I can't," he replied. "I've tried everything."

Although I was eventually able to help this sophomore turn the problem around, I have no idea if he reverted to twilight viewing. Nor is there research to show how many other students have related addictions. One of my student advisees did confess that her reason for not taking afternoon classes was to watch soap operas she "couldn't miss." A neighbor admitted he missed local PTA meetings because it "conflicted with *The Office*." At least three of my colleagues will not answer phone calls when online, so we play telephone-cum-computer tag with voicemail *and* E-mail. Voicemail might begin with "Did you get my e-mail about...?" or vice versa.

During my undergraduate days at Harvard, I encountered three peers with print addictions so severe they would read at meals, until dawn, in the bathrooms, and even walking to class. To my knowledge, only one of these ever discovered that both his reading retention and comprehension would improve with balanced living—consistent sleep, well-digested meals, steady exercise and counter-balancing activities.

Perhaps talking is the greatest communication addiction. Most of us have met people who would rather give up their freezer than their right to unlimited chatter. The syndrome is reflected in staggering phone bills, urban drunks offering disconnected soliloquies, and our picturesque idioms: "windbag," "chatterbox," "grandstander," "hot air," and "couldn't get in a word edgewise." I will discuss the limitations of "talking without speaking" and incessant verbalizing in Chapter Ten.

THE SUBTLETIES OF HABITUATION

One definition of the word *habit* is "act that is acquired and has become automatic." *Addiction* carries the additional connotation "devoted to" or "given up to" or "controlled by" a specific habit. Usually, a habit forms *prior* to an addiction to *that* habit. For example, I might consciously eat ice cream periodically late at night. It is only when I eat it consistently and eventually *automatically* late at night that it becomes a *habit*. If I become conscious of the habit from time to time and decide to go without ice cream, I "break the habit" at will. When I discover that the habit can no longer be broken easily or will bring discernible consequences (depression, headaches, eating ice-cream substitutes late at night, etc.), the *habit* has become an *addiction*.

Implied in the nature of *habituation* is invisible slavery to a preset piece of behavior. Prolonged habituation becomes deep, persistent, subconscious and transparent. Thus, when bringing in the mail one may habitually spot and begin reading an interesting magazine article. While riding in a bus one may unknowingly begin tapping a foot to a radio song the driver has selected. While working out in a health club I often find myself using the piped-in music as a metronome for jogging, machine workouts, swimming or lifting weights.

It is impossible to think of a medium that is not habit-forming. The next time you are in an airport, try *not* to observe sexy billboards or advertising, *not* to skim any headlines or magazine covers being read by passengers or on display, *not* to discover what is playing on TV in an airport bar if you go in, *not* to pay any attention to background music and Muzak wherever it is secreted by the environment. Our habits of unconsciously drinking in such media fragments, often only momentarily or subliminally, are deeply entrenched yet largely unnoticed.

The media addict will cite the ubiquity of media as one reason for not being able to "kick the habit." He may blame society for corralling us with a media "obstacle course"—there seem to be video stores on every third corner, newspapers and magazines at every supermarket checkout counter, advertised products on most shelves, and music blaring out every tenth window, eighth car and sixth restaurant. How could anyone stop tasting these?

Because the media surround is omnipresent, we take it for granted and become unaware of more subtle effects. Other quotes from the NPR *TV Addicts* broadcast demonstrated some of the ongoing *side* effects noted by heavy viewers: "I have a picture of the way my woman is supposed to act from TV." "Like when I go to sleep I can still see images…in my mind…it puts a real deadener on my motivation and energy." "This [TV] is America's largest business. How can you stop it? It takes control of me." "No one gives you flack for watching TV…it's [a vice that's] really acceptable." In short, peer socialization, attitude formation (including sexism and racism), commercialization, hegemony and anomie are other surreptitious processes that accompany viewing.

We may also habitually *neutralize* our environment with a media surround. One friend of mine states that she sleeps with the radio on. When questioned about the habit, she says, "Well at least the music is more soothing and predictable than the sirens, barking dogs, yelling and other city noises it drowns out." In this regard, it is interesting to note that the boom box, Phil Spector's "wall of sound" music mixing, the headset, and the electrification of music, primarily through rock and roll, all compete favorably in shutting out urban noise and sound overload.

Thus, new habits not only usher more media into the foreground but increasingly push other sounds and media into the background, including *human* communication. As actor and director Alan Alda put it: "TV has the power to suck you into its vortex. It can stop *any* conversation…." It can also obliterate the gentler sounds of the birds and the breeze.

THE OTHER FIVE FREEDOMS

In discussions of communication, the freedoms most widely saluted are freedom of the press, freedom of speech and freedom of assembly. These three freedoms are actually quite meaningless without the five underlying Freedoms I will call freedom of thought, freedom of emotion, freedom of action, freedom of identity and freedom of perspective. If a culture's thoughts, emotions, actions, perspectives and identity are controlled, then freedom of speech, press and assembly can only permit expression of what those in that culture have been told. Of what use are my freedom of speech, assembly and the press if I have already been drugged, hypnotized or indoctrinated? That is, if my freedom of thought, for example, has already been censored, so too is my freedom of outer expression automatically censored to the same degree.

Similarly, invasion of privacy is discussed as trespassing on private property or on private situations, such as when a person is in his bathroom or bedroom. However, if one's consciousness has already been invaded by sounds of radios, TVs and stereos while one is *still in the womb*, what greater invasion could possibly occur later? Infants, toddlers, and even embryos, hear the electronic thoughts and rhythms of the media environment long before they can think about the meaning of such sounds.

At the age of two, my daughter could recite songs and jingles from her immediate radio and TV environs. Was such speech *free*? Was the privacy of her thought invaded? If she publishes her thought in a "letter to the editor" in ten years and her thoughts are further colored by the two hundred thousand ads, programs, songs and articles she will ingest by then, and if the same is true for the thoughts of the editor of the paper, which paper itself runs thousands of ads, in what sense is that press *free*?

FREEDOM OF THOUGHT

If Heidegger is considered to be a (or the) leading thinker of our century and he is not certain that true thinking can take place, why do we feel free to think that we think freely? Which thoughts are unshackled of past or outside influence? Which thoughts are deliberately chosen rather than randomly recycled? Which thought flows from an inner reservoir rather than erupts from the stored hazardous waste of horror memories and replayed news atrocities?

During my fast, I cruised with one hundred other passengers on a commercial jet. For several minutes I looked out at the fluffy cumulus clouds and meditated upon how insignificant the scurry of human events seemed below. Time stood still and I could choose my experience—to see shapes in the clouds, to identify bodies of water below them, to feel one with it all, to prepare for an upcoming talk, to meet the passenger next to me, to...

Suddenly my thought was broken by the flight attendant's voice: "The movie today will be starting soon and the sound can be heard on channels one or two, found in your armrest. Please close your window shades so that other passengers can see the screen." Immediately my freedom of thought seemed interrupted by an "outside" controlling communication. I could have chosen to ignore it but, since some messages from the pilot and crew are safety related, I was conditioned to listen.

All around me passengers were donning headsets, like sailors grabbing life jackets during a ship emergency. Others were closing window shades, including myself, like guards securing a palace. What surprised me was not so much the uniformity of action we gave the flight attendant—such obedience is typical of our tacit social agreements—it was the high number of passengers who chose to see the movie which shocked me, possibly ninety percent. Although the film was above average, and I might easily have watched it myself before or after the fast, it seemed to me that the real show was outside the window—billowy clouds of great beauty; patchwork landscapes light-years away, dotted by tiny microbes inching along winding trails, called highways; infinite rich blue expanses above a silvery wing; a tiny toy airplane reflecting a sliver of lightning-bright sunlight, perhaps a mile away. What could be more picturesque or inspire more creative meditation? I erased all this as I dutifully brought down the window shade so all could view the movie.

I was aware that there was a close relationship between freedom of thought and freedom of experience. One is often free to choose to experience each thought and think about each experience in a variety of ways—innocently, skeptically, analytically, neutrally, enthusiastically, randomly, etc. As I saw the headsets pulled on, the shades pulled down automatically, and darkness fall within the plane, it seemed such freedoms were being consciously limited, if not thwarted. The same intravenous sound was being pumped into many heads. Most passengers seemed to *stare* dumbly, as a baby does once pacified, rather than look at or examine the screen. The boob tube, or glass teat, had suddenly swallowed our collective consciousness for two hours.

FREEDOM OF IDENTITY

The interpretations of modern behaviorists, such as B. F. Skinner, have led many to believe that we are the products of our conditioning. Skinner's testing of animals led to the notion that behavior may be modified by positive and negative "reinforcement." Put simply, the view holds that we tend to repeat those actions for which we are rewarded, and avoid actions for which we are punished. Although it is unfair to Skinner to say he opposed free will or obliterated the notion of freedom, the view of "operant conditioning" does promote the idea that our environment controls us, and not we ourselves.

Such a view can lead to human beings imagining they are merely the sum of all influences acting upon them. Other variants on this "imposed identity" concept are: "I am the product of my education." "My religion shaped me." "Society predetermined my behavior." "I am the outcome of this political and economic social structure." Innis, McLuhan, Mumford and many others also gave credence to the notion of *media determinism*; that is, that people's actions and attitudes are controlled by the evolution, nature or content of mass media. Such a concept typically maintains that we are never free of an identity shaped by the implements of communication. One medium makes our society more tribal, spiritual or cultic, depending upon who you ask. Another medium makes us more individualistic, logical, secular or structured. Watered-down forms of such identification include "I'm from the TV generation." "I see it this way." Or "As a scholar born in the age of literacy, I'd be wary of what you *hear* on the news." Or "Cyberspace is free and open; I don't think Bill Gates is controlling us."

Various simple forms of this environmental identification reduce to "You are what you eat." "You are what you read." "You are who you know." "You are what you watch." "We are what *we* watch."

During media fasts, I become aware of being someone else—not just my programming, enculturation and intake. It seems likely that actual identity is obscured by identities imposed—i.e., by socialization or by identities worshipped—such as media stars and heroes. It is difficult to find a child who will not model the behavior of several favorite characters, even during adolescence, and who will not try to purchase toys associated with such heroes.

Conditioning by media, education, parents and other social forces is so pervasive it seems impossible to imagine a "pure" identity, unsullied by role models, two-dimensional idols and social imprinting. Answering the basic eternal question "Who am I?" seems especially challenging in a world and consciousness populated by who I am not.

FREEDOM OF EMOTION

As a child I saw a film, reportedly about ancient history. Both my parents and I thought the movie would be educational, since I was becoming an avid history buff. During one scene a warrior queen unexpectedly asked one of her soldiers to volunteer to sacrifice himself. He was asked to demonstrate the use of a lethal instrument of torture, so that a visiting diplomat could see how it worked. If he chose to serve the queen in this way, he would die a patriot's painful death. If, on the other hand, he chose not to volunteer, he would be executed by his peers as a traitor.

In choosing to serve his cruel queen, the soldier "volunteered" to descend a giant slide by straddling what amounted to an enormous razor-blade that divided the slide. Thus the soldier was asked to honorably bisect and disembowel himself while descending the slide, or to be dishonorably executed. I will never forget the impression both his fate and dilemma made upon my young consciousness. The piercing scream he made (or Hollywood post-dubbed for him) haunted my nightmares for weeks. To this day, when the image and sound resurface in memory, I feel a sharp pang and, for a split second, identify with the pain and horror of his dilemma.

Such emotional poisoning once again challenges the notion of "freedom." Much of what we have seen and read occurred long before we were selective, if in fact we are, or before we could understand its meaning or its "make-believe" reality. Even the emotions I consciously chose to have manipulated by watching Hitchcock's *Psycho* or Begosian's *Talk Radio* or Stephen King's *IT* or by reading *The National Enquirer* color present experience.

Often one has no intention of subjecting one's feelings to a "high" or a "low." For example, when I saw a solitary Chinese citizen stop a row of tanks on national television, I was watching "in neutral" but momentarily felt thrilled. However, when I learned later that the same citizen had possibly been executed, I felt both shock and grief. The same emotions were felt worldwide, even though the street scene could have been staged or the reported execution might have been inaccurate. Teenagers faint at horror films, whether or not the special-effects crew employed animal blood or paint on the severed bodies. Heart attacks occurred during *The Swarm* (of bees), despite other audience members just a few rows away murmuring under their breath, "It's just a movie."

We seem less alarmed by the "positive" emotions manipulated within us. Nevertheless, during the late show when the long-lost orphan is reunited with her parents or when Quixote sings "The Impossible Dream" en route to his fate or when the town cynic finally falls in love or when true lovers hold hands in freezing water beside the sinking Titanic, we cry *against* our will. The violins swell, and so too do our tears.

Are these emotions genuine? Do they serve a purpose? To what extent are they voluntary? How do they affect our nervous system? Which ones will be replayed when triggered in the future? Do they upset the endocrine glands? Does this affect our emotional expression in the "real world"? Our emotional stability? No one seems to be asking or answering these questions with authority.

In any event, the notion of emotional freedom seems totally naive. Most human beings are already controlled by emotional underpinnings we frequently fail to monitor, understand or, when valuable, to express. The even subtler shades of emotional manipulation by vivid image and sudden sound, haunting headline and tear-jerking strings challenge the credibility of the First Amendment to the U.S. Constitution. The three freedoms of communication—of speech, the press and assembly— comprise what is in fact an oxymoron: "free expression." Who is actually wise, liberated or discerning enough to express what they actually feel, *free* of hidden influence?

FREEDOM OF PERSPECTIVE

Sustained media intake often engages audience interest in the details of day-to-day drama. Conversely, the ancient wisdom—whether of Buddha, Lao-Tzu, Plato, Heraclitus or others—taught a greater detachment from detail, so as to observe larger patterns and cycles of social flux.

The virgin viewer of a football game might enter it with a similar transcendent perspective—"What's the meaning of this?" "Is this a metaphor for man's latent animal instincts or a discrete form of war?" But upon the fiftieth screening of a football game, the questions are likely to be more pedestrian and controlled by the event itself: "What's the score?" "Is Brady injured?" "How much time remains?" We become hooked by the detail. If I want to learn about U.S. television's unique qualities, I ask someone with perspective, such as a Nigerian or Russian teacher observing it for the first time. To ask the same person for their insights after they have observed U.S. TV for twenty years is unlikely to present such useful insights—they, too, are asking: "Will Charlie Sheen make it with that model?" rather than "Why are the programs interrupted every six minutes?" or "Do people actually find these stories credible?"

News is supposed to widen one's perspective. But who will widen one's perspective from the news? I once decided to produce a news program which began "Today seven trillion planets were born, eight billion blades of grass bloomed, ten thousand baby humans were born, and...." Such a script immediately shows how narrowly what is called "news" focuses upon a restricted range of surface events important to some members of the human species. These surface events, shown devoid of context and process, and severed across both time and space, may actually narrow, rather than broaden, our understanding of the human condition, the many levels of reality, the forces behind events, and the relationships among life's components.

Freedom of perspective means the ability to choose, rather than have chosen; whether one will, in any given instant, view one's world or any part of it in close-up, long-shot, or from a distant "master-shot." Media make these choices for us, deciding at what distance and for how long we should view events, or, in print, deciding how much analysis and context and how many points of view should be provided within a "story."

One of the greatest lessons of my media fast was understanding that at any time I was free to gain or switch perspectives on anything, even on my present perspective. The detached bystander, who is not hooked on whether the U.S. should commence trade with China or whether the Cleveland Indians should fire their current coach, may ultimately be more perceptive by virtue of his distance and uncluttered state of consciousness.

After all, as I found out when interviewing his students, Harold Innis often noted that "Opinion is the lowest form of knowledge," which is in turn a lower form of wisdom. As presently structured—particularly in their worship of the editorial, talk show, chat room, gossip and infotainment—most media subconsciously mandate that we live in a world of opinion. Minds full of unsubstantiated opinions, however, may blot out perspective, which in turn may distort vision. And without vision, it is said, the people perish.

FREEDOM OF ACTION

Throughout the various fasts, I was fascinated with how media worshippers were governed by rigid schedules. Already we have noted how the length of programs, commercial breaks, one's "need to keep up" via cybernews, segmented radio slots, etc., can orchestrate a person's or even a society's actions—just as one aerobics tape can cause twenty people to move in step. A late-breaking news bulletin can cause hundreds of people about to leave their cars to run their engines longer, and even drive around the block, until the bulletin is completed.

Such action becomes robotic, entrapped by the time segmentation reported in *TV Guide* and other program schedules. One colleague of mine contends "I don't know who I am until after my morning cup of coffee *and* my morning paper. In Max Weber's terms, what was originally a unique action has become *routinized*, and eventually we become a one-person bureaucracy.

Like many humanists, I became enamored with the work of Jean-Paul Sartre and other existentialists as a student. Sartre seemed to be saying that the opposite of habituation could also be obtained; that is, that at any given moment I can be free if I see that I am free and take action. For example, I am free at this moment to commit suicide or murder, no matter how much my conditioning is to the contrary. I am free to drive on the wrong side of the road in one instant and to revert back or drive the car in reverse in the next. Even if jailed for my actions, I am free to speak Pig Latin, wake up at 3:33 a.m. daily, recite nursery rhymes or invent a new alphabet in jail.

Such thinking suggests that, whether we live in the "free world" or not, none of us have experienced total freedom. Most action—wearing clothes, eating food, sleeping at night, writing right- (or left-) handed, and exchanging money for objects—is endlessly and mindlessly repeated. Following Sartre's line of thought or, to be even more liberated, following my own line of thought, why not periodically challenge any or all of one's actions? "What am I doing here?" "Is there a purpose in this?" "What was my intention?" "What effect might this have?" "Am I *free* in this action or following the well-worn rut of custom?"

One of the saddest executions committed by mass-media habituation is murder of the spontaneous. Freedom means seeing new possibilities in each moment. However, mediated communication automatically structures experience, simply by virtue of the machines and other tools required to package sounds, print words, and record images. Broadcasters speak of themselves as fundamentally conservative and publishers describe themselves as being cautious about unknown commodities. *Glasnost* and *perestroika* are welcome as media content—after all, they increase the ratings—but not as process. That is, they are not welcome in the form of drastic internal change and openness within most media industries.

The "freedom of action" to reverse direction, change speeds or gears, or "move with the flow" seems essential if one is to break addictions, understand habits, contribute to a seemingly dying planet, and exert positive influence. It is of interest that three of the most popular dramatic productions in U.S. media—*It's a Wonderful Life, A Christmas Carol,* and (in theater) *Our Town*—use the same literary device to reveal the value of one individual's *influence.* In each case, the leading character is brought back—as if from the dead, by an angelic presence—to note with new eyes how his life affected others. Scrooge (in *A Christmas Carol*) realizes his destructive impact; Emily (in *Our Town*) realizes her prior insensitivity; Jimmy Stewart's character (in *It's a Wonderful Life*) wakes up to his own significance for those he supports.

Freedom of action implies that one may (and perhaps *must*) live as if one might die tomorrow. It implies the freedom to act with understanding, rather than with ignorance, about one's influence on others. Perhaps the three dramas cited above are popular because they remind us of our impotency when addicted to self-preoccupation and our potency when free of it. Fasting from any substitute for living can be liberating and empowering. The transition from consumer to creator can increase effectiveness and influence simultaneously.

However, total liberty to the contrary, I am not advocating abandoning *all* habits—such as swallowing food after chewing it or watching television right-side-up rather than on its side, so as to be "liberated." Liberation lies in the conscious inspection of *all* habits, not in the arbitrary changing of *any* of them.

If there can be media addiction, then there can also be media liberation. But media liberation does not necessarily mean liberation *from* mass communication. Rather, it means liberation from the rigid attitudes, manipulated emotions, frozen thoughts, assumed identities and truncated perspectives that both contribute to and result in media addiction.

However, addiction and habituation cannot be "conquered" by bold acts of revolution, glasnost or emancipation. The causes of addiction are often extremely deep—feelings of loneliness, alienation, worthlessness and emptiness do not completely vanish through symbolic gestures. Instead, it is consistent engagement in the creative process that allows such feelings to recede and be replaced with the joy of discovery, beauty, creation, engagement and self-worth.

The ultimate freedom rests in seeing that one has a choice—to identify with the creator or the consumer. Becoming the creator does not mean mindlessly bashing the media any more than mindlessly digesting it. In fact, one of the easiest, cheapest and most creative ways to publicize your liberation is to create a Web site or printed article about your creations.

BUT WHAT ABOUT THE CHILDREN?

In *The Journal of the American Academy of Child and Adolescent Psychiatry,* an article entitled "Pathological Preoccupation with Video Games" stated that some video-game manufacturers "deliberately promote habituation." A similar article, "No, You Can't Have Nintendo," published six months later in *Newsweek,* expressed concern that "killing" video games were proving far more attractive to children than "learning" video games, which seem boring by comparison. The Lloyd Garner article noted that one Los Angeles teacher even forbade his students to mention the word *Nintendo* because "that's all they were talking about." Concerns about children's habituation and addiction have become widespread.

Educators are disturbed because they see portable games replacing forgotten textbooks, both in the book bag and in the child's head. But this is just the tip of the iceberg: "As an educator, I'm concerned about growing childhood obesity and heart disease, which is often caused by a sedentary lifestyle," said Steve Schulten, a physical education teacher in Portsmouth, New Hampshire, "and I'm concerned that conversational English is declining because so many people just sit passively in front of their sets." (Gaines, 1995)

Many doctors are no less anxious. Susan Johnson, M.D., and Professor of Pediatrics (UCSF/Stanford) is concerned about media effects on children's moods, motor movements, play, nerves, imagination and thinking. Researchers, such as Healy (1990), Pearce (1992), Buzzell (1998) and Winn (1982) suggest that it is the actual act of viewing TV that is more damaging to brain development than TV content. Miles Everett, Ph.D., observes that we train children *not* to talk to strangers but every day we let total strangers from advertising agencies set standards for what is good, desirable and real inside children's brains and souls.

Healy's 1990 research suggests that television may be related to children's attention and learning difficulties. In one sense, TV is a multi-level form of sensory deprivation that may stunt the growth of children's brains. The combined research of Poplowski (1998), Gross (1999), Mander (1978), and Scheidler (1994) remind us that children are not just watching programs or surfing the Net, but are staring into flickering, radiant computer monitors and into fuzzy cathode-ray electron guns.

Johnson (1999) synthesizes this research to show what common sense might dictate: since repetitive screening allows functions of the corpus callosum, cortex, neocortex and limbic system to atrophy, children become more mentally lazy, uncoordinated and underdeveloped. She concludes that what children truly need to develop their minds are purposeful activities using their hands, feet and whole bodies; much exposure to nature and imaginative books; and much less media.

It is one thing for us to become media addicts ourselves, and another for us to allow such addiction among children. They are frequently not old enough to realize that childhood habits can last a lifetime and that media-controlled patterns in elementary school can mean drop-out or failure tendencies in high school or college. Over the years I have informally discovered a high correlation between students who are heavy media consumers and those who procrastinate, arrive late, submit poor assignments and flirt with failure.

More than anyone, parents and teachers may explain the difference between the "consumer" and the "creator" to children. The music classes, sports programs, summer camps, family outings, and educational or therapeutic hobbies in which we enroll our offspring pay lifelong dividends.

However, those who are addicted cannot bring others out of addiction. Since children are watching us for leadership and example, our own habits will loom large to them. In that regard, Ralph Waldo Emerson's persuasive quotation applies as much to what adolescents see in us as to what they see in the hidden optical patterns in TV, video and computer screens. Emerson stated: "Do not say things. What you are stands over you the while and thunders, so that I cannot hear what you say to the contrary."

CHAPTER FIVE

LESSONS FOR SOCIETY

Media Waste, Nuclear Waste, Wasted
Minds and the State of the Planet

At the outset, I stated that one purpose of the fast was "to save resources, money, space and time." In one sense, I meant this personally—I did, as an *individual*, conserve hours, dollars, battery life, electricity, mental and physical "space," paper, and much more during July. But in another sense, since no one is isolated from the universe, I had also meant that I would, in my own small way, be saving the *earth's* substance and resources as well.

Some of these savings are more readily seen at the *individual* level. For example, most adult individuals spend thousands of dollars each year on DVD and video rentals, software, Internet fees, movies; cable, magazine and newspaper subscriptions; book, tape, record and magazine acquisition; equipment, such as TV sets, satellite dishes, DVRs, radios, sound systems, CDs, lap tops, iPods, blackberries, cameras and accessories; electricity; and maintenance costs. Nor is such an expense ever complete. There are upgrades, maintenance plans, applications, new channels, memory sticks, power strips, warranties, and more. Most of us also spend as much time consuming media as we do in *any* other activity. If all this hard- and software could be converted to a single aggregate natural resource, we would discover that many of us consume more of it than we consume food.

Although price varies across countries and regions, the cost of major home acquisitions has grown from $400 U.S. for a large TV to $4,000 U.S. for a deluxe HDTV widescreen; $2,000+ for a good computer/color printer; $1,000 for a sound system; $1200 per year for mid-tier cable; $600 per year for moderate Internet (plus) provider; not to mention maintenance and keeping up with the neighbors. While some costs are dropping, the overall cost of owning an ensemble of gourmet en vogue media has risen sharply and will increase. Every year new products— digital cameras, intelligent agents, 900-channel satellite services, omni-platform (combine all media into one home system) packages, and desktop publishing software all compete for our attention.

Equipment owned by a standard TV- or radio station usually weighs more than all of the people within it. For that matter, the mass media (TVs, books, stereos, computers, etc.) stored in one home sometimes outweigh the occupants. Usually the floor space consumed by such media, although often transistorized, is greater than the floor space occupied by residents. Each American adult alone owns over five media machines, a fact easily grasped when one realizes that the typical single adult owns four *radios*—one in the car, one in the bedroom, and one at the office or one within the home entertainment system, or in the clock alarm, study or elsewhere.

The waste and unused capacity at this individual level is staggering. Consider, for example, a newspaper subscription owned by a single person or family. Less than one fifth of the average newspaper is actually *read*. Although much more is skimmed, frequently many entire sections are discarded, lump sum, into the garbage. In other sections, only headlines are given a cursory glance until eventually part of an article, cartoon or ad is digested.

Although families often read or browse through different parts of a newspaper, and while a few users read an entire paper, most newspapers are "sampled" by only one person (compare this to a well-circulated library book), if by anyone. Every day millions of surplus or unread newspapers are discarded as trash, many of which are not recycled. Multiply this individual waste by the three hundred and sixty-five times a year such papers are wasted.

To add to this, "Nothing is so old as yesterday's newspaper," as Harold Innis quipped. Once they are old hat, their relatively minuscule secondary use to line bird cages, doghouses and fireplaces does not alter the huge waste-to-use ratio. Sunday papers now weigh up to ten pounds each, only one pound of which is closely perused by many readers. Imagine how we might respond if most people threw out ninety percent of their groceries, spilt nine-tenths of their gas, or used only one room of their houses.

Even when a paper is read almost cover-to-cover, as smaller tabloids sometimes are, there is no guarantee that the quality, accuracy and originality (portions of papers are redundant of other information sources) of the *entire* product will educate, enhance or elevate the reader. Is padding, news filler, serialization (of stories in which nothing new has happened), inflating headline and photo size another form of waste?

So the individual reader of a newspaper might be said to ingest twenty percent of the *lean* part of a product, which is perhaps twenty percent to eighty percent *fat*—depending, of course, upon the paper. When viewed globally, this excessive newsprint (and magazine and book) consumption adds steadily to the depletion of forests which, in turn, threatens earth's supply of oxygen.

Other media permit us to be equally excessive, if not gluttonous. Millions of personal books sleep unread on dusty home library shelves, rather than circulate at public libraries; millions of unused radios are stored in drawers, attics and closets; and billions of Xeroxed pages, articles or chapters are discarded, permanently filed, or skimmed by one lone reader.

Consider the challenge facing institutions that try to meet the expectations of news consumers. When this book was written, one such paper, *The Washington Post*, in order to supply over eight hundred thousand weekday and one million one hundred thousand Sunday readers, was using over two hundred seventy thousand tons of newsprint each year. According to their own fact sheet, this annual consumption "is enough to encircle the globe 360 times." One way to visualize such a quantity is to envision that almost every day of the year, *Post* paperboys would paper the entire equator with its pages. If all the other publications printed on any given day were added to the process, the entire earth would be quickly papered daily. Perhaps such an image is an appropriate metaphor for what is actually happening through global deforestation.

At the time of writing this book, *The Washington Post* also spends over $3,000,000 per year on eight million pounds of ink. When it is considered that such ink is oil based, the oil spills of Exxon seem minuscule relative to those spilling opinion around the world by the press and by printers. Large quantities of metals, grease, plastic, chemicals, electricity, coffee and sugar are among the other resources consumed by newspaper institutions.

However, many products ingested by large media institutions are found almost universally throughout American society, and thus seem invisible. For example, media professionals, by and large, worship at the coffee urn. Coffee stands are topped with sugar, milk, cream substitutes, plastic stirring rods, and non-reusable paper, plastic or, more typically, Styrofoam cups. Styrofoam, in turn, is frequently reported by the same news institutions as a leading contributor to the earth's ozone contamination or depletion.

Of equal interest is the omnipresent telephone throughout the communication industries. *The Washington Post*, for example, houses sixty miles of telephone and twenty-four miles of Teletype cable within its headquarters. To follow those lines, which connect sixteen hundred telephones within that headquarters to nineteen bureaus, twenty-two foreign columnists, and thousands of sources, advertisers and customers daily, is an astronomical exercise. According to Pool's *Forecasting the Telephone*, such wiring on a global scale has frequently threatened the earth's *copper* supply and pricing.

Moreover, there is no disentangling the crossed lines of over-consumption by a variety of media institutions. Pool states that the telephone industry has also contributed to deforestation. As early as 1936, telephone *directories* were using twenty-five thousand tons of paper per year, and the large demand for telephone *poles* was already viewed as an eventual threat to the supply of suitable trees. Indeed, virtually all industries employ not only lumber but plastic, chemicals and metals for furniture, packaging, correspondence and equipment. No one escapes responsibility.

Waste is not confined to those who purchase supplies for newspapers. It is a way of life for most communication professionals: three *Post* photographers, for example, might be assigned to take nine hundred photos of a Washington Redskin football game, only one or two of which photos might actually be used. Although many internal items at some newspapers, including *The Post*, are recycled, nothing is more easily discarded than an internal memo, an in-house newsletter, or an extra napkin at the cafeteria. Multiply this process a million fold nationwide... and then there is the computer on every desk, the Teletype, the power needed for printing presses, diskettes, cartridges, office supplies and water.

I do not mean to single out *The Washington Post* but, rather, to ground my observations with at least one typical case study. Indeed *The Post* provides many valuable services of quality that might be better catalogued in another context. What seems more revealing than the amount of paper devoured by that paper, is the fact that the editor of *USA Today*, when asked, had *no* idea how much paper his national daily consumed. When presented this question in a room shared with other *USA Today* staff (which I observed as a guest), Peter Prichard replied "I doubt if *anyone* in this room knows the answer to how much paper we use."

There are no more attempts to scapegoat Prichard than Ben Bradley at *The Post* or the editors of *Time, Newsweek, The New York Times* or others. Many of Prichard's ideas and policies are impressive and he promised that his paper will eventually recycle. Nor is it worthwhile to condemn the newspaper for waste far larger than any single institution. Indeed, ignorance is abundant: newsletter, journal and magazine publishers seem little more aware of their own role in the state of the planet. Filmmakers and photographers, by and large, do not regard celluloid, negatives, and the chemicals used to develop them as potential toxic waste. Computer manufacturers may not regard themselves as accessories to earth rape by furthering the plastics explosion. Television and radio engineers probably have little idea that they are upping the voltage of a giant electric blanket of the air, which affects crops, livestock and, via cathode radiation, people. Finally, which industries, including mass media, do not contribute, in one way or another, to global pollution?

THE INTRICATE ECOLOGY

All of these spill-over effects are related to the growing list of global environmental concerns—resource depletion, the greenhouse effect, nuclear waste, oxygen suffocation, ozone contamination and destruction, acid rain, endangered and extinct species, nuclear arms, Omnipollution, overpopulation, hazardous waste, starvation, radiation leaks, economic fragility, and countless others. The combined interaction of these problems has moved beyond Meadows' warning about the limits to growth, to Maskell's caution about the limits of sustainability. Indeed many experts no longer debate *if* life as we know it is sustainable but, rather, debate *how long* it is sustainable.

A common bleak prediction is omnicide. For mass communicators the additional danger has been caused by the myth of journalistic apartheid. Since communicators often pose as neutral and emotionally distant commentators upon human activity, they frequently view themselves *apart from* rather than *a part of* the increasingly fragile human condition. The bogus but insightful headline "Earth to End Tomorrow—Pictures at 11" well illustrates the tragicomedy. In thinking themselves somehow amputated observers of mankind, communicators have been slow to notice their own functioning as an over-stimulated nervous system in the larger human body and as equal contributors to the issues and problems they report.

Ecologists are forever pointing out the subtle unity and intricacy of all life systems. Upsetting one system leads to devastation of another. This logic would lead to a less obvious "solution" to the present conundrum. If all systems are related, so too are their abuses. There is no point in treating each one—acid rain, hazardous waste, ozone depletion, etc.— piecemeal via separate conferences, commissions and isolated Band-Aid remedies. If the underlying causes of these problems are ultimately human avarice and fear, why not fast from those, rather than add to the array of solutions that create more problems?

PERSONAL RESPONSIBILITY

Observing excessive waste (such as homeless seaward garbage barges) raises questions about how much consumption is what Veblen called "conspicuous" and is what Pavlov called "conditioned." Similarly, fasting from spending, which I employ when approaching possible debt, raises the question of why nations cannot similarly hold back. That is, why not break the addiction to spending? Could not any such condition be reversed with sufficient self-control? Cannot fasting from any excess exert a counterbalancing vector to the seemingly dangerous vector called "runaway"—runaway economy, waste, information, speed-up or pollution? As Aristophanes depicted in *Lysistrata*, enough people making concrete changes in attitude and behavior can have profound influence upon any "runaway." In that theatrical case, women fasted from sex until their men agreed not to fight wars. The strategy proved effective.

If, for example, the entire global economy is a shaky house of cards resting upon the wobbly table of government loans and securities, why add more cards to the house or shake the table with increased debt and spending? Similarly, if global communication systems are reaching the point of human saturation and stripping the environment, why not pull back rather than add another two hundred channels? Why insist that scholars publish (more unread books) or perish rather than distribute their best work in simpler manner? If the white-collar world claims information is excessive, redundant, explosive and technical, why not abridge it and make it user-friendly? If all of these systems—economics, communication, environmental, etc.—are closely interrelated and their master system is close to collapse, why add to the overload of *any* system?

Thus the answer to Lenin's famous question "What is to be done?" is "*Internal* revolution"—pull back. Abstain from excess. Observe the situation carefully and consistently. Out-pressure any counter-veiling pressure. Hold steady. Communicate creatively and only as necessary. Assume total individual responsibility to follow through. Watch how this action is reflected in the larger environment, without becoming enamored with the results.

This process seems too simple to succeed. However, empirically and historically it is the other approaches that have failed. To follow the approaches that have produced failure at this point in our history would guarantee mega-failure.

What viable alternatives exist? Dreamers always maintain that new technologies will solve our geometrically increasing problems. For example, fiber optics will solve the need for more copper in telephone wiring. Electronic news will now fully replace the newspaper. All will be well!

Historically, such an approach has proven comical. Have contraceptives that were developed to curb overpopulation been effective or free of unexpected effects? Have explosives, theoretically invented to assist in mining, been free of other uses? Did the airplane, in helping us go everywhere faster, create a safer, quieter, cleaner world? Has replacing steam transportation with oil energy improved the planet? Has evolution from horsepower to nuclear power cur(b)ed world problems? Will fiber optics and electronic news require *no* natural resources, bring *no* unforeseen effects, and remain incorruptible by mankind?

The individual-responsibility approach begins with the premise that I have neither credibility nor effectiveness without practicing *before* I preach. Indeed, preaching is often self-defeating. For example, what authority would this book have if I had not actually conducted fasts? What credibility would this chapter have if I had not consistently compressed and abridged chapters to save paper, ink, glue, and our mutual time and money?

Similarly, what is the effectiveness and authority of nuclear protesters, who themselves radiate poisonous attitudes? What is the impact of those who join movements to save the whales but forget to feed their cats? who fight for peace? who babble to sort out the confusion? who communicate to cover their own inner voice? who kill to live? who pollute to progress? who destroy to build? who gobble media to think freely?

Such questioning catalyzed my fasting. After all, how may I speak to the question of overconsumption as one who is mentally fat? This overarching vision—that substance outweighs surface—was inherent in the little-understood dictum that "All the world's in your own back yard" and was the cornerstone for the most famous speech of all time—Russell Conwell's "Acres of Diamonds." In essence, if the entire world *is* contained in one's living, then environmental alternatives begin with my sending more succinct memos, photocopying only according to need, and utilizing the backside of used syllabi and handouts as scrap paper.

In this full assumption of personal responsibility, one widespread addiction to be broken is the customary belief in a controlling "they." "They"—usually the government, all media, some hidden conspiracy, or society are at fault for the insane global condition. However, ultimately, I have found no "they." When visiting *The Washington Post, The New York Times* and *USA Today*, each person I met breathed the same air I did. She could just as easily have been, in another context, a parent of one of my students, a fellow juror serving trial duty, or a customer standing in line with me at a supermarket. "They" dissolve into "us" when a larger perspective is employed.

Even if "they" do, at *one* level, seem to exist as autonomous minds and bodies, how could I possibly change them other than through my example? A parent quickly learns that children imitate what is done, rather than obey what is said. And the mass media are particularly noted for observing this distinction between verbiage and behavior, for peering behind our outer front into our private actions. Politicians, celebrities, athletes and public spokespersons know this syndrome only too well. Cover-up, camouflage, evasive rhetoric, sunglasses, official releases and public statements are red flags to journalists.

Thus, unless I implement what I advocate, I have little chance of communicating with influence. Ultimately, my audience will doubt me, the media will expose me, and even my children will replicate my hypocrisies.

In 1983 I started an informal organization based upon this simple premise: If I wish to see a more responsible media, I and those who join the organization must first be responsible ourselves. That philosophy found application in this manner: If I object to the sensationalism of tabloids, such as *The National Enquirer*, I must stop gossiping. If I become tired of journalists taking target practice at world leaders, I must examine my own attitude toward leadership, or for that matter toward these leading journalists. If I am concerned that media addiction is becoming the largest dependency of the 1990s, why not limit my own consumption or experiment with fasting?

As the organization grew to include worldwide membership, a president (Barbara Coffman); co-sponsors and co-hosts, such as AT&T, the Radio Television News Directors Association, the National Academy of Television Arts and Sciences; and advisors, such as Vladimir Pozner and Bruce Allyn, we kept this assumption central. No matter how visible or transparent our activities, we maintained the notion that "this is an inside job." To restate that view in suitable terms for more adversarial lobbying groups who were crusading after some scapegoat—advertisers, producers, liberal or conservative writers, the FCC, etc.—to blame, our motto would read "We have seen the adversary...and they are us." Instead of becoming another vigilante corps tilting with corporate windmills, we elected to support whatever *positive* utterance we heard in all forms of communication—producers with integrity, programs of quality, writers of vision, inspiring musicians, and anyone who backed their words and work with consistent living.

Such an approach grounded in individual responsibility seemed opposite McLuhan's view that it is media, and not we ourselves, who create our consciousness and social patterns. Indeed, what I am saying seems to also contradict other leading voices in mass communication studies of our day—Goodman, Christians, Gerbner, Postman, Meyrowitz and others—who have noted that mass communication has pronounced impact on our way of seeing and acting.

However, as the first chapters of this book indicate, I strongly endorse such conclusions. Unless and until individual responsibility is fully assumed by large numbers of people, we *will* believe our own fantasies writ large, we *will* become dependent upon intriguing toys of perception, and we *will* swim in a program-infested collective subconscious. Unless the single switch is made, we will be bought and paid for frequently within the accelerating whirlwind of changing media ownership.

WASTED MINDS

One often hears the conventional folk wisdom that we human beings only use three percent of our brains. Whatever the actual figure, I wonder if most of what is used stores old episodes of TV shows, radio promos, ads, cyber-junk and pop tunes.

In the previous chapter, a selected survey of research was presented which suggested that children's minds may lay dormant, damaged or developmentally retarded due to excessive exposure to media. But it is not only children who are vulnerable to media-induced epilepsy. What Emery (1986) calls "cortical slowing" has shown a relationship between the brain's inability to process either radiant light or excessive signals and the TV cathode ray tube (CRT). Amalgamating research by Sommerhat, Silberstein and others, Emery noted that the CRT (television) epilepsy is not restricted to epileptics. As we innocently stare into a mosaic of dots, our brains are scrambling to make sense of them.

Lawless (1977) demonstrated how our blindness to hidden technology effects might prove hazardous to society. He cited one hundred examples of how a new technology or product created an environmental, genetic or public health disaster. The birth defects caused by herbicides and thalidomide, the cancer associated with hexachlorophine "wonder soap," the lung cancer associated with asbestos, and on and on, are well documented. As Clendenning (1990) put it after studying DES, Agent Orange, toxic waste and related problems, "Our health is traded off for the economic health of corporations." Why then should it surprise us that computer radiation may be related to birth defects, cell phones to possible brain cancer, flash animation viewing to epilepsy, and headsets to loss of hearing?

Mander (1991), who initially introduced arguments for the elimination of television and of advertising, has now launched a campaign against the computer. He is concerned that, due to the high volume of acids and solvents used by computer manufacturers, related occupational illnesses are three times higher than those of other manufacturers. The acids disposed of in toxic dumps, and the trichloroethylene leaked into Silicon Valley drinking water, remind us that little within the cyberworld is environmentally friendly.

Far more concerns about the computer appear in Mander's *In the Absence of the Sacred*. Citing the type of surveillance, centralization, rate of acceleration, automatic global warfare, conceptual change, personnel layoffs, quantification and health hazards already associated with computers, he wonders out loud if they do not cause far more harm than good.

However, computers are just the front office of a crumbling skyscraper that disturbs Mander—technology. He argues that society does not know how to test new or existing technologies: immense unwanted side (or full frontal) effects show up years after a new technology is introduced.

Part of the problem is that we suffer from "technology somnambulism." Since manufacturers introduce new technologies in their very best light, we sleepwalk into the future. Once asleep, we are numbed to the reality that techno-optimism is created by those with a vested interest.

Although we would never buy new foods or drugs that had not been tested by the FDA, we rush out to buy the latest communication device, often due to advertising. By and large, we have little or no awareness of what kind of virus, environmental damage or health hazard it might bring.

What is most troubling about the lack of testing is that it is coupled with the lack of thinking. Canadian biochemist Ross Hume Hall in *Food for Nought* (1974) revealed that most food testing analyzes only one food additive at a time. Hall's research showed that when two or more additives are introduced into a food, they may create untested and unexpected toxic or nauseous by-products.

Hall also noted that short-term testing usually will not detect the gradual buildup of carcinogens that become multi-generational. In other words, a food preservative might test harmless. But the buildup of that preservative in a mother could unexpectedly damage her unborn child ten years later, or her granddaughter forty years hence.

Attempts to test the media environment have proven equally

shortsighted. The personal computer's real effects (eye diseases, brain tumors, ADD, who knows?) may not show up for another two or three decades.

Similarly, the real social problems associated with media may not show up in one media additive alone. Often it is the interplay of media, rather than one technology, which creates a transformed social climate. Application of the Ross Hume Hall effect suggests that the combined effect of BlackBerries, satellites, fax, PCs, DVDs, VCRs, cable, the Internet, print, audio, ATMs, intelligent agents, et al—is vastly different from the sum of their parts.

The new media ecology is constantly changing. Since multiple media signals saturate the polluted ocean in which we swim, it is hard for us to see clearly through the water to conduct tests above sea level. To think about all this, we must empty our minds of stored laugh tracks and dialog, to let them fill with fresh insights and key questions.

BEYOND THEORY

For many years, scholars in my field have bemoaned the lack of a comprehensive theory that accounts for the nature of communication. After all, Smith, Ricardo, Marx and others undergird economics. Weber, Parsons and James, among others, bolster sociology.

If I were to construct such a theory of mass communication, it would show that implements of communication, which Innis and others posited as *primary* forces of history, are only *tertiary*. Human beings have in fact been the *secondary* forces that create and maintain technologies of communication. It has always amazed me that theorists have given printing presses and televisions the full weight of Aristotle's *first* and *formal* cause; that is, of stating that these machines *cause* everything that happens.

Moving beyond theory to reality, I have never been able to find a media machine that created a person but have known many human beings who produced or manufactured media equipment and programming. In my study of communication history, I have not discovered one word or implement of communication not attributed initially to consciousness.

109

Looking strictly at the evidence and the laws of physics, media-centric cosmologies seem to adopt the nature of the media they worship—that is, both are tempting fantasies.

Individual actions and responsibility allow people to play this secondary role of creating tertiary media. People who abandon awareness, however, and become sleepwalkers, find themselves enslaved by the mesmerizing nature of media. The hypnotized subject will believe one fiction as easily as another. In ceasing to create, such a subject is created in the likeness of his teachers, electronic or otherwise.

The *primary* force of creation is neither human beings nor their artifacts. It is, rather, what Shakespeare called "a tide in the affairs of men," what Hegel posited as "the forces of history" and Bergson called *élan vital*. That is, the animating force *behind* human behavior—by whatever name it is known—creates forms that include both humans and their technologies.

Those who lean toward the metaphysical and theological end of the spectrum have always labeled such a force, or forces, by some divine title, such as God, the Gods, Source, or similar. Toward the more empirical end of the spectrum, scientists have employed terminology, such as the laws of physics, the principals of nature, or universal forces. Philosophers have sought to surround the phenomenon with terms such as *ontology*, *being*, *essence*, *substance* and *existence*.

I am not so much interested in naming this ubiquitous energy as in viewing it as primary to communication. If Einstein was correct that energy and mass are constantly changing place beyond our perception, it is foolish to insist that either we or our artifacts control the weave of life. Both are one.

At this point we realize that, in one way or another, *all* theory is speculation. In moving beyond theory, one returns to the authority of *what is* over human guesses at *what seems to be*. Given the limitations of our senses, inventions, the astigmatic nature of our perception, and both the enormity and eternity of that surrounding us, theory seems overrated.

TO PRACTICE

Grounding theory in practice implies that the end of this chapter should come full circle to its practical beginning. At this moment, enough nuclear warheads, pollution, resource rape, famine, war, deforestation, hazardous waste, nuclear spills and other conditions exist to dwarf other subjects and concerns by comparison. All the information, theory, technology and culture currently being developed will come to naught if we continue to avoid personal change or cling to studying just one piece of the puzzle. In the age of Al Gore, the media themselves proclaim this *Inconvenient Truth*.

Personal responsibility means making *current* changes. For example, I had originally intended this to be three books: one for the general public, one for teachers leading classes on media fasts, and a third for their students. It now seems much more practical and more respectful of our friends, the trees, to compress the three projects into one.

I had also planned originally to make each chapter about the same length, for the sake of continuity and style. Indeed I have more notes to develop to form a conclusion to this chapter, which would enlarge it to the average length of other chapters.

However, upon close inspection I note that much of what I have to say could already be inferred from what has been said. If I am genuinely interested in saving your time and mine, in saving resources such as pulp and ink, in empowering thought with action, in saying only what needs to be said, and in letting my microcosm of behavior influence the macro-mess, why not bring change now, rather than fantasize about a changed tomorrow? Why not end this chapter *now*?

PART III

GROUP FASTING

CHAPTER SIX

GROUP FASTING

Taking Your Group, Family or Class On a Fast

As you will see in the chapters that follow, group abstinence is neither new nor temporary. As Chapter Seven details, some subcultures—such as the Plain People (Amish, Old Order Mennonite, Hutterite, etc.)— avoid all electronic media as part of their way of life. Others, such as the Dani people of Irian Jaya and the Rapa Nui of Easter Island, have unique minimal media contact and are the subjects of Chapter Eight.

This chapter is about more temporary group fasting, such as experiments by community groups, families and classes. As in Chapters One and Two, I provide practical tips for informal experimentation; only in this case you can cluster with friends, family or peers.

COMMUNITY GROUP EXPLORATION

A wide diversity of groups may explore media abstinence. Civic, religious, organizational, hobby, and other groups—from a Boy Scout pack to a bowling league, from a knitting circle to a Young Democrats club—may explore fasting.

There are unlimited creative approaches. For example, one seniors community group met twice per week. They would see a play on a Friday night, then discuss how it differed from the movie version on Monday night. The following Friday night they would attend a children's ballet (one couple had grandchildren participating), and then Monday they would discuss the differences between the live and televised ballet they had seen prior to the fast. To break with routine, they then took a guided bus tour to a famous Civil War historical site. The following Monday night, they discussed and compared their previous *media-made* impressions of the Civil War.

Not every group can devote as much time and money to the experiment. But a tried-and-true formula for most groups is to read one chapter of this book per week and meet, say, every Tuesday or Wednesday, to discuss insights and breakthroughs.

Each group can customize the experience to their own approach. For example, Rotarians meet for lunch and feature weekly guest speakers. So one week they coordinate the fast with the guest appearance of a local television producer, who speaks on "fast media," and the next week they feature a neighboring monk, who speaks on what it is like to fast full-time. Meanwhile, an overall fast/study leader from the Rotary Club coordinates the actual experiment.

Many groups, from bridge clubs to prisoners, seek an interesting change of pace from their routines. Social clubs and hobby groups (from the Audubon Society to elite blue-blood societies) may already have members who are media teetotalers.

One of the easiest ways to conduct a group fast is to follow the outline of this book. Participants should read the Introduction and first two chapters during three consecutive meetings prior to the experiment. During that time the group leader should make clear the type (blackout, fast, diet) of experiment the group will conduct or explain that every step may be debated and decided democratically. Whether to break into subgroups, include a speech fast, invite spouses or guests to participate, or plan field trips in advance are all questions for the group leader, which she in turn may wish to discuss with the group.

It is important for group leaders to be flexible. People occasionally must fly out of town for emergencies or forget to bring their diaries to meetings. Sometimes a participant will forget she is even on a media fast for five to ten minutes and habitually listen to the car radio. It is not appropriate to chastise the person but more important that she realize *why* she unintentionally broke the fast, and let the group learn from the experience.

Sometimes, especially in extreme situations, participants with great impatience, withdrawal symptoms or antisocial personalities will criticize the group leader or the experiment. It is useful to welcome their feedback, consider it, and, at the same time, remind them that abstinence is not for everyone and that the rewards of fasting are not usually immediate. Sometimes it is important to make adjustments to truly hear and consider a participant's perspective and dilemma, such as a student with a media-addicted, insensitive roommate. When the leader is malleable, typically (almost) everyone completes the fast and reports a victory. The success of any group situation is almost always in direct proportion to the preparation, pro-social methods and fluidity of the leader.

FAMILY FASTS

Family fasts seem different from others, since participants usually share more daily contact. Indeed, if the family decides to go camping or traveling for their adventure, they may well be in close proximity most of the time.

Consequently, there is opportunity for daily learning, work, play, creativity and exploration. If alone in the woods, a family may learn about a different animal, plant or natural wonder each day. They may pitch tents, cook, play games, take silent nature walks, canoe, work out family problems, create and tell ghost stories, learn self-defense, enjoy astronomy by night, and explore dozens of other activities.

Fasting at home is an entirely different experience. Visible computers, CD players, TVs and radios seem to cry out for attention. Neighbors and friends will invite you into their noise-filled homes. But a home fast can be productive if at least two family members work together. When only one is an enthusiast, she or he may come across like a dictator ripe for assassination.

Questions about "what to do" in a home family fast are more easily answered after reading an excerpt from an *Atlanta Constitution* article by John Rosemond.

The next time your child watches television, look at him instead of the screen. Ask yourself, "What is he doing?" Better yet, since chances are he won't be doing much of anything, ask yourself, "What is he not doing?" In answer, he is <u>not</u> scanning; practicing motor skills, gross or fine; practicing eye-hand coordination; using more than two senses; asking questions; exploring; exercising initiative or motivation; being challenged; solving problems; thinking analytically; exercising imagination; practicing communication skills; being either creative or constructive. Also because of TV's insidious flicker (every four seconds on the average, and laterally in time, not to mention from subject matter to subject matter), television does not promote logical sequential thinking.

So what? Well, interestingly enough, the deficiencies noted above are characteristic of learning disabled children; children who don't seem able to "get it all together" when it comes to learning how to read and write. Since 1955 (about the time television became a mainstay in our children's lives), learning disabilities have become epidemic in our schools.

If a TV child is deprived of all these activities, a fast provides a great opportunity to focus upon them. Games, conversations, sports and activities that emphasize questions, motor skills, personal imagination, solving problems, using more than two senses, being challenged, practicing communication skills, creating et al are essential to counterbalance the hours, days, months or years that children, if not all of us, waste.

Family fasts require additional planning, since there may be multiple ages or even generations involved. Some of the reported activities families have chosen to experience include a whale watch, making a tree house, co-authoring a poem, playing miniature golf, compiling journal entries into a book, worshipping, singing, playing card games, enjoying badminton, using board games, planning family events, playing horseshoes, building an igloo, cleaning the attic, phoning sick relatives, hosting a party, volunteering together for charity work, attending a town meeting, writing letters to old friends, making an ice-cream bar for supper dessert, taking everyone shopping, donating toys to an orphanage, enrolling in a wine-tasting course (not for *younger* families), visiting a carnival, seeing the zoo, creating a garden, writing and staging a skit, perusing family photo albums, writing letters to the city council about neighborhood issues, co-authoring a family declaration of purpose, and taking a trip to Disneyland.

It is important that adults not only supervise but also learn from the experience. If everyone (old enough to write) keeps a diary and talks about her own feelings and thoughts, the adults will model what is required for other family members.

Within some families there may be children too young to comprehend this book. Adults should thoroughly explain the highlights of Chapters One and Two; and then, should they choose, lead discussions periodically based on the appendices and other chapters. Since family habits run deep, due to years of programming, explaining forthcoming behavior changes is not enough. It is essential that adults iterate and demonstrate all new paths of discovery.

Sometimes a small group can create group purposes, guidelines and ground rules (see Chapter One), rather than ask individuals to do so. If that approach is taken, it is not a bad idea to tape these common goals to the door, or wherever they may be seen, so that periodically they may be read aloud or skimmed by passersby.

Upon completing a family fast, it is great to have some form of celebration—eating out, throwing a (music at last!) party, or even watching your favorite TV show (finally!). However, preceding the bash or binge, it is wise to conduct a final conversation about what you have learned, what changes you will make, and even who you are as a family (or similar). A final talk *in depth* can be healthy, bonding and empowering.

CLASS FASTS: TIPS FOR THE TEACHER

Some aspects of your media fast will depend upon the age, number and media habits of your students. Other aspects may depend upon how often your class meets, whether you choose to make this primary or secondary curriculum, and how formal or scientific you wish your methods to be.

Much of the fast will also depend upon how well you know your students and their age group, and thus have a feel for how much freedom vs. control to extend throughout the experiment. Only you know how much homework they can handle, at what intervals, and with what degree of commitment.

However, whether your students are in graduate school or are sixth graders, there are many common questions all teachers will want to answer when designing the fast. Reading the checklist in Appendix One (for the general reader) should help. Rereading the introduction and the first two chapters, particularly the sections on purpose, motivation, ground rules and guidelines, should also be helpful.

Since you and this book are already present, let's examine your respective roles first. How much do you wish to utilize this book and what will your role be in discussing it? For example, with many high school, college and graduate-level students you may want them to read the entire book before the fast. On the other hand, since I have divided the book into logistical (Introduction and Chapters One, Two and Six) and essay/discussion chapters (Three through Five, Nine and Ten), you may wish to read and discuss the Introduction and the first two chapters before the fast. If so, then it is wise to conduct the fast while discussing the other chapters during and following the fast.

If your students are in elementary or junior high school and you sense that parts of the book are beyond their reach, you may wish to try another approach, such as to use the book as a springboard for a series of handouts at their level. Or you may choose to read only the essential sections of this book in class. You may wish to simplify the entire text into an exercise manageable for their age group or have them read the book alternately aloud in class and discuss new words and concepts.

However you use the book, you will need to determine if it is required reading, suggested, or whether you will paraphrase it for their level.

Your personal action as a teacher is significant. If you have already conducted a fast, the teaching will naturally carry more weight and credibility. You will also need to decide whether you wish to fast during the class fast, so as to genuinely relate to their experiences. Or you might prefer to be a media user during the fast, so as to be a comparative voice or to debate with students or inform them about what they are missing or simply be a different frame of reference.

You, or some of your students, might wish to role-play the parts of media owners and producers. Being a devil's advocate for those who might disapprove of media fasting can create thoughtful controversy. It is always fun to have young surrogate celebrities in the room, whether Bill Gates, Ted Turner, Sherry Lansing or others.

Methods require advance consideration. Will you want the entire class to take the fast? Or should part continue their normal habits to serve as a control group? Would you learn much if half fasted from electronic media and the other half from print? There are many creative possibilities. Do you wish to give students the option of *not* fasting? What might prejudice their experience? Would reading the entire book before the fast tend to set up expectations that could bias their findings? Must you as teacher be careful not to say *too* much prior to the fast, which might influence their expectations? Should they refrain from discussing their experiences with others during the fast, lest their discoveries foster imitation? Or would such discussions during the fast help students learn what to look for and help them better articulate a new idea?

In rereading Chapter 2, note that you will wish to help focus group thought at three different times: 1) before 2) during and 3) after the fast. Will you wish to make up a handout on each of these three areas? or lead discussions then? or reread those three sections of Chapter Two out loud or as homework?

If you do wish to work with the class at all three stages, be sure to cover the following areas beforehand: purpose, motivation, ground rules, guidelines, methods (will notebooks or dairies be used? graded?

how?), length, assignment length and due date, and all questions raised by students.

During the fast you may wish to use five types of questions to provoke discussion, help catalyze thought about their home experience, or to be completed for homework. These are:

1. Questions raised throughout this book: every chapter has "question clusters," which are easily spotted by the question marks at the end of several consecutive sentences.

2. Similar questions not found in the book but which *you generated* when reading this book or during your fast.

3. Queries I have designed for student exercises, term papers, dissertations, etc. (to be individually approved by you) in Appendix II at the end of this book.

4. Questions that the students themselves raise during the experiment, possibly through moments of debate or discovery.

5. More personal questions, designed to make sure they are comprehensively monitoring their fasting experience. Such questions might include: "Are you discovering media residue or afterimages playing in your head?" "What programs or habits seem to be nagging at you or tempting you?" "How would you best describe any new experiences?" "Are there any changes in your schedule? activity?"

After the fast, you may pose other questions about the nature of their "reentry," about comparing before with after, about how media now seem, about whether old habits seem to be returning or if they are more selective, restrained, etc. After the fast, you will also wish to determine how they will best present their highlights to the class. Will they sit in a circle while you call on people to answer specific questions? Or will each make a brief presentation (be careful about endless redundancies)? Will you set up debates about the value of the experiment or, at a larger level, about whether society needs mass media or similar? There are many options here and much space for imaginative pedagogy.

Diaries may be collected for grading or used for oral presentations, in which students briefly share their "purple passages" (i.e., most interesting material). They may have tape-recorded or even videotaped their projects, created dramatic or other formats, or divided into team debates. Inspiring them to make their summary projects creative, thought-provoking and engaging is essential.

You may wish to use tally methods in class. For example, you might choose to ask:

1. How many feel that you discovered you had an "addiction," based on the book's definition of the term?

2. How many of you feel you discovered you were "habituated" to a mass medium, based on the book's definition?

3. How many felt you were neither addicted nor habituated to any mass medium?

4. How many of you are uncertain as to how to answer these questions? Why?

You may wish to design other surveys, informal polls, formally scrupulous empirical questionnaires, or "voting" methods to give to the class. If you used a control group, you can contrast the findings between groups and share the statistics with the entire class. Naturally, I would appreciate a copy of your results and methods.

If you discover that your first media fast has some methodological glitches or that some questions do not appeal to your students, note these limitations as feedback. Before trying the fast with another class or section, make the necessary adjustments, possibly deleting or changing the parts that were the least effective.

Over the semesters or years, you might wish to alter the fast in a variety of ways. For example, you may elect to divide your class into five groups, one fasting from film and video (visuals); another from all tapes, radio, CDs, etc. (audio); a third from books, magazines and newspapers (print); and a fourth from speech. The fifth group might serve as a control by continuing their media as usual.

You may wish to try the fast with different students at different ages or stages or in a different context. Adding field trips, lengthening the fast, and varying the media mix also provide engaging opportunities.

You might also elect to utilize different types or lengths of fasting yourself or encourage such activity among individual students, say as an independent study, "over-the-summer homework" for an exceptional student, informal optional assignments, one of many options for term papers, etc. Since the fast itself is not as important as the thinking it inspires, it might be useful to follow up each fast with discussions of the essay chapters of this book, say reading one per class or per week, depending upon the age and aptitudes of your group.

Students may also wish to read some of the other books to which I refer; for example, Postman's *Amusing Ourselves to Death*, Meyrowitz's *No Sense of Place*, Huxley's *Brave New World*, Heidegger's *What Is Called Thinking* (for more advanced students), Buber's *Elements of the Interhuman*, and many others. In a two hundred-page bibliography, *TV and Ethics* (G. K. Hall, Boston), which I co-authored in 1988, at least one tenth of the eleven hundred entries refer to some of the issues raised in this book. Indeed, so much has been written about media effects, media ethics, mass communication and society, journalism ethics, etc., that this fast could spark a reading list which could easily take a term, year, or graduate literature review to complete.

Naturally, as a teacher myself, I greatly respect your insight, creativity and personal autonomy in the classroom. Hence all the suggestions above are intended simply as starting points for thought. As you think, fast and experiment, many other creative teaching ideas should emerge. I would be grateful to hear from you about these, about your classroom experiences and about your own observations and findings. I will conclude below with a few of the pedagogical techniques that have worked best for me during twelve years of experimentation.

MY APPROACH

After years of trial and error, I have discovered that dividing a class into three groups works best. One third take the practical media fast; one third choose a specific media diet; the final third serve as a control group by keeping detailed diary notes about their ongoing media activity.

Please note that this approach only works if you have fifteen or more students in the class. Groups with fewer than five students each are poorly represented on days of poor attendance. If you have a smaller group, you might try dividing into two groups—one as a control group to those who take the practical fast.

When I use the five-week approach, students cover two chapters per class as homework while working simultaneously on their diaries. They must read the first two chapters immediately preceding the experiment. During each class every student must make a two-minute presentation about specific questions drawn from homework and include a brief check-in about overall experience. During the class break I spot-check all class diaries and help students with their questions.

Because students know that both their diaries and their participation will be graded, they take the experiment seriously. They also realize that they must give an intelligent update during each class, which incorporates the latest reading. Consequently, both their reading and their diaries are typically completed on time.

Although I understand the rationales of very strict and very relaxed teachers, my approach to the fast is moderate and case-by-case. It is reasonable to give students as much choice as possible about which group they will enter and to grant exceptions to some of the rules—after all, some students work in video or computer stores, TV stations and movie theaters. On the other hand, unless you set and enforce a high expectation level for individual participation at the outset, you will find some students taking major shortcuts.

When students give summary presentations during the final class, we review the most intriguing conversation points, such as the "five freedoms" (Chapter Four), a composite list of what they have saved (Chapter Five), and discussion of how their thinking and lives might change (Chapter Ten). Each student takes notes about what the others have learned and are aware that a final examination question could derive from the aggregate group learning.

Consequently, each student pays close attention to the others.

Every student is important. The first two weeks of any experiment I deliberately arrive early and stay late to have quick one-on-one sessions with each person. Some need questions answered; others need a word of inspiration; still others wish a sounding board for ideas and insights.

It is essential that each student realize that what is important is the restoration of her own independent thinking process. So the teacher must emphasize that, in one sense, there are no homogenized "right answers" or perfect experiences to be had on any given day.

What is far more important is that each student use the experiment to truly *think*, rather than regurgitate answers, whether from electronic media or from standard textbooks. The true goal of group fasting is to retrieve and transmit *le gai savoir*, the joy of learning.

CHAPTER SEVEN

GROUPS THAT PERMANENTLY FAST

The Amish and Other Plain People

Throughout the world many groups of people permanently fast from mass media. For some the word *fast* may be inappropriate because they have little or no awareness that media exist. Such groups include highly remote Pacific Islanders, the Kogi people of Columbia, and other isolated indigenous communities discussed in the next chapter.

For others, such as many varieties of Plain People, abstinence from most media is a deliberate practice. The most widely publicized Plain People are the Old Order Amish, famous for their horse-and-buggy transportation, uniform sober clothing and beards. In Pennsylvania, in Lancaster County alone there are twenty-two distinct groups of Amish, Mennonite and Brethren that abstain from virtually all electronic media. (Kraybill and Scott, 1984; Scott, 2000) Television, film, radio, VCRs, CDs, audiotapes and the Internet are forbidden, although some communities accept limited or full use of the computer and telephone.

Unlike the media fasts taken by urban vacationers, the Amish, many Mennonites and some Brethren have been abstaining from mass-media consumption for decades. Six important questions about this fasting and these groups will be considered in this chapter: 1) Who are the Plain People? 2) To what extent do the twenty-two selected groups use mass media? 3) What are their theological justifications for fasting? 4) What are their other reasons for abstaining? 5) What if these Plain People are right? 6) What may we learn from them?

WHO ARE THE PLAIN PEOPLE?

From a distance the Plain People seem like one homogenized American counterculture that shuns all technology, preserves ancient agricultural and social European traditions, and adheres to one narrow dress code. However, in truth there are Plain People in numerous countries with many shadings of lifestyle, theology and wardrobe. What they share in common are European Reformation ancestors who fled religious persecution to establish isolated farming communities. Given the large scope of Plain sects and resettlement, this research will focus upon only those groups in Lancaster County, Pennsylvania, which abstain from electronic media.

The Amish take their name from their seventeenth-century leader Jacob Amman and are the largest and most socially conservative group of Plain People. (Scott, 1988) Although all Amish disdain electronic media, progressive (Beachy and New Order) Amish groups have adopted electricity and some basic electronic technologies.

Mennonites take their name from leader Menno Simons, who converted from Catholicism to Anabaptism in 1536. (Durnbaugh, 1968) Like the Old Order Amish, Old Order Mennonites maintain a horse-and-buggy lifestyle, while some reformist, more urban Mennonite communities use cars and media.

The Brethren movement started in Germany in 1708. Due to their practice of baptism by immersion, they received the nicknames "Dunker" and "Dunkard" (Scott, 1988). Although some branches of Brethren faith have embraced modernity, the Old German Baptist Brethren (excepting some of their youth) shun electronic media. Although treated as kindred in this essay, the River Brethren/Brethren in Christ family of churches and the Dunker/Church of the Brethren churches are distinct groups.

All three groups—the Amish, Mennonites and Brethren—are classified as Anabaptists (rebaptizers) because their founders advocated that each individual should freely choose baptism as an adult, rather than be involuntarily baptized as an infant. The three traditions may also be categorized by what Max Weber called "the believers' church," a "community of personal believers who are 'reborn.'" (Durnbaugh, 1968)

Of the many tenets shared by believers' churches, two which help to explain media avoidance are 1) separation from the world and 2) scripture-based heritage. The believers' interpretation of scripture, and need to be isolated from worldly values, are key factors in their condemning of electronic media.

"Plain Peoples" have received their name from their belief in utmost simplicity, humility, sobriety and a distinct dress. Jewelry, makeup, fashionable clothing and amusements all detract from a climate of simplicity and piety. Thus radio, television, the Internet and film also pollute such an atmosphere of silence and the sacred.

Perhaps the best known and most diversified clustering of Old Order groups exists in Lancaster County, Pennsylvania, where over eleven thousand Plain People have banned electronic media. The attitude of these seeming social hermits might best be described in this discipline of the Old Order Mennonite Church: "Let us be plain and humble in our homes, clothing, carriages, and everything we own." (Kraybill, 1998)

WHICH PLAIN PEOPLE USE WHICH MEDIA?

Although many progressive Mennonite and Brethren congregations permit the use of electronic media, there are twenty-two sub-groups, (including all Amish groups in Lancaster County and many others elsewhere), which do not. Some groups ban only the visual media (TV, computers, film, photography) and at least two Old Brethren groups are in a transition period in which many of their youth listen to radio. (Kraybill and Scott, 1984; Scott, 2000) Not surprisingly, there is a high correlation between those who abstain from electronic media and who also ban automobiles, musical instruments and many automated conveniences.

Not all technologies are treated identically by these groups. For example, debate about photography has led to a mixture of acceptance and rejection in different Amish, Brethren and Mennonite settlements. (Kraybill and Scott, 1984) Similarly, telephone use is neither universally adopted nor, where used, universally domestic. Some groups restrict the use of the telephone to businesses or to telephone booths at the end of farm lanes. (Umble, 1996) Tape players, although banned by some groups, have been used to record sermons and *a cappella* music by others. (Scott, 1996)

Other media have had a checkered career. For example, the largest group of Mennonites took a strong stand against radio in the 1920s, experimented with limited radio programming of their own in 1936, despite controversy, then finally sanctioned and fully utilized radio in the 1950s. Similarly, in some Mennonite groups—although television was banned in the 1940s—TV was clandestinely watched in attics and basements throughout the 1950s, until some groups lifted the ban in the 1960s. (Scott, 1996)

The computer had an innocent introduction within many groups but was later proven guilty by association. In the Old Order context, computer monitors resembled television and could house video games and film, all of which were persona non grata. (Kraybill, 1989) Moreover, by the 1990s Old Order groups had heard about the Internet and did not want the serpent that brought this venom onto their property. However, in many communities compromises have been made: several groups allow word processors, and still others permit business computers that are not linked, or restrictively linked, to the Internet.

More than any other media, print—newspapers, magazines and books—have been acceptable in Old Order life. Indeed, to outlaw print would mean to ban the Bible and other pillar texts, upon which Plain life is established. Old Order groups have their own internal publications; i.e., weekly newspapers such as *The Budget* and *The Message* (*Die Botschaft*), which differ greatly from most outside publications. For example, in the outside world news is usually that which *disrupts* the normal, whereas in the Plain publications news is largely that which *conveys* the normal. (Byrne, 1998)

Other print media, such as *Family Life, Mennonite Weekly Review* and local newspapers have been popular, although much local news seems too sensational, violent or sexual now that it must compete with news from radio, television and the Internet. One Amish minister, who wished not to be identified, said "We used to subscribe to *Time* and at one point to *Newsweek*, but both became so extreme in their pictures and subjects we cancelled the subscriptions." (Anonymous, 2000)

A fascinating media debate occurred around the telephone. Initially the phone was seen as an improvement for rural life, because it allowed farmers to order supplies, contact remote veterinarians and doctors quickly, seek relief during fires, and stay in touch with community events. (Umble, 1996) However, when the phone also proved to be an amplification of gossip, worldly contact, and disruption of family rhythms, it was banished. (Kraybill, 1998) Yet due to the practicality of telephones for business in both small shops and on the farm, a compromise emerged in many communities—phones could be housed in barns or booths outside the home or they could be used in the homes of neighbors.

To outsiders it would seem that "media free" Old Order life might be bereft of enjoyment. However, life was filled with what many might consider "old media"—magazines, library books, games, toys, puzzles, singing, family outings, conversation and prayer. (Scott, 1990) It is also important to Old Order philosophy what work and worship should of themselves be highly fulfilling activities.

In many communities there are also minor exceptions to full-time fasting—some Plain People encounter media while working away from the community, others while staying in hotels when traveling, others in their experimental teen years, and still others by smuggling media into their barn or attic.

SCRIPTURE AND MEDIA ABSTINENCE

Although much Plain lifestyle is simply traditional, some Old Order living may be traced to a strict specific interpretation of the Bible. Thus, when new media inventions appeared in society, they reminded church leaders of evils to be avoided, as described in the Bible. For example, the advent of the mechanically reproduced photograph summoned forth the second of the Ten Commandments:

> Thou shalt not make unto thee any graven image or any likeness….
>
> (Exodus 20:4A)

Television, film and the Internet only served to make these likenesses more lifelike, and thus more dangerous. With the advent of glamorous images from Madison Avenue and Hollywood, coated by seemingly endless cosmetics, hair coloring, special lighting and effects, those who were Plain avoided those who seemed vain.

Almost every medium violated some injunction. Radio disturbed the "quiet in the land" (*Psalm 35:20*) and Satan had been biblically described as "the Prince of the air." (Kanagy, 1997) As recently as the spring of 2010, a Brethren minister preached against the evils of Christian lyrics married to a rock beat because the "very electric rhythms were from Satan." (Name withheld by request, 2010)Many core scriptural prescriptions of Old Order theology transcend particular media and point toward their common secular content. Old Order leaders refer to this sensational, commercial and sensual entertainment as "worldliness." In direct opposition, the New Testament teaches:

> Love not the world, neither the things that are in the world…
>
> (I John 2:15)

And again:

> …friendship with the world is enmity with God.
>
> (James 4:4)

Thus the Anabaptists insist that one must keep oneself "unspotted from the world." (James 1:27) Hence, Old Order life has sought to draw an invisible line of apartheid between its remote bucolic communities and the violent, urban landscape.

Such behavior is in response to the New Testament commandment:

> Come out from among them, and be ye separate, saith the Lord, and touch not the unclean thing, and I will receive you.
>
> (II Corinthians 6:17)

Obviously contemporary leaders may interpret the "unclean thing" as film or pop music or the Internet. However, the "unclean thing" is also an entire larger modern way of life they wish to keep at arm's length from their communities.

More than any other Bible verse, Romans 12:2—"Be not conformed to the pattern of this world; but be ye transformed to the renewing of your mind"—is quoted as the divine command which the Plain People obey. Deliberate, socialized nonconformity has led to decades without electricity but not, in their view, to decades without light.

WHAT ARE THE CULTURAL REASONS FOR FASTING?

Kraybill (1989) has amassed some striking statistics about Amish family life. The average family has 6.6 children. Differing studies suggest that between seventy-six and eighty-eight percent of Amish children eventually join the church. (Kraybill, 1989) Strong family and community emphasis keep the Amish and other Plain families large, functional and efficient as a labor force.

Plain communities are aware that media are a threat to family fusion. In secular neighborhoods children eventually replace their parents with headsets or video games, while parents gravitate toward adult programming. Plain people do not welcome this programmed "generation gap." Family outings, conversations and silences are eventually drowned by endless noise and enlarged images if great care is not taken.

Nonviolence is another key tenet of Plain life. Historically, one reason that led these Anabaptists to separate from other religions was obedience to biblical pacifism. Thus a Hollywood film such as *Witness* (1985) adds insult to injury by both *mis*representing the Amish way of life and featuring scenes of lethal violence and seminudity within a celluloid Amish community.

Despite a wide spectrum of "wholesome" media—educational documentaries, children's features and informational Web sites—the Plain People are not impressed (although some Brethren and Mennonites have produced films and videotapes). The very nature of acting is more than suspect—"the actor is a professional liar and thus to be shunned." (Gerbner, 1990) In theater, television and film

> An actor is seen as a phony, playing the part of someone else. In the Amish mind, playing the role of a character in a drama is the equivalent of a lie because the actor puts on the mask and deceives the audience by pretending that he's someone that he's really not.
>
> (Hostetler and Kraybill, 1988)

The Plain People have taught themselves to be content with life as it is and to give thanks for their every blessing. Media, however, seek to teach consumers that "more is better," "bigger is superior," "faster is best," and other commercial values that would break the commandment not to covet. Notions of time-saving and speed-up are not necessarily healthy to people who find great worth in their slower, steady pace of manual work. Work builds character and community, not just health and home. (Hostetler and Kraybill, 1988)

In many ways electronic media seem like a symphony of sacrilege. Web sites poke barnyard fun at Amish customs, pornographic videos are available in neighborhood stores, while amoral "cop-killing" music comes into the home. Much pop media paints a mustache on what is deemed holy—from the church to matrimony to life itself. Plain People do not wish to be mocked or to see God's creation taken frivolously. It is not one scriptural passage that the media disobey. They often ignore or ridicule all of them lump sum.

At the heart of the Amish Order is the German notion of *Gelassenheit*, which has several levels of meaning—submission, obedience, thrift, humility and simplicity, among others. (Kraybill, 1989) It means letting one's individual will be yielded to and guided by the church. *Gelassenheit* keeps the individual meekly integrated within the community purpose, whereas the media portray numerous (super)heroes who champion rugged individualism, aggressive competition and ego assertion. Often those heroes become role models for children and teens—role models who are unattractive to Plain parents.

To Plain People, life is holistic—all parts affect each other, and thus the whole. Thus an Old Order Mennonite would not tolerate this line of reasoning from a city cousin: "Why should I worry if my child sees a horror movie on a Saturday, so long as his homework is done during the week and he goes to church on Sunday?" For the Plain person, once the psychological damage has been done and the child's innocence destroyed it can never be restored to an unsullied state. Each day of the week affects the others and each person affects the community. Atomized individualism and fragmented behavior are not acceptable.

The colorful expressions of Plain People, albeit often anonymous (many do not wish to be identified), give a more graphic view of media content:

Hollywood is the outhouse of society. Why would you want to link up a pipe to bring that sewage right into your living room?

(Amish deacon, 2000)

It's not just the destruction of our community spirit which media bring, but you can see it is already destroying the entire American country just by reading a few newspapers. Kids seem to be imitating movie killers, and everyone wants more and more consumer goods until the earth runs out of resources—what kind of country does that build?

(Amish minister, 2000)

TV is a brainwasher for sure. It is certainly no good for the young mind.

(Retired Amish farmer, 2000)

The internal literature of Plain People is equally damning, as these excerpts from conservative Mennonite tracts suggest:

> Radio and television provide no respect for God's order of one man and one woman...and present a world in which pleasure, lust, greed, and hate are predominant...there is enough unavoidable evil that we must see and hear to fight against without tubing into our precious homes...
>
> (Moore County Mennonite Brotherhood, n.d.)

> TV may not destroy the strong, but weak parishioners lose control and become addicted...and missionaries note that when TV is introduced to a town, church attendance goes down.
>
> (Rod and Staff Publishers, n.d.)

> As Judge Kronenburg has noted, "TV is a subtle form of American brainwashing...its main themes are sex and murder...."
>
> (Free Tract and Bible Society, n.d.)

It is not surprising that rejected media technologies are primarily one-way transmitters. Television, film, the VCR and radio primarily import the values of outsiders to insiders without insiders being able to reply in kind. When the insiders did decide to reply, those few groups that adopted minimal radio use created limited evangelical programming. The controversies surrounding e-mail, business Web sites, the telephone, and photographs in advertising demonstrate more tolerance to "talk back" media, which enhance opportunities for better farming and business.

It is important to note that not all edicts from conservative Plain groups amount to media prohibition. For example, the *Rules and Discipline of the Southeastern Mennonite Conference* caution against misuse, rather than use, of radio:

> We commend and encourage those who refrain from (radio) ownership and use for the spiritual safeguard of their homes. We caution users against the indiscriminate use of the radio for

both secular and religious broadcasts. Furthermore we lay the responsibility upon users for control....

(Scott, 1996)

The *Rules and Discipline of the Mid-Atlantic Mennonite Fellowship* similarly note TV's potential but nevertheless advocate prohibition:

While television is used sometimes to promote worthy causes, yet by far the greater part of what it brings into the home is entertainment, propaganda, and commercials... we believe that the evil influence of television greatly outweighs that which is good...members who are responsible for the use and ownership of television forfeit their membership....

(Scott, 1996)

When Plain groups do use electronic media, it is primarily for cultural reinforcement, social cohesion and insularity. As Byrne (1998) points out, marginalized groups employ media, whether ethnic publications or evangelical radio stations, to ensure, not invade boundaries. Byrne's analysis of the Amish newspaper *Die Botschaft* reveals how that internal social publication provides two-way boundaries: 1) it employs dialect and description of outsiders as "strangers" and "English," which reinforces the solidarity of readers; 2) thus it proves dull reading for outsiders.

Among outsiders there is a commonly held notion that communication technology is "value free." This view suggests that any medium is neither positive nor negative, but depends entirely upon who is using it and for what purpose. Conservative Plain folk disagree. For example, it is hard to imagine what positive uses technologies of torture might have and it is similarly impossible to imagine which technologies of deception (TV, film, movies, the Internet) might create "positive" lies.

The "value-free technology" argument is dismissed by Umble (1996) when discussing the telephone.

The telephone is not merely a neutral instrument. Its use intrudes into already established patterns of communication, potentially reorganizing and reordering practices that have long held "the world" at bay. Community rituals of worship, work, silence and visiting strengthen community identity and articulate the edges of community. The telephone, however, makes the community permeable to new information and introduces new methods for information gathering, association, and interpersonal interaction. The telephone brings the world to your door, a reality welcomed by some and shunned by others.

(Umble, 1996)

Although many saw the telephone as practical or "value free," below are fourteen discrete, albeit overlapping, ways it seemed to disrupt a sealed community. The telephone

1. funneled worldliness as a conveyor belt of unwanted news and perspectives

2. magnified and further exaggerated gossip

3. disrupted the flow of family activity

4. interrupted silences

5. extracted conversation from a shared multi-sensory context

(Kraybill, 1998)

6. increased contact with individualism, pride, vanity, materialism, and other corrosive values

7. ushered in intrusive, unwanted strangers (epitomized by telemarketing, pollsters, etc.)

8. polluted sacred home atmosphere

9. provided greater association with "unbelievers"

10. increased "jangling" (cf. idle chitchat, Umble, 1996)

11. provided an avenue for youth to dissipate spiritual time

12. shocked nerves of people and animals with loud ringing bells

13. contributed to "uncontrollable drift," in which one technology, innovation or conduit to the world leads to another, then another

14. diminished face-to-face communication, and often interrupted it

Silence is very important to most Plain People, just as it is to Quakers. Sundays should be free of workday sounds, and silence begins and ends every meal. Generally services are punctuated with periods of silence, whether in prayer, meditation or transition. Wisdom is frequently equated with silence, as in the anonymous proverb "It is better to be silent and appear ignorant than to open one's mouth and remove all doubt." So many communication tools interrupt or eliminate silence that there is a fear the basic pauses of life will be lost forever.

Not only the pauses but also the overall tempo of life seem irrevocably altered by the introduction of many media. For the Old Order Plain People nothing should be rushed, save in an emergency. Media invite an accelerated racing by thriving upon police chases, adrenaline-pumping action, "fast women," and fast-talking deejays. Advertising emphasizes fast cars, fast food, and the opposite of everything paced by nature. Even the technology and programming itself has seemed obsessed with speed-up—faster modems, faster MTV-style storylines and accelerated editing.

Hence the concern about media intrusion into Plain life is more than scriptural. It feels, and is psychologically alien, to a placid, heterosexual, oral/aural culture. Plain People understand that there are economic, structural, amoral and rhythmic forces attached to media that have the penetrating power to transform, erode, and even erase Plain life as they know it.

Summarily, although there are numerous scriptural reasons for abstaining from media, the cumulative prohibition list is much longer.

While many of these rationales overlap, it is important to see how extensive are the voiced objections to a mediated lifestyle. Although the following thirty-eight objections could be collapsed or enlarged, and include some of the fourteen objections to the telephone, their collective weight is staggering. They suggest that there is little to no hope for media managers who wish that some of these twenty-two Plain groups are long-term potential markets.

In the aggregate, most electronic media are shunned because they

1. promote individual and ruthless competition

2. introduce unwelcome negative values/lifestyles—cynicism, relativism, existentialism, postmodernism and nihilism

3. with few exceptions emphasize secular over sacred atmosphere

4. foster consumerism—"more," "bigger," "new," "improved," "better"

5. promote fragmentation above wholeness

6. inspire laziness and idleness (cf. couch potato)

7. promote higher education and non-scriptural knowledge (for Amish, youth education terminates with eighth grade)

8. deplete, diminish or spoil national resources

9. waste money

10. waste time

11. interrupt family activity, priorities, communion and rhythms

12. invade community privacy

13. increase dependency upon advertised products and electronic stimuli

14. promote sexual promiscuity, violence, nudity and sensationalism

15. encourage stereotyping and prejudice, including toward Plain People

16. convey sacrilegious and blasphemous attitudes against religions and deities

17. commercially exploit the images, sounds and culture of Plain People for profits typically not shared with Plain People

18. create electrical (sometimes seemingly deafening) noise, drowning silences and natural sound

19. foster unnatural speed-up

20. violate community philosophy (Gelassenheit) and conduct code (Ordnung)

21. present acting ("professional lying") and other deceptive and hypocritical presentational forms

22. show forceful methods of conflict resolution (e.g., war, fist fights, martial arts, gunfights) rather than nonviolence

23. lead to a conforming to worldly behavior

24. invite greater association with nonbelievers, including celebrities, deejays and talk-show hosts

25. pollute the consciousness of youth ("converts their bedroom into a bar or boxing ring")

26. stir those base and lower emotions that lead to lustful and greedy behavior

27. cultivate imitative behavior, whether copycat crimes, alcohol indulgence or fashion trends

28. lead to media addiction among the weaker and younger community members

29. brainwash or propagandize innocent minds

30. destroy the moral fiber of the United States as a world power and home for religious freedom

31. seduce humans to prefer the vain to the plain, the spectacular to the ordinary, the cosmetic to the genuine, and the glamorous to the modest

32. intrude within and reorganize patterns of community and family communication (visiting, prayer, dialog, silences)

33. increase idle chitchat, misinformation, slander and hearsay/gossip

34. minimize and interrupt face-to-face interaction and nonverbal communication

35. undermine work ethic, business frugality with Mecca/mirage of labor-saving, amusement-driven society

36. introduce corporate one-way mass communication, which can increase spending patterns and the homogenization of thought

37. lead to the worship of graven and glamorous images

38. expose the community to non-normative non-Anabaptist behavior: homosexuality, trans-sexuality, pedophilia, Satanism, bestiality, Mafia, KGB, prostitution, Nazism, CIA, terrorism, polygamy, etc.

Many other variations on these themes could be listed.

WHAT IF THE PLAIN PEOPLE ARE RIGHT?

Such a long list begs the question of whether it is the Plain or the mainstream that is "backward." Indeed the outside world must take note that Plain People have a very low rate of poverty, divorce, crime, suicide, pollution, mental illness and defection. (Kraybill, 1989) Theirs is primarily a world of functional families and communities surrounded by an increasingly dysfunctional global community. Indeed their children are welcomed, loved, grow up bilingual and are taught skills useful to their community.

Moreover, their approach to electronic media suggests that *they* are in control of technology, and not vice versa. Unlike the U.S. government, which dissolved its Office of Technology Assessment, the Plain People are diligent about assessing the possible impact of each technology before it becomes widespread in the community. Nor are they hesitant about removing a technology or removing its applications. Questions such as "How *might* this technology truly benefit or erode community harmony and practices?" are crucial to any technology trial. Even if a technology is assessed as harmless, it can be banished or reinstated later, when unforeseen effects are detected.

One does not have to be religious to agree with Plain People that mainstream approaches to life are not working. The world encounters crises at every turn—resource depletion, economic collapse, widespread mental illness, waves of refugees, endless war, famine, nuclear threats, global warming, hazardous waste, terrorism, and a growing list of others.

Not only do complex global problems seem unattractive, but many outsiders are finding the Plain lifestyle increasingly attractive. By March 1995 *The New York Times* published that over five thousand families had subscribed to *Plain* magazine and that in 1995 several hundred homeowners in Ohio alone had abandoned their city jobs for an "Old Order" country lifestyle but had not necessarily joined one of the Plain churches. (Schneider, 1995) That pattern is magnified in many other agricultural areas worldwide.

What is behind this ongoing urban and suburban exodus? Keith Schneider of *The New York Times* concluded that

> prompting this movement is the sense that people are losing control of their lives, largely as a result of the increase in stress and alienation bestowed by technology. "We've moved to a whole new speed in how we live...at electronic speed..." said Scott Savage, a 35-year-old former librarian. "We're being crushed by the way we live, and it's on everybody's mind."
>
> (Schneider, 1995)

It is also important to understand what is happening within other remote groups, which were until recently media free. Ogden (1993), Varan (1993) and many others have noted how Pacific Islands—such as the Cook and Marshall Islands—have changed after the introduction of television, video games, boom boxes and headsets (see Chapter Eight). In some cases, elders are treated as "stupid" by island youth, since they are out of touch with the latest pop culture.

Human interaction is replaced with technology (TV and personal computers) in the evenings, and spiritual values are supplanted by commercial ones. (Ogden, 1993; Varan, 1993)

A large literature about the effects of technology suggests that these Pacific cases are not isolated examples. For example, the average American child spends more time with media than with parents, fears she will be mugged more if she is a heavy rather than a light user of television, seems more likely to be aggressive if a mega-consumer of violent programming, and seems to have an overall decreasing attention span. While the precise effects and the causal nature of programming and technologies may be debated by scholars, no serious researcher can doubt that media has a pronounced impact upon society.

The Plain People cannot predict exactly what could happen to their communities if various media were introduced, nor do they frequent remote Pacific Islands. But they read enough and see enough of their Pennsylvania neighbors to know about suicide, divorce, abuse, pollution, poverty and crime rates in neighboring communities that do not police runaway technologies.

Whether or not there is a direct causal relationship between television and violence or between the Internet and individualism, Plain People have not seen examples of one without the other. Indeed, all of the comparative hard evidence to which they have been exposed suggests that Plain People may only preserve their way of life, goals and values by abstinence from electronic mass media.

WHAT MAY BE LEARNED FROM PLAIN PEOPLE?

In 1938 Aurand wrote: "Nothing is rushed among the Amish." He also suggested that theirs was a more relaxed and natural way of life, which was less stressful. Implicit within such assumptions are notions, such as that the best things in life are worth waiting for and that the Old Orders hold their lives in harmony through proper pacing and balance. (Aurand, 1938) Over sixty years later, their pace remains gentle.

In interviews, modern business executives and media professionals have confessed to the author that they now move too quickly to consider ethical factors before making important decisions. Gleick's important book *Faster* (1999) demonstrates many other social perils of a society moving at breakneck speed (see Chapter Nine). Similarly, Kovach and Rosenstiel in *Warp Speed*, an analysis of the new blitz media, note the unhealthy time pressures and problems suffered by competitively sprinting journalists. (Kovach and Rosenstiel, 1999) Error, burnout, lost focus, superficiality, poor health, ethical dilemmas and overall imbalance all increase with speed.

Aside from maintaining a natural pace, one may learn from the Plain People how to take control of one's own community and the technologies that transform it. What may best be adopted is not who they are but, rather, that they *know* who they are and know how to maintain that discrete identity.

Are there serious problems among the Plain People? Of course.

For example, some communities are located just a few miles from the Three Mile Island nuclear power plant. Without electronic media and automobiles, it seems likely that high numbers could suffer seriously from a nuclear accident.

But what of interior self-inflicted problems? People who leave the strictest communities often complain of unbending social rules; oppressive lives, especially for women and children; parochialism; straight-laced workaholism; fundamentalist narrow-mindedness; the micromanagement of human lives; and lack of exposure to alternative philosophies and perspectives. Nor can any people, Plain or otherwise, transcend universal problems, such as community politics, scandal and disease. Even "worldliness" has crept into Plain communities in the form of occasional drug dealing, alcohol dependency, and "sowing wild oats" among the youth. No people are perfect.

Yet, in the final analysis, Pennsylvania Plain People are global role models in overall social stability and in "walking their talk"; that is, in exemplifying their philosophy. Whether or not one agrees with any of their dozens of reasons for media fasting, one must admire their ability to implement and consistently maintain the fast over decades. Many people who undertake to diet, let alone to fast, cannot withhold the temptation to break their control after just a few hours or days.

Without a dictator, and with minimal politics, the Plain People have effectively created a "media-free zone" for decades within many differing cultures and countries. As a society, if not as individuals, they are surprisingly in control of their own lives and technology. Through a well-controlled media fast, they resist fast media.

CHAPTER EIGHT

GROUPS THAT ARE BREAKING THE FAST

The Kogi, Dani, Rapa Nui, and Others

Far from Lancaster County, Pennsylvania, are many other intentional and unintentional media-free zones. Pacific Islanders, desert bushmen, remote mountaineers and impoverished nomads are among those who have never seen a computer or television. In this chapter, several groups are mentioned that are "breaking their fast"; that is, they are being exposed to media for the first time.

Each group and each "break fast" is different. I have selected some of the most interesting examples. The first moments of exposure to a medium are highly instructive. Just as *you* may learn much when you return from your fast to normal life, even so communities learn much about their previous state when a new medium enters society.

THE KOGI PEOPLE OF COLUMBIA

Perhaps the most dramatic example of "breaking the fast" occurred in 1989, when the hermetic Kogi people of Columbia permitted a BBC television crew to produce a feature documentary about their unique way of life. Denizens of the high equatorial Andes, the Kogi people had evacuated into seclusion after European explorers arriving between 1514 and 1600 began to control what was later to be called Columbia. Slavery, death, rape and disease were the fate of many indigenous people who encountered the Spanish. So the Kogi elected to flee persecution to the high Sierra Nevada, where they preserved a highly spiritual, ascetic culture as descendents of the Tairona priesthood. (Eriera, 1990)

Although the Kogi had been exposed to reading and writing, they chose not to adopt any process that might alter the "spiritual and intellectual organization of their world." (Eriera, 1990) They also feared that reading and writing English might also erase their own language. Thus theirs was a deliberately imposed abstinence from literacy and from some, but not all, sixteenth-century European technology. Since they had no way of knowing about electronic media, their abstinence was not from each communication technology but from an entire civilization that seemed most uncivil.

Ironically, the BBC production about the Kogi indirectly called attention to the glories of media. It demonstrated how video could "boldly go where no man has gone before" by presenting not only a pristine tribe but also taping and distributing the disturbing Kogi warning message to the outside world.

Because the Kogi could observe the fading and yellowing of vegetation at the top of their mountain home, they were certain that life below the mountaintops would also fade and die. Thus their simple yet dramatic warning was "Unless you do something, the world will end." (Eriera, 1990)

For that reason, the 1990 BBC production, directed by Alan Eriera, was entitled *From the Heart of the World: The Elder Brothers' Warning.* Since the Kogi people preceded the European "South Americans," they call themselves "the elder brother" and label all imported cultures— Portuguese, Spanish, English, etc.—"the younger brother." Thus the *elder* brother warned the *younger* brother to stop stripping the earth of precious metals and other practices that lead to omnicide.

The Kogi people constitute an exceptional media case study for two reasons: 1) more successfully than perhaps any group, they shut out the outside world and its media and 2) ironically, they realized that to reach a substantial portion of the outside world, they must welcome and use media. By one set of values they are the worst receivers and best transmitters of electronic communication, since 1) their only transmitted media message involves the survival of the planet, and 2) they have never received a media message.

Moreover, the Kogi's deliberate resistance to print is notable. A profound literature—including works by Innis, Hall, Havelock, McLuhan and others—demonstrates that when an oral culture adopts print, it does not become an oral culture *with* print. Instead, it becomes a print culture. Hence the Kogi have not simply resisted a technology; they have both resisted and preserved an entire way of life.

It is significant that, following the production by Eriera's BBC crew, the Kogi have fully returned to their life of isolation. At the end of Eriera's videotape we see Kogi leaders close the gate to their bridge. One leader says to the camera crew, "That's enough now. Don't come back." The Kogi have returned, perhaps permanently and most deliberately, to a world without literacy and electricity.

THE DANI PEOPLE

One must guard against the notion that humanity responds to media in predictable, monolithic ways. For example, near the beginning of the nineteenth century some French audiences ran out of a theater when they saw a film about a train entering a station. Some Americans supposedly ducked under their seats upon seeing the same film.

But some indigenous audiences were uncertain how to respond, since they did not know what a train was. Still other audiences stayed in their seats, having been told about the illusions created by cinema.

Anthropologists have reported that some first-time viewers of photographs turned over the photos to look for the back of the person's head. Similarly, members of some tribes have been reported to try to walk behind a movie screen to see where the actor goes upon exiting. Legend has it that two middle-aged European men tried to peer over the edge of a filmed bathtub to see the woman bathing inside it. Significantly, they saw instead their own shadows silhouetted against the screen.

The Dani people of Irian Jaya (formerly Netherlands New Guinea) had a unique response to Robert Gardner's photographs and the movie *Dead Birds* (1964). Although a few of the Dani might already have seen Bibles and photographs owned by missionaries and explorers, most of the Dani had never been exposed to print, photo and film. Within this context, ethnographic filmmaker Robert Gardner conducted an interesting experiment.

Having taken many photographs of the Dani while filming *Dead Birds* (1964), Gardner published a book of photos in 1977 and elected to return to visit the Dani people twenty-five years after his initial filming. His informal experiment involved showing both the documentary film and the book of photographs, *Gardens of War* (1977), to the people who were depicted within the images one quarter of a century later. He filmed their responses as an audience to *Dead Birds* at a time when some not only saw film for the first time but also saw themselves in images of their forgotten youth.

As Gardner showed the Dani *Gardens of War*, a book filled with images of their warrior past, he noted more than the usual curiosity and interest which first-time viewers have for film. Since the images were of themselves, specific Dani were fascinated to remember how they appeared long ago, especially as a form of moving magic.

However, what was most arresting was the Dani hunger for their heritage. Since they had been forbidden to fight by the government of Indonesia, and since their proud ancestry as warriors had not otherwise been preserved, the book was a treasure chest of memories. Gardner found that copies of the book were in great demand. (Gardner, 2000) Similarly, the Dani watched *Dead Birds* with a strong interest, curiosity and longing for a lost way of life.

Such a response is in marked contrast to the Amish view that love of graven images is to be shunned as vanity. It is also in contrast to the conventional wisdom that media will be embraced or shunned, based upon a community's response to consumerism and sensation. In this case, it was cultural pride, if not tribal narcissism, which led to the embracing of artificial images—not the longing for consumer goods or for narrative entertainment.

Indeed, the narrative elements of *Dead Birds* were not understood by the Dani. The editing of shots taken from multiple angles and distances, and the collapsing of real months into cinematic moments, was unlike anything in the natural world to which first-time audiences may relate. My neighbor's young daughter shuddered when she saw, for the first time, the extreme close-up of a human eye at the movies. To her it seemed like the huge, possibly twenty-foot-tall eye of a one-eyed monster. Undoubtedly, the codes and rules of media interpretation must be learned via socialization over time.

Hence the initial impact of mass media is not just that of the technology. Media content was very important to what the Dani wished to see and what the Kogi wished to say.

EASTER ISLAND, RAPA NUI, AND THE ONE-TRACK MIND

In 1975 the first pre-taped television programs were shown in the remote Pacific island known as Rapa Nui by its indigenous Polynesians, also known as Easter Island to much of the outside world. The small population of three thousand mostly congregates within a single village, Hanga Rao.

Hanga Rao mayor, Pedro Edmunds, has hailed the advent of TV on the island as a welcome breath of fresh education, culture and news. (Edmunds, 1998) Others, such as the island's vice rector for education, German Merino Vega, are concerned that the values depicted on television—such as commercialism, promiscuity and violence as problem-solver—have nothing to do with Rapa Nui culture. (Vega, 1998) Equally troubling to hotel-keeper Patricia Ramirez is that locals often become envious of the lifestyles and possessions of televised others, who live oceans away.

Beyond these pros and cons is a concern unknown to many populations on the planet—Rapa Nui has only one source of information. Without radio stations, movie houses and local newspapers, residents have seen and heard just one view of the world for over a quarter of a century. This one source, the official national television channel of mainland Chile (which annexed Rapa Nui in 1888), is the only electronic mass medium most of the three thousand residents encountered until a few VCRs arrived in the early 1990s.

Although a few residents import magazines and newspapers, the news is often days late. Thus the Chilean national television news has the only widespread impact. It could be said that the consumer of Easter Island's TV has a "one track mind," or a one-channel brain. This syndrome has also been said to persist in many other countries in which government-owned programming has brought citizens basically one perspective—whether on one channel or on several—the party line.

But what is this one track? Does one source or one channel constitute narrow-mindedness? Or might not one hundred channels also constitute many variations on a single wavelength? A diversity of channels is supposed to represent a cornucopia of ideas. However, what if together all channels speak only the same dialect, such as commercialese or infotainese or sensationalic? Are two hundred versions of the same message ("Buy this product"; "Laugh when you hear laughter," etc.) all that different from one "track" on Easter Island?

The Rapa Nui people have a different "track" than conventional media. According to Pedro Edmunds, traditional islanders wish to preserve their language, culture and history in a world that is quickly becoming homogenized. The question facing such peoples—the Rapa Nui, the Native Hawaiians, the Kogi, the Dine, the Yap, and many others—is "Do we preserve our culture *with* mass media or *from* mass media?" Some tribes and peoples have preserved their songs, dances and other cultural forms on videotapes and compact discs, while others have sensed that the very presence of videotapes and compact disks would adversely change their lives and families.

Canoeing instructor and tour guide Cesar Huke feels that the encroachment of television values upon the Rapa Nui people is wrong. "The danger of television is that it changes minds" away from Rapa Nui culture Huke believes. There is much evidence to suggest that television does "change minds," attitudes, values and priorities.

It is interesting that we train *brain surgeons* for many years and give them examinations before they operate. Yet we do not give *mind surgeons* (TV writers and producers) any training about the anatomy of the human mind. Yet they have license to erode consciousness and erase culture, to "change thought," as Cesar Huke declares.

The final word on whether media is good or bad for Rapa Nui has not been spoken. Educator German Vega warns that media bring a message of "too much freedom," unlimited sex, alcohol, drugs and weapons. But Mayor Edmunds points out that communication technologies bring great advantages to islanders—for example, small islands are extremely vulnerable to tsunamis, and good TV reports allow residents to evacuate or move to higher ground. But Patricia Ramirez notes that television is the only consistent entertainment on Rapa Nui (aside from a discotheque open for a few hours per week). Thus TV becomes an easy habit for children. In fact, during Easter Island's rainy season, television has a surefire captive audience, even when the programming is poor.

Always encouraging education, Pedro Edmunds would love to see the Internet flourish on Rapa Nui. It would bring islanders into much closer contact with the outside world and show children innumerable perspectives, species, galaxies and cultures. But what will happen when these same children find adult Web sites, become glued to video games, and use computers to avoid homework rather than complete it?

In that regard, Easter island will have much in common with the Orkney Islands, the Marqueses Islands, the Aleutian Islands, Fiji, Guam, the Canary Islands, and too many others to list. And it will have much in common with the celestial island called Earth.

THE REMOTE CALIFORNIANS

It is easy to see why small bands of distant low-income people in remote locales, like the Dani, Rapa Nui and the Kogi, would not be priority markets for mass media. However, "media" hermits exist everywhere—within major cities, in highly developed countries and in intentional communities.

153

For centuries the people of Taos, New Mexico, have lived without running water or electricity. Several of the alternative "communes" of the 1960s, and thereafter, declared a creed of self-reliance by growing crops, weaving cloth, baking bread, and leaving mass media behind.

Other mainland communities *accidentally abstained* from television and radio—not due to remoteness *from* the mainland but, rather, due to remoteness *within* a mainland. Indeed, since *remoteness* is a relative term, almost everyone initially seemed remote *from* new technologies. China, Canada, Russia and the United States had major sweeping expanses—some packed with mountain, glacial and tundra obstacle courses. Small population pockets remained unwired for years, and even decades, until the telephone, cable or the Internet became local.

In that context, it is interesting to select a "typical" isolated U.S. town and examine the advent of television at the moment of impact. Such was the goal of *The Impact of Television* (1980), a film sponsored by the *Encyclopedia Brittanica,* which chronicled the arrival of television in the small (population of one hundred) town of Essex, California, in 1979. Television invaded Essex three decades after it had been reintroduced in the U.S., and two decades after it had blanketed both major and minor U.S. population centers. Initially, the high mountains of the Mojave Desert prevented television signals from reaching Essex.

What is instructive from filmed interviews is that Essex viewers, as they inspected television, found their own lives reflected through a largely distorted mirror. For example, after watching the police show *Chips,* a policeman commented that the program compressed, or even crammed, events from a real policeman's year into thirty minutes. Similarly, a housewife observed TV housewives and said, "They've sure got a lot of sex. They're always a kissin' someone's neighbor.... We don't do that around here...we don't even shake hands." (Britannica, 1980)

Although police know they are unlike TV police and housewives know they are not like TV housewives, to what extent do people from other backgrounds and countries know how much each media stereotype is distorted? To what extent do American audiences realize that many people see terrorists as freedom fighters or that some Cubans might view Castro as an excellent leader? If one watches only television, it is hard to know if there are Sicilians who are rocket scientists rather than Mafia thugs, or if there are nonviolent martial artists. We may never know, if television is our only guide.

Not every Essex citizen viewed the coming of television the same way. Some welcomed TV news as a means of keeping tabs on the outside world by viewing wars in progress and recent traffic accidents. Others thought such information could reach the community by less graphic means.

Whatever their stand on television, some Essex citizens knew that adding television to their homes, businesses and bars was unlike adding any other piece of furniture. Indeed, those making the documentary presented the view that Essex would be very different once television became a permanent fixture. What is feared by the Plain People in Pennsylvania—that television could irreversibly change their lives—is borne out by the police and housewives of remote California.

THE ISLAND PACIFIC

To the tourist, the romantic notion of South Sea Islands often includes only Fiji, Tahiti, and of course Hawaii, as dream vacations. Yet there are thousands of other islands, often huddling in galactic packs, which are largely unknown to the outside world. Kiribati, Tuvalu and Vanuatu are such clusters of obscure dots and microdots on maps of the Pacific. There are many other slightly better known families of islands, such as Melanesia, Micronesia, Polynesia, and others.

Pacific Island specialist Albert Hulsen, of the East-West Center, notes that there is just one weekly newspaper and some radio in parts of Kiribiti, only one monthly paper and one radio station in Tuvalu, and only speckled shortwave and print throughout large chains of neighbor islands. (Hulsen, 2000) There are more (eight hundred to nine hundred) languages in Melanesia than the rest of the world combined. The difficulty of translating large quantities of news and entertainment into that many languages for small, secluded, often poor, low-technology audiences seems impractical, if not impossible, within the foreseeable future.

Within many smaller indigenous islands there are groups that have not seen electronic media. These include Marshall, French Polynesian, Melanesian, New Guinea, Solomon, Cook, Micronesian, and other island groups.

Nor are telephones commonplace throughout the Pacific. As of 1997, only one in forty people in Kiribati had a phone, one in twenty in Tuvalu, and one in fifty in the Solomon Islands. As early as 1991, there was a telephone waiting list of over eleven thousand in Fiji and two thousand in Western Samoa. (SPF, 1991) Often the installation, like the introduction of a technology in many Pacific islands, moves at a tropical pace.

Unlike the Amish or the Kogi fasting, island Pacific media abstinence is not by choice, although Fiji did attempt to resist media infusion initially. (Chu, 2000) Some women in Fiji wish that this resistance had been more successful; they are now feeling ugly relative to the ideals of televised beauty imported from New Zealand. (Hulsen, 2000) Many Fiji females feel that they look bulky and plain by imported advertising standards. (Hulsen, 2000)

Internet use in the Pacific is relatively low but is growing quickly. (Ogden, 1999) Islands such as Guam, Fiji, Papua New Guinea, and the Solomons supported over one thousand Internet users by 1997. (Biddle, 1998) Nevertheless, there are numerous smaller islands without telephones, where residents have not yet heard of the Internet.

What is known of the relationship between fast media and those islands that fast from mass media? There has been much concern about cultural intrusion, homogenization of diverse cultures, and a yielding to advertising pressures by those living on these islands who cannot afford consumer goods. (Topping, 1993)

Nor is literacy viewed as necessarily benign. The rise of European languages in the Pacific is associated with the erosion of Polynesian languages. Moreover, a change from oral culture to literacy usually means a shift from holism to an analytic way of thought. Finally, the introduction of media "has accompanied if not caused radical changes in belief systems, ways of governing, teaching, learning, and notions of law and authority." (Topping, 1993)

Some reactions have been extreme. In the Marshall Islands one man "smashed his TV to regain some control over the household." (Ogden, 1993) Many women in the Marshall Islands left the room when feminine hygiene products were advertised to mixed audiences. Highly embarrassed, they did not return. (Ogden, 1993)

Some Marshall Islanders became concerned that they were losing their cultural identity. As more of their neighbors became obsessed with products and electronic titillation, they feared that they were "becoming more like the Americans." (Ogden, 1993) Cultural amnesia about their traditions and ancestry began to settle in. Life in Palau followed a similar pattern, since TV displaced gardening, fishing, family activities, storytelling and handicrafts.

If they could talk, the Cook Islands could tell similar stories. Due to late-night media fixations, Cook students became quite tired in their classrooms. (Varan, 1993) Concerned parents also noted that traditional games were replaced with video Ninja Turtles violence and that girls began to chase impossible standards of beauty. (Varan, 1993)

Indeed, the government itself became concerned and found that culturally erosive television was

> more influential than the church, the family, and the school put together in redefining the customs, habits, attitudes, values, and lifestyles of Rarotonga youth.
>
> (Ministerial Task Force, 1990)

Many of those in the Cook islands witnessed decreasing family and community communication as independent individualism replaced communitarian values.

One important factor in "breaking the fast" is rate of change. Some groups have been able to sustain the slow introduction of new media, while others seemed psychologically stampeded. When Nii-ki Plange asks whether Fiji is "fast-forwarding into the future," the term *fast forward* raises many questions. (Plange, 1993) Does an influx of media, whether TV, the Internet or other media cause a society to skip decades? Does a culture adopt outside perspectives too quickly to absorb, understand and assimilate them? Even if a medium is benign and an entire society chooses to adopt it, is there a proper tempo of introduction?

Marshall McLuhan once quipped that the Soviet Union had no nineteenth century. (McLuhan, 1975) By that, he meant that Russia and other Soviet states were forced to modernize instantly, rather than gradually, following the Russian Revolution. Jumping from serfdom and Czardom to socialist industrialization, they seemed to leapfrog over the Industrial Revolution.

While McLuhan's claim may seem exaggerated—certainly Russia experienced *some* aspects of the nineteenth century—one sees his point. As Pacific islands, one by one and group by group, break the fast, will they be forced to leapfrog the entire twentieth century to enter the new millennium? Will they fast-forward?

Such questions have important social consequences. As Sukarno pointed out, his Indonesian populace interpreted imported Hollywood films as colossal ads for consumer goods—goods they could not afford. In imported feature films, movie stars paraded through kitchens stuffed with relatively huge appliances, which upstaged the dialog.

Peasants, among others, wanted these huge machines before Indonesia could manufacture them, thus opening the door—or at least the demand—for Western manufacturers. Often such hidden media messages foster a fast-forward or leapfrog effect. As satellite, Wi-Fi, cable, fiber optic, VCR, fax, CD and DVD technology are being slam-dunked into the Pacific, will islanders pole-vault the twentieth century? At what cost?

SUMMARY

Breaking the fast from mass media has many variations. It can be reversible and "transmission only," as with the Kogi, or irreversible and reception only, as with Essex, California, in 1979. It may lead to an ongoing "one track" society, as with the Rapa Nui, or to fleeting fixation, as with the Dani.

The ongoing consequences of dancing with the media are unpredictable. Paradoxically, the Kogi, who wished above all to be obscure, are now minor celebrities. Although the arrival of filmmakers and photographers adulterated the Dani lifestyle, ironically the films and photographs are now their *least* adulterated memory of that warrior lifestyle. For the Rapa Nui, media held the promise of freeing them from a single point of view. Paradoxically, their single channel has now introduced them to another single point of view: national Chilean television.

Tragically, there are no national or international safeguards against implementing media untested for their possible social effects. Drugs are tested; weapons are tested; and foods are tested for their effects. They are all scientifically researched prior to their release into the market, but not mass media.

It is *after* widespread computer use that we discover that monitors are associated with the radiation poisoning of expectant mothers and embryos. It is *after* years of reported hearing damage that we inspect CD headsets. Similar controversies surround cellular phones and brain tumors, computer keyboards and carpal tunnel syndrome, television screens and radiation, etc. Many effects cannot be detected prior to implementation—and there is *in*sufficient research given to finding those effects that can be predicted.

When an island or society breaks the fast, no one can say how fast media will transform a media fast. However, ethically the argument can be made that someone should know what *might* happen. Presearch; that is, preventive research, should be required about the possible effects of any medium before it is introduced. Inventors, executives, parents, ethicists and civic leaders should all meet to discuss the possible effects of media implementation. It is especially important to inform each new "market" about the known effects a technology has had upon other markets where it was inserted.

In *From the Heart of the World: The Elder Brothers Warning*, the

Kogi people warn "younger brother" that, based upon their observation of the death of the High Sierra, the end of the world is coming. Unless something is done about hurting "the Mother" (Earth), the Kogi believe that "She" will die. Environmentalists have also become increasingly concerned about the blacktopping of the world, a concern about the likelihood that someday we will have more concrete than green surfaces on many sectors of the planet.

Simultaneously, another phenomenon has developed, which might be called the electric blanketing of the earth. Around the globe is a highly trafficked halo of satellites, electronic transmissions and vibrational residue. Linked to this is the heavier ring of actual electronic generators, power plants and transmitters encircling the earth's surface. The two concentric circles grow in heft and intensity each year. Already, doctors and civic activists are concerned with the effects of high-voltage generators upon plants, animals, and especially upon people. The larger problem associated with both global blankets is that someone keeps turning up the heat.

It is hard to know what effect this hot-blanketing will have upon the world's diminishing forms of life. It is also impossible to know how many people will be fasting from mass media fifty years from now, whether by choice or by isolation. Will any archipelago or atoll escape the electric blankets? Will the Kogi, who have lost part of their land to power plants, survive? Will the Dani survive television?

Will those who fear the advent of omni-McDonalds find that the McGlobe has become one comprehensively McWired McWomb? Will even our language clichés and idioms reflect mass media's imperialistic initiative to invade?

Stay tuned.

PART IV

THE ULTIMATE CHOICE

CHAPTER NINE

SPEED-UP AND ITS EFFECTS

This Is the Way the World Ends?

Although most of us think we have to "keep up"—an image bolstered by media themselves, we do have a choice to live as the Plain People or Rapa Nui. We can also vary our home and business tempos more than we often realize, without living backward in time.

Of course there are always trade-offs when we change gears. This chapter describes the world of speed-up and many of its hidden effects. The following and final chapter contemplates the world of contemplation, of slow-down, of silence and stillness...a world that includes yet transcends media abstinence. These two chapters are about choice, about whether or when to speed, about whether or when to be still, and about the means between these extremes.

Since media themselves are closely associated with speed-up, in this chapter I will consider their role in teaching us how we must live an ever-faster life. However, it is vexing to extricate media from their larger social context, one that embeds speed as a value within our very language. For example, what do these idioms and clichés within our everyday language mean and imply?

"There isn't a moment to lose."

"We don't have all day."

"Time's running out."

"Twenty-four-hour shopping."

"Step on it."

"Daylight Savings Time."
"The rat race."
"Sorry, I'm multitasking."
"I'll have to squeeze you in."
"Time-sharing."
"I'll have to take the red-eye."
"Must save time."
"Get a move on."

These phrases, upon close inspection, depict a world of "hurry sickness" inhabited by multiple Mad Hatters "late for a very important date." If intelligent aliens were to visit this planet, we might seem much the same as Gulliver did to the Lilliputians—they thought his watch was his God because he seemed to worship it.

SPEED THRILLS

Indeed, there *are* social sectors and professions that seem to worship speed. Race-car drivers, swimming and track stars, fast-food entrepreneurs, photocopy shop owners, pizza delivery vendors, photo-development lab managers, dry cleaners, team athletes, manufacturers, Federal Express employers, modem suppliers, sales managers and sports-car enthusiasts all seem driven by speed.

As James Gleick's book *Faster: The Acceleration of Just About Everything* makes clear, speed has always had its champions. For example, the Futurists of Italy were enamored with machines of velocity. Futurist author Filippo Marinetti wrote:

> We declare that the beauty of the world has been enhanced by a new beauty—the beauty of speed. A racing automobile with its bonnet adorned with great tubes like serpents with explosive breath...a roaring motor car which seems to run on machine gun fire.
>
> (Gleick, 1999)

Military leaders have always shared a similar lustful passion for quicker weapons. Faster-loading muskets, crossbows, rifles, artillery or missiles have always provided a life-and-death competitive advantage.

THE ACCELERATION OF ACCELERATION

Indeed acceleration is at the heart of most social "progress." Almost anything manufactured one hundred years ago can be made much faster today. Even acceleration is accelerating. Trends, fashion and entertainment fads all shift far more quickly than in medieval or Victorian days. The media themselves constantly change skins. In our great-grandparents' day, people were surprised to view one "gee whiz" phenomenon, such as photographs or movies, in their lifetime. Today we take for granted that *our* great-grandchildren will see several, if not dozens, of such breakthroughs. We ourselves have watched the CD, color TV, PC, DVR, VHS, satellite dish, TIVO, pocket calculator, portable TV, HDTV, Internet, wireless (cell) phone, World Wide Web, intelligent agent, BlackBerry, iPod, iPad, iPhone, satellite radio, microchip and digital camera become widespread.

We have observed another new contraption, the remote clicker, make it possible to speed around the entertainment audio-visual universe. The polished "sound bite," which has had all the "uhs" and "ahs" edited out of our voices, compresses *individual* thought into higher velocity, while the telephone, TV or Internet opinion poll reduces *collective* thinking to rapid relief. We have also replaced ourselves with AVATARS who travel virtually for us, and with various aliases, in chatrooms, cybergames and E-identities.

GLOBAL AMPLIFIERS

Social interplay is not only accelerated but *amplified*. The tabloid press, now accelerating across the TV and Internet landscape, amplifies gossip and sensation. Ads, which once barely punctuated TV and radio, now seek to dominate the programming and writing of many magazines, channels, news venues and Web sites.

Entertainment and news themselves have skyrocketed from breakfast or weekend treats to round-the-clock obsessions. With the amplification of information and fun comes the shadowy side of "blow-up"—distortion, anonymous sources, character assassination, hardcore pornography, noise pollution, invasion of privacy, consumerism, violation of confidentiality, censorship, commercialism and propaganda are also amplified worldwide. "Blow-up," like "speed-up," seems omnivorous.

Just a few of the phenomena currently being amplified include:

1. Production

2. Buying and selling

3. Population

4. Trade

5. Invention

6. Speed-up

7. Amplification itself

8. Marketing

9. Mediated emotional display

10. Polling

11. Advertising

12. Consumer research (demographics, psychographics)

13. Environmental, economic and energy depletion

14. Travel

15. Manipulation

16. Communication conduits (channels, media, formats)

17. Events (amplification = spectacle, such as Super Bowl, Woodstock, hyped Olympics, WWF, Academy Awards, March Madness, etc.)

18. The image—logos, icons, public relations

19. Sales pyramids

20. Digital processes

21. Debt

22. Invasion of privacy

As many of these processes grow (blow-up), they simultaneously accelerate (speed-up). This twin increase creates the impression of a Grade B sci-fi movie monster, which comes to earth as an embryo and quickly takes on colossal size and velocity.

Such changes alter the way things *seem*—or, in other words, our psychological reality. People say: "It all goes by so quickly." "That seems ages ago." "That's ancient history now." *Ancient history* once meant thousands of years ago and might mean only a few days ago today. Even "the good old days" used to mean one or two generations back. Now it can mean last decade or the time preceding a current trend or technology.

The perception of *future* has also drastically altered. Henry Kissinger stated: "Next week there can't be any crisis. My schedule is already full." So, too, is the schedule within the best-selling magazine in America, *TV Guide*, which has quadrupled in size and cost.

Day-Timers, desk and hank-held calendars, and PC planners have skyrocketed in sales in the age of a precise, if densely populated, future. It is our appetite for this chock-full future that leads to trampling over the present to "get there."

WHICH REALITY?

Thus, our perception of reality is shifting. The test pilot does not see the same world as the pedestrian. In *Cyberia: Life in the Trenches of Hyperspace*, Douglas Rushkoff writes:

Because the nature of knowledge changes so quickly, as does our inability to track and map it, and because the forms of communication change so quickly by which we perceive knowledge, "reality" is up for grabs, and in increasingly more cultures.

Indeed, in some ways reality has become "virtual," which means we may be speeding toward a world in which art literally imitates life. Like John Hinckley, Ronnie Zamora, and others trapped between the "real world" and the "*reel* world," we may someday no longer know the difference. This limbo state between two perceptual atmospheres can contribute to a sense of confusion. Indeed it leads us, in John Barlow's parlance, "to embrace confusion as a way of life," "to surf the white water," and to painfully adopt "the learning curve of Sisyphus." (Rushkoff, 1994)

FASTEST MEDIA

As Gleick notes, even already-fast media are boosting into warp speed. He labels MTV videos "the three-minute movie," and notes our impatience with vintage classical music: one can now buy the abridged "greatest classical hits."

The same is true of Sir Walter Scott's classic novel *Ivanhoe*, once beloved for its hundreds of pages of vivid description. At one third its original length, it is often now reduced to action and dialog and can also be found in comic-book form. In an age of speed-reading, movies and pop culture, literature is being re-cut from the cloth de jour.

Educators bemoan a shrinking attention span in an age when movies, already compressed from '30s-style transitions to hit-and-run editing, are fast-forwarded on DVD players to the "good parts." The bad parts often involve slow tempos, character development, beautiful settings, philosophical dialog, and clothed actors.

The Internet's history and process involve breakneck speed. Software cycles have shrunk from two years to a few weeks or months between upgrades. Film used to require developing and mailing; now it is placed on the Internet as video, so it can be everywhere instantly. (Gleick, 1999) The number one problem plaguing Web site lovers is time. Minutes, and even hours, seem lost in downloading images, software and mega-sites. The craving for greater speed catalyzes inventors and designers to create breakthroughs with greater velocity. Appetite begets speed-up begets blow-up begets keep-up.

The telephone, itself a time-saver, also offers a plethora of time-shavers. Automatic redialing, teleconferencing, one-button dialing, beepers, portable extensions, multifunction cells, directory service, voice mail et al buy us seconds, minutes and hours. Perhaps the most hidden truncation of time comes in the computerized processes that delete the "pleases" and prepositional phrases to save bites in recorded messages. Even the hidden spaces between our words and e-mails are converted into hidden electronic conveyor belts for other e-passengers. Not to mention that all devices are tirelessly morphing and merging into polyglots.

Such over-automation has always epitomized America, the home of Charlie Chaplin's mechanized, robotized *Modern Times*. On at least three different occasions, U.S. president Franklin Delano Roosevelt alluded to an American obsession: "Slowness has never been an American characteristic." Roosevelt also remarked that "lost ground can be regained—lost time, never."

Nowhere does the race to "beat the clock" show up more than in workaholic culture, which is now considered an illness. In Juliet Schor's *The Overworked American* (1991), she noted that by 1990 the average employed American worked an average "extra month," compared with 1970. The additional time is spent commuting, moonlighting, working overtime, working at home, independently contracting, and coming in early or staying late at the office.

Schor suggests that one motivation for workaholism is to look indispensable to the firm: "The more time you have on your hands, the less important you must be. So sleep in the office." Greed is another obvious motivation for overwork in an age when lawyers, electricians and mechanics all charge by the hour.

THE NEW MATH—MULTIPLICATION AND PENETRATION

Cable companies, Internet providers, direct satellite providers, fiber-optics manufacturers and many others can quote you how much *penetration* they have into residential and business districts. A cablevision manager in my home district told me: "We have fifty-four percent penetration in your city." Telephone companies, Internet vendors and telecom giants are all hoping for an amplification (blow-up) and acceleration (speed-up) in their penetration; that is, the size of their slice of the communication pie.

All the telecom players seem concerned with this new combined speedometer-odometer. On January 25, 2000, ABC news anchor Peter Jennings reported "Only four percent of U.S. homes have Internet service *faster* than the telephone." Growth rates, coupled with speed, are inferred to be indices of success. One day earlier an article in *The Honolulu Advertiser* stated: "A recent survey of the world wide web has turned up at least one billion unique web pages, underscoring the startling growth of the internet during the last few years." Futurist Richard Worzel, author of *The Next Twenty Years of Your Life*, estimates that by the year 2015 there will be one thousand bits of data for every fact in existence. (Olafson) Info-penetration!

If there is a speed-up in penetration, then there is a blow-up in growth. Indeed, by 1967 Galbraith had already argued that corporations were not so much motivated by profit as by *growth*. Growth is needed to obtain the competitive scale to leverage profits later. Growth itself now occurs at a far greater speed. When Gutenberg's printing press was introduced, it took decades, even centuries, before the book reached majority populations, in part due to illiteracy. But at the time television was introduced into society "it took less than five years for ten percent of households to adopt TV, and in less than twenty years, over ninety percent of households had television sets. VCRs were the second fastest to diffuse, followed closely by radio, which was in ninety percent of U.S. homes in about twenty-five years." (Lievrouw, 2000) By comparison, it took telephones over seventy years to reach the ninety-percent penetration mark, while earlier technologies (such as newspapers and magazines) had an even slower adoption rate.

SPEED-UP + BLOW-UP = KEEP-UP

One of the consequences of speed-up is that individuals feel pressured to "keep up." Anyone in America who relied on e-mail in 1988 was an anomaly. But by 1998, any professional who did *not* use e-mail felt like an anomaly. By 1996, Professor Jay Gillette was promoting the building of an "information city" in Ft. Hays, Kansas, where everyone from granny to junior was encouraged to learn and use the cyber-world. Simultaneously, the electronic village in Blacksburg, Virginia, ushered in the advent of cyber-democracy. President Clinton and Vice President

Gore promoted and demonstrated the potential of the Internet in inner cities and outer hinterlands. Anybody who was anybody needed to be *online*...and "big-time."

But it is not only individuals who feel the relentless pressure to upgrade. Corporations also find that "speed-up plus blow-up equals keep-up." Often corporate mergers are coerced by the fear of falling behind. Indeed, several communication company mergers have been driven by the changing markets and technologies of information, not by the initial urge to co-create with partners.

The instantly famous AOL-Time Warner deal was a high-profile example. As described in *Newsweek*:

> The internet boom has eclipsed politics—and everything else for that matter—as the nation's most captivating playing field. A perfect marker for the new millennium, the (AOL/TW) deal brings home the way the internet has moved from the margin to the mainstream. It has realigned the corporate landscape, forcing worried corporations to respond—sometimes hastily— with new ventures and huge deals.
>
> (Roberts, 2000)

INNER SPEED

So at every level—the corporate, the community, and the individual— "keep-up" is the offspring of "speed-up" and "blow-up." Even at the micro-level, we increase our heart rate, breathing, hormonal secretions and metabolic rate. Caffeine, sugar, nicotine, Jolt, SURGE, steroids, power bars, Red Bull, amphetamines, sweeteners, "uppers," mega-vitamins, "bennies" and a host of other stimulants are consumed in *huge* quantities to sustain our keep-up.

Doctors and psychologists who treat heart problems, burnout, ulcers, drop-out, nervous disorders, strokes, breakdowns, workaholism and attempted suicides know the problems manifested by "keep-up." Just as a rat on the treadmill runs faster to "get there," we too have fallen for the illusion that artificial inner speed-up will help us master outer speed-up. Instead, the two become interlocked in a vicious circle, somewhat like two dogs chasing each other's tails. Eventually, as the music plays faster and faster, there is exhaustion rather than conquest. And a host of unintended side effects follow in the wake.

THE EFFECTS OF THREE UPPERS

"When I was faster, I was always behind" is a catchy refrain from Neil Young's "Slow Poke." (Reprise Records, 1999) Young's apercu suggests that there are unintended and ironic consequences due to speed changes. As a child, I would play the long-playing 33 1/3 rpm records at the faster speeds of 45 rpms and 78 rpms with my friends. We found there were comic, absurd, and even fascinating effects at the faster speeds. But we could no long understand the song's *meaning*. Is it the same for society?

If so, the death of meaning, or of the time to find it, could be one of the most tragic unintended effects of the three "uppers"—keep-up, speed-up and blow-up. Virilio describes other effects, such as that "where," "what," "who," and especially "why" lose priority to "when" as society hits overdrive. Virilio is also concerned about "the end of the human"—a time when the computer replaces many human functions at an alarming rate.

Such consequences are the footprints of a giant body of changes. Consider this partial list of "triple-up" effects:

1. Fatalities (vehicle, airplane, Titanic, train crashes; industrial accidents, heart attacks, etc.)

2. Information anxiety (paper overload, e-turmoil, burnout)

3. Stress (health, interpersonal, career problems)

4. Human error (multiplied by millions of moments, machines and dollars)

5. Frustration (confusion, lost purpose, missing pattern)

6. High blood pressure (early retirement, stroke, disease)

7. Travel illnesses (jet lag, flight-attendant syndromes, car sickness, spread of contagious illnesses)

8. Lost time (2-3 million person hours lost in L.A. last year alone, due to traffic delays)

9. Impatience (increase in accidents, interpersonal tensions, pressure, anxiety)

10. Compression (nutrients squeezed from food, context squeezed from news, indigestion, fragmentation)

11. Digests (arts, classics, epics, aesthetic depth reduced to Cliffs Notes, Beethoven's "hits," and TV spin-offs)

12. Multitasking (loss of focus, quality, accuracy, attention to the job at hand)

13. Diminished attention span (ADD, superficial conversation, incomplete tasks and processes, error)

14. Instant gratification (Domino's Pizza, Burger King, Dunkin' Donuts, Starbuck's Coffee = end of nutrition, health, balanced thinking, etc.)

15. Deadline fixation (no time to think, discuss, consider ethical issues)

16. Psychological dysfunction ("Never enough time"; "Job is killing me")

17. Insomnia and sleep deprivation (Perpetuates poor job performance, grogginess, nervous breakdown)

18. Drug and alcohol dependency (Escape, coping, induced slowdown—conflicting body drives due to dependency on uppers for work and downers for sleep)

19. Many others

Any of these effects could be highly elaborated. However, to focus upon just one, it is notable to consider the world of sleep. Since the "triple-ups" have contributed to round-the-clock work cycles, overtime and strange employment schedules—such as the "graveyard shift" or "night watch"—there is an overall increase in the state of human drowsiness. The President of the American Sleep Association notes that fewer and fewer people sleep well, due to the obsessive and disjointed rhythms of human activity. Without knowing it, large portions of humanity have accrued a kind of semi-permanent jet lag, due to violations of natural, nocturnal sleep cycles.

In such a world, we have shifted from what Ed and Mildred Hall call monochronic time—completing one task at a time—to polychronic time, in which we take on multiple tasks and multiple interruptions. (Hall, 1990) Polychronic, or "P-time," well known to a working single parent, seldom permits one to follow the adage "Once a job has been begun, never quit until it's done." Consequently, in P-time people feel they cannot concentrate, must truncate and collapse assignments, and suffer "incompletion anxiety." There seems to be an endless fragmentation of tasks and confusion of cycles, which lowers productivity and invites alienation. The triple-ups almost always force P-time upon both groups and individuals.

P-time can change an entire profession. In the world of faster media, for example, Kovach and Rosenstiel note the immense impact of speed upon journalism. In *Warp Speed* they assert "Journalism is in a state of disorientation brought on by rapid technological change, declining market share, and growing pressure to operate with economic efficiency."

Responding to these factors and many others, competitive speed-up transforms and damages journalism in several ways:

1. Sources gain power over journalists

2. The gatekeeper is increasingly eliminated

3. There is a never-ending news cycle

4. Argumentation and opinion become more attractive than reporting (newstalk is everywhere)

5. Verification becomes more difficult

6. Anonymous and third-party sources become more attractive

7. Error is more likely

8. Unsubstantiated allegations are more tempting to report

9. Coat-tailing (all but Xeroxing stories and leads without double-checking) and piggybacking (media-on-media stories, spin-offs) multiply

10. Overall standards lowered re acceptable information

11. Decision-making time compressed: fewer facts and factors weighed and studied

Consequently, Kovach and Rosenstiel infer that the public, journalists, journalism and the truth all are cheated when time is accordioned to meet deadlines.

According to Gleick, another group cheated by speed was the food and drug testing professionals, who, in turn, unknowingly cheated the public. Under pressure from the pharmaceutical industry, the U.S. Food and Drug Administration adopted fast-track procedures so that more drugs could be placed on the market in the 1990s. A disturbing number of such drugs were recalled shortly after their approval. Reportedly, drugs such as Duralt, which were hastily approved, were later associated with problems as severe as kidney failure and death. If experts are correct, lives could have been saved by more thorough and deliberative testing. The accelerated drug test reviews, incidentally, were financed by the drug industry.

Journalism and drug-testing are only two of many processes in the fast lane. Who would have thought that speed-up affects even this process in which we are now engaged? Eric McLuhan's research indicates that writers of the fourteenth century averaged sentences of about seventy words each, whereas current authors average less than twenty words per sentence. Choosing exceptional writers from each century, such as Chaucer, Austen and Gibbon, McLuhan tracks the declining attention span to today's world of harlequin romances and detective mysteries.

Keeping that research in mind, is it not entirely possible that if I were to start writing gargantuan Medieval sentences now in this book, you might prefer turning on the television or boycotting my publisher? In McLuhan's view, speed has created a world in which less is more. Unfortunately, it is less substance that is equivalent to more time. Indeed, the expert scholar who now wishes to be quoted on television, radio or the Net had best learn to compress substantial insights into hit-and-run sound bites.

TRIPLE "UPS" AND ETHICS

Speed-up, blow-up and keep-up often create a haste-makes-waste climate. What is wasted within the opportunity to reflect are questions such as "What are the ethical dimensions of this decision?" "How might innocent bystanders be affected?" "Could this choice cause unforeseen side effects?" "Do my vested interests in this decision allow me to see clearly?" "What choice might I make if I had more time?"

Ethical challenges increase when you consider how rapidly each new technology is implemented. Communication tools are *not* tested for possible hidden effects or for the ethical issues they may introduce or intensify. Since every new technology amplifies or creates new ethical dilemmas, "speed-up," "blow-up" and "keep-up" compound the problem.

For example, within the United State, if a technology poses ethical challenges, such as children's access to pornography on the Internet, it may take Congress months or years to adopt (or vote down) suitable policies. However, while one medium is being debated, or even two media (such as a rating system for cable TV), other technologies, such as intelligent agents or face-recognition imaging, are being developed and introduced onto the market. These innovations introduce other problems. Often technology effects, such as radiation poisoning, privacy invasion and noise pollution are not discovered until months or years after a communication tool has widespread use.

In the area of video surveillance alone, there are now controversial applications introduced into society every month. Here are some that Steve Mann has catalogued in *Leonard*:

1. Security video cameras in department stores

2. Hidden cameras in employee locker rooms

3. Automatic face-recognition computer systems (allow criminals—or anyone—to be traced

4. Hidden TV-top box cameras (so cable companies can track audience response in each home)

5. "Smart spaces," where employees under surveillance can be helped long distance via monitor when they have problems

6. "Experimental bedroom," which sees you wake up and automatically starts brewing your coffee, turns on your lights, etc.

7. Bathroom mirror camera to automatically examine your skin and moles for danger signs

8. See-through security cameras to detect theft hidden by clothing, etc.

Rapidly developing and implementing such surveillance devices short-circuits ethical discussion by the public. If cameras will be installed in public bathrooms to catch possible drug dealers, should not citizens debate the privacy issues first? If cameras might be installed to see through clothing for the detection of stolen or smuggled goods, why not have both Congress and the public weigh the pros and cons in careful deliberation *before* citizens feel violated?

What becomes obvious is that questions of policy and ethics often follow the runaway engine of innovation, like a distant caboose. Unlike the Plain People and those indigenous groups that collectively consider the likely impact of a new medium upon their culture, we often procrastinate or feel too busy to convene experts and citizens alike. "Keep-up" can make ethics a distant or deceased priority.

THE LIMITS TO SPEED-UP

Phenomena, like "speed-up," start slowly, such that we barely notice. But by this third millennium, all three rings of a circus seem to be orbiting us...faster. Part of the backlash to this world, seemingly out of control, are micro-worlds which are also out of control—road rage, serial killings, drive-by shootings, hosts of hostages, school massacres, and other random acts of violence cannot all be explained by the usual analyses. People who cannot or do not wish to catch up to a runaway society are finding unexpected ways to say, "Stop the world. I want (you) to get off."

In *Faster: The Acceleration of Just About Everything*, James Gleick notes that social acceleration is not uniform. Following a specific algebraic curve, "blast-off" or "lift-off" looks inert at first, then slow, and then quickly accelerates out of the picture. In Gleick's words:

> Not only does all exponential growth look the same, once the scale is properly adjusted, but it looks scary. For all that time something is at zero. Then it starts growing. All too soon the growth becomes impossibly fast. At the end, it rises like a wall— the limit, the present, right now. Is it any wonder we develop a sense of our future as a thing curtailed? Surely we will hit limits imposed by physical laws.

Such limits seem obvious when you consider an isolated process. The limits for test pilots pushing toward speed records are blackout or bail-out. The limits for astronauts include nausea or fiery disintegration.

The limits on automobile speedsters who push the envelope in the salt flats are spinouts, blowouts, rollovers, and explosions.

In the limits-to-growth research of Dana Meadows and others, it became obvious that one cannot accelerate population growth, pollution or resource depletion without the dire outcome of omnicide. The death of all consequential life seems the logical conclusion to a rapid stripping and swamping of the planet. Are there limits to all forms of speed and expansion?

If "this is the way the world ends," not with a whimper but with a crash, must not alternatives be investigated? Even if major global systems survive, what of the increasing numbers of people who crash on the sidelines? The "ups"—speed-up, blow-up and keep-up, invariably lead to the "outs"—spin-out, drop-out, blackout, blow-out and bail-out. Psychologically, the most dangerous "out" is "out of control." People fear loss of control and succumb to numbness, confusion, anxiety, anomie, and the syndromes of the post-Post-Modern world—Attention Deficit Disorder, social autism, perpetual dizziness and global carcinoma.

There are trade-offs that accompany speed. Speed thrills *and* speed kills. Speed can be practical, efficient, and humane—as when firefighters *rush* to a fire or ambulances *speed* victims to hospitals. But gratuitous, thrill-seeking speed-for-greed writ large can lead only to a runaway roller coaster. And the safety engineer for that amusement ride has become the Mad Hatter. Surely there are alternatives.

CHAPTER TEN

SLOWDOWN, SOUND, AND SILENCE

Dropping the Mask

In finding an alternative to the "triple-ups" and to media saturation, it may be important to ask why we love speed, growth and media. Motivations and factors, such as "socialization" (keep-up), greed, power, fear and competitive drive have already been mentioned with speed.

There are many benign and pro-social reasons why people love the media. Scholars as different as George Gerbner and A. A. Berger, among many others, have noted that the uses and gratifications of particular media include consumer amusement, catharsis, therapy, inspiration, learning, escape, sexual stimulation, aesthetic enhancement, etc.

THE WORLD WITHIN

Sometimes during a period of fasting, individuals also discover some of the less romantic reasons why they, or perhaps we, love the media. Consider journalist Linda Weltner's brutal honesty about her mirror just prior to TV Turnoff Week, as published in *The Boston Globe*:

> If you're anything like I used to be, TV isn't optional. You need it because silence makes you uneasy, or because your mind is full of negative thoughts you want to avoid. You need it because you're too tired to cope with other people's demands all the time,

or because it's too upsetting to look closely at how things have turned out. You need it to absorb your anger, or to distract you from a myriad of fears. You need it because you can't get along without a buffer between you and your life.

This deeper auto-psychology suggests that there are parts of ourselves we like to hide, even from ourselves. The media can help us provide cover-up, diversion, anesthetics and a buffer zone.

Economist Herbert Stein seems to be wearing similar X-ray glasses when he watches urban creatures put cellular phones to their ears. He does not believe they are engaging simply in the exchange of information or in anecdotal reality. Instead

it is their way of keeping contact with someone, anyone who will reassure you that you are not alone. You may think you are checking your portfolio, but deep down you are checking on your existence. I rarely see people who are with other people on the sidewalk using cell phones...it is being alone they can't stand.

So it is just possible that speed-up and media addiction may pertain to connectivity.

For some the media, speed (i.e., the consumption of more) and growth are an antidote to emptiness and alienation, or, as Max Beerbohm said of radio, it is a "friend in one's room." The eternal undertaste of inadequacy, insecurity and existential loneliness are combated or avoided as we "reach out, reach out and touch someone...."

SLOWDOWN

Slowing down to meditate often allows us to think about what lies behind some latent inner shadow. Such work can be productive and helpful in finding a promising insight, or even ourselves. Additionally, in slowing down we can also rediscover different levels of enjoyment, the nature of ease and flow, and what it means to be at home inside our skin. Gleick comments:

May suitable doses of guaranteed sensual pleasure and slow lasting enjoyment preserve us from the contagion of the multitude who mistake frenzy for contagion.

Indeed, dampening one's speed may prove to be more efficient. Overwork does not automatically produce a better product, and overconsumption does not create a better life. In *Why Things Bite Back: Technology and the Revenge of Unintended Consequences*, Edward Tenner writes:

We need a retreat from intensity. Not every software upgrade may be worthwhile. Not every increased workload creates more profit.

All of these thinkers create a strong case for simplifying our lives. Indeed when Thoreau said, "Simplify, simplify, simplify!", one "simplify" would have been sufficient.

Of interest is the fact that *Avatar* is now the most popular, best-selling celluloid story of all time. It is the story of the retreat from intensity to a world of indigenous simplicity, beauty, slow-down and organic rhythms. Ultimately, the exploitative, artificial and rapacious forces of commercialism-gone-wild, symbolized by speeding military helicopters, are evicted from the garden planet called Pandora. Is this humanity's secret wish?

SLOW IS BEAUTIFUL

Media critic Jerry Mander, in his book *In the Absence of the Sacred*, writes, "If small is beautiful, why isn't slow?" Slow-motion photography allows us to see otherwise hidden beauty and processes. Slow dancing lets us know our partners more intimately. A slowly served full-course meal gives focus to each taste and smell, such that we savor the evening and the company.

Of course, advocating "slow-down" is not the same as advocating laziness, procrastination, delay, or avoidance. Many peoples and cultures move at a slower speed than the industrialized sprint cult and yet accomplish their goals in balance.

One secret to such organic productivity might be called cooperation with the natural cycles. Many indigenous and other groups find that coordinating with seasonal and daily energy pulses guarantees *both* work efficiency and quality of life. Such understanding is the difference between perpetual paddling upstream against breakneck currents and turning one's canoe around. Going with the flow transports the canoeist further via natural propulsion with much less effort, although navigation and paddling skills are still involved. Ironically, by following the right currents, the canoeist arrives faster, healthier and better rested for tomorrow.

SLO-MO PERSPECTIVE

In sports, the "super slo mo" video playback of an action often allows viewers to appreciate the talented magic of an exceptional athlete. Slowing down one's life can have the same effect. The infinite ocean inside a conch shell, the subtle light patterns reflected upon a wall, and the complex activity around an anthill again become arresting.

While living near and often visiting the Amish people of Pennsylvania, I had eye-opening experiences. Having driven automobiles since the age of sixteen, I had always taken cars for granted. Such vehicles do not seem fast or unusual to the driver.

But as I walked along the Pennsylvania farm roads, I put myself in the shoes of the permanent pedestrian. To the walker, or to the Amish horse-and-buggy driver, the automobile zooms by like a catapulted cocoon. Car passengers seem like fly-by mannequins from a universe fully isolated from nature and humanity. There is an unintended condescension from those who live in auto culture, suggesting gross insensitivity to the kingdoms of plants, animals, cultures that live at other tempos, and to the earth blacktopped beneath them.

After days or weeks away from media, I would hear the blaring radio of a passing car as a portable subculture of amorphous noise and blinding blur, hurdled like a roaring comet through my day. I saw, heard, smelled and tasted a different planet while breathing the fresh air and enjoying the exercise my commuter life had banished. Every speed has its magic.

SLOW-DOWN AND THINKING

Urban societies seem to teach that fast thinking is superior to slow thinking. Indeed, rapidity of thought, such as by someone who can quickly solve difficult math problems, is often seen as genius. And yet our language is also padded with precautionary idioms about jet-think. "Jumping to conclusions," "Not so fast," "Wait a minute," "Let's backtrack a little," and "Leaping from a false premise" are phrases that suggest that quick thinking is not automatically correct thinking, let alone substantial wisdom.

When I was privileged to study with Shuswap Native Canadians, I was told of a problem Shuswap children faced in Westernized classrooms. Canadian and U.S. teachers who were imported to teach the Shuswap would labor in vain to convince these children to quickly put up their hands to answer questions. Behind closed doors, teachers would complain to each other about how slow and ignorant the Shuswap were—a painful insult to the parents and tribe.

What the teachers did not realize was that the Shuswap children had been taught that talking back quickly was disrespectful and that real thinking must *precede* speech. To speak quickly was foolish, for it showed that one had not taken time to think carefully. In short, teachers were condemning students for being intelligent and courteous. Western guest professors have encountered similar cross-cultural embarrassments in Asia, the Pacific, South America, and most indigenous communities.

Who is to say if there is a correct speed thought should travel? When Descartes suggested the necessity of an *un*learning process, when Russell invited a cross-examination of hidden premises, when Socrates instructed "Know thyself," when Aquinas and Emerson recommended the contemplative life, when Gilligan advocated more feminized moral standards (nurturing, caring, connection), when leading spiritual and religious leaders have prescribed inner peace as a path to enlightenment, it does not seem that they had speed-thinking in mind.

185

A contemporary problem that accompanies speedy thinking is the later regret that we have made the wrong choice. Car sales managers, time-share salesmen, airline employees and bankers all exert pressure upon our thinking speed when they say, "I can only guarantee this price today" or "The interest rate may change tomorrow" or "There's only one of these left in stock." We are supposed to make snap decisions about large sums of money, possible debt and purchases forecasting our quality of life. Quickthink, like groupthink or mediathink, has a decisive downside.

SLOWDOWN AND CHOICE

Rushkoff is concerned about precisely this problem in *Coercion*, his potent book about how the persuasion experts manipulate human behavior. It is not only sales, marketing and advertising professionals who are trained in these techniques but also children collecting funds door-to-door, smart beggars, evangelists, telemarketers, fundraisers, and many other benign and not-so-benign "coercives" who know strategies to force quick decisions. An advocate of slow-down, Rushkoff concludes that

> we may choose to take the time to distinguish between what we're told and what we really want. We might even find a way to think for ourselves…. We can come back and buy that TV tomorrow. We have the prerogative to stop, to think, and disengage.

Reclaiming one's ability to thoughtfully choose is an important option, both in fasting and in slow-down. One can even choose between speed-up and slow-down. They are not "good" and "evil," "right" and "wrong," or "life" and "death." Instead, they are more like fire and ice. Each can be helpful or dangerous, depending upon use and upon timing.

The same is true of thinking. Fast thinking is no more inherently virtuous or dangerous than slow. As Yale psychologist Robert Sternberg notes, "The essence of intelligence would seem to be knowing when to think and act quickly and knowing when to think and act slowly."

Indeed, knowing when to think slowly or quickly would seem to be a higher order of wisdom than either one considered independently. As with driving a stick-shift car or ten-speed bicycle, intelligence does not reside in a particular gear but, rather, in knowing *when* to use *which* gear.

A BIAS OF BALANCE

It follows that slow-down is no more virtuous than speed-up. Similarly, perpetual fasting is no more intelligent than social immersion. It is the interplay between the two that provides balance and maximum learning. Knowing when to fast or diet and for how long, and knowing how to apply what one learns to everyday life, become a higher order of awareness than either fasting or immersion alone.

My bias is balance. The balance between reasonable speed-up and reasonable slow-down, between practical fasting and sensible immersion, between accelerated thinking and measured contemplation, elevates thinking to wisdom and existence to living.

PUSHING THE SILENT ENVELOPE

During my first fast, refraining from speech was the final stage of my abstinence. Since I had to attend meetings, answer phone calls, and care for my child from time to time during that week, I adjusted to a *practical* speech fast; that is, I spoke only when spoken to. Simultaneously, I fasted from food and conducted a juice "cleanse" throughout the third week, as supervised by health professionals.

This process of purification was extremely healthy in many ways, particularly as overeating and speaking were two pervasive habits. I also concluded a second one-week food fast during the final week and a *total* speech fast as I wrote up my conclusions.

There is nothing new about fasting from speech. Trappist monks and other religious orders have adopted full-time or part-time lives without talk, frequently in remote seclusion. The famous Trappist Thomas

Merton let his book speak for him. Thoreau's existence at Walden Pond did not permit much conversation. Martin Exeter's moving lecture "Communion and Communication" began with a reminder that some Native Americans sat in silence, sometimes for days, until the time was ripe for speaking.

Many countries and cultures, particularly ancient tribes and indigenous peoples, have valued the role of silent periods, rituals and ceremonies. Even our own noise-dominated Western society is occasionally punctuated with "a moment of silence," usually to honor the dead, or with havens of silence, such as libraries, sanctuaries and monastic retreats.

The reasons for abstaining from chatter have been many—to commune with nature, to worship, to avoid distraction, to remember the deceased, to focus one's thought or work, to heighten group- or self-awareness, to perpetuate a tradition, to enhance listening and to evoke a discovery process. In a library, silence may be requested to protect mental concentration. In religious or spiritual meditation, silence may help free the mind from such concentration and bring it "into the present moment." Prayer, depending upon its denominational context, often originates from or perpetuates some degree of silence.

In my case, the further movement away from a noise-laden society helped me better perceive the uniquely artificial rhythms of many mass media. The glib conversation of talk shows, the slick presentations of game-show hosts, the fast-lane chatter of AM disc jockeys, the terse prose of journalists, stood out like bagpipes in a symphony when I returned from the speech fast. To be sure, I greatly enjoyed many forms of communication and can still appreciate the honed skills of such public communicators, particularly having hosted programs myself. Nevertheless, my return from silence to media observation reminded me of tuning my radio from a clear station to static or of returning from the seacoast to Manhattan.

It is obvious that the nesting places, movements and timing of many species have been altered by human conquest of the planet. So I had no romantic illusions about rediscovering *totally* natural rhythms by retreating to wildlife preserves or distant islands. Nothing on earth has escaped the residue of Chernobyl or the distant rumblings of nuclear testing. Nevertheless, I found that even a walk through the Goldsmith natural park in *downtown* Memphis, Tennessee, or around the shrubbery of my yard in *suburban* Lawrence, Massachusetts, had much to teach...if I would but listen. More natural rhythms are available everywhere, even within one's own heartbeat and breathing, when external involvement recedes.

Much of the ancient wisdom began to make sense in deeper ways—silence *is* golden; those who *know* don't say and those who *say* don't know; a picture (viewed in silence) *is* worth a thousand words; actions speak *louder* than words. Similar simple phrases took on greater meaning—the sign "Silence Spoken Here" that I had seen in a friend's office; a quote by T. S. Eliot about being at "the still point of the turning world"; another friend's workshops about "the lost art of listening"; Buber's emphasis upon "being rather than seeming to be"; "the sounds of silence" rediscovered by Simon and Garfunkel; the biblical command "Be still, and know that I am God"; and a favorite ancient adage, "It is better to keep one's mouth closed and *appear* the fool, than to open it and remove all doubt."

PERSONAL SILENCE

Such personal silence emphasizes not so much what is *absent*, but rather hidden dimensions of self which suddenly become *present*. I am not suggesting that "enlightenment" or "wisdom" are *automatically* more available to the silent than to the loquacious. After all, a zombie seems silent; a corpse is still. But if the stillness is purposeful, consistent, focused, intelligent, and deliberately connected to a creative process, a larger awareness can appear, step-by-step.

Part of my own awareness vis-a-vis media was that our programming resembles the most adventurous customers in a pancake house. Such customers freely layer their pancakes with maple, strawberry, blueberry and other syrups simultaneously. Similarly, who we are has become so smothered by layers of radio, TV, print, education, religion, and domestic conditioning, we have perhaps moved beyond Erikson's "identity crisis" to an "identity absence."

189

Buried beneath the syrupy muzak and soaps of modern media is a *self* impossible to discover without stillness. With this word *self*, of course I am referring to the one Socrates invited us to "know" and the one to which Shakespeare (via Polonius) invited us to be true. Ironically, when I once asked a class of communication students at the University of Maryland what Socrates meant by "self" in the phrase "Know thyself," their first, lengthy answer was silence.

FROM SENSATIONALISM TO SENSE

One of the common protests of the age of media-ocrity is that journalism, entertainment, advertising, public relations and other forms of mass media have become too sensational. Hype, spam, gratuitous violence, tabloids, "X-rated," spectacle, glitter, infotainment, T&A and "Tinseltown" are all terms which indicate the public communicator's penchant for preferring surface to substance, for shocking or seducing our senses to beat his competition. A trend appearing at the forefront of "threshold programming" (Jerry Springer, Howard Stern, Sally Jessie Raphael, Geraldo Rivera, Morton Downey, Jr., Dr. Ruth, etc.) has been called the "trash, flash, clash and slash" movement. "Cash" is the apparent motivation for its appearance.

In the same vein, throughout history we have discovered how to captivate and dazzle the human sensorium. Babies have long been enticed and engaged by colorful, bright objects. Adults are more customarily enticed by aromatic perfumes, incense and colognes. More recently, Madison Ave., Hollywood, Paris, and worlds beyond have become fascinated with the visual trinkets and acoustical perfumes which will entice the full spectrum of potential buyers.

When the senses are freed from such obsessions, when the tongue is liberated from soliloquy, and thus the mind is relieved of concocting incessant verbiage and interpreting constant stimuli, what other forms of sensation are possible? My experience is that when senses are no longer saturated, they become enhanced and re-sensitized. Stopping to smell the roses may mean more than bending over for a moment for personal pleasure. Each individual flower and species may have some fragrance or other message to communicate, which may take a lifetime of gardening or hiking to discover. When one stops gawking at each accident along the roadside, you finally go somewhere.

Anyone who has ever taken a top-flight course in music or art history knows there is infinitely more to be sensed from the arts than is immediately grasped. So it is with life at large and all the sensory powers. For example, Hugo Zuccherelli's research notes that listening may extend far beyond the notion of merely *hearing*. It includes an outer-directed, sonar-type listening which we have not known how to utilize.

We mention seeing "between the lines," "hearing with radar," "sniffing out the situation," "hearing what she was *really* saying," "seeing through to the bottom of this," "smelling a rat," "seeing with new eyes," "feeling it out," "seeing other dimensions of the situation," "listening with your heart," "touching another level," and "keeping my antenna out." Intuitively, we *sense* that when our head and portals (eyes, ears, etc.) are not clogged, they have space to fulfill a fuller range of functions and fine-tuning. Phrases such as "common sense," "I sense that," "in another sense," and "makes sense" indicate that subconsciously we know how much we rely on intuition, not just analysis.

Lest anyone think I am suddenly advocating "extrasensory perception" (another subject for another time), I emphasize that the power of stillness lies in "*intra*-sensory perception." To simply discover the range and function of natural sensation is a lifelong enrichment program. Similarly, while many advocate that enhancing the senses leads to better *sub*liminal awareness, my emphasis is on *super*liminal discovery; that is, what resides *above* the range of awareness. We are reminded of this range of sound when a dog picks up his ears in response to frequencies we cannot audit. Such unheard sounds are but the tip of the tip of a mountainous iceberg.

In propaganda wars, much is said about the ability to "jam" the transmission of rival or enemy signals. For example, since the Cold War, Radio Free Europe, its Soviet counterpart (Radio Moscow), and similar broadcasting systems reported the silencing, scrambling, descrambling or "jamming" of their signals. It seems likely that our own senses are

191

jammed by external devices to varying degrees, such that we no longer listen attentively to inner signals.

Perceptual psychologists may extend the list of inner senses beyond the usual five. Sometimes they mention a possible "sense of direction," "sense of time," "sense of proportion," etc. But I have reference to even deeper "senses," which reside at the core of self—a sense of home, a sense of truth, a sense of (well-)being, and a sense of purpose, among others.

THE VALUE OF TRANSCENDENCE

The value of transcendence is the difference between being in a centrifuge and above it. To be spun around by outer events is to lose orientation, perspective, self-control and homeostasis. To view what spins below is to learn from its actions, remain undisturbed, and be able to shift one's gaze wherever necessary. This is the lesson of Edgar Allen Poe's story *A Descent Into The Maelstrom*. The sailor who remained calm and detached as his boat spun downward in a whirlpool was able to first observe the flow of the currents, then the rising of the flotsam to the top. He then hurled himself into the whirlpool and spiraled upward to safety. His partner, tormented by fear of the maelstrom, sunk with his boat to instant peril.

Whether maelstrom or centrifuge, it may be understood with greater clarity and less danger from above than below. The point of transcendence, however, is not merely perspective and protection. When cooperating with the currents and winds, any skipper joins a larger field of influence and ease. The deeper roots of addiction and identity, previously illusive, become more visible. At that point truly substantial understanding and changes may occur. If this work is done with irreversible initiative, the need for future fasting fades. Hence transcendent vision and a sense of overall context is essential.

When clichés are liberated from our overuse, we discover in *stillness* the *deeper* meaning of "still waters run deep." No matter which Martin one reads—Buber, Exeter or Heidegger—*being* is the central ingredient of such depth, and the core of such stillness. Of course, when one stops over-reading and listens to other martins, and indeed invigorates one's own expression, yet another level of being is known.

What is discovered in these depths, or paradoxically at these heights, might be called *being fully present*. Fasting from all distraction, including one's own post-dubbed narrative over the sounds and images of life, allows a sense of anchoring in this *ground* of being...present. The answer to the question "What is present when my programming is absent?" is "I am."

Thinking also becomes *present*. In wondering why professors are caricatured as *absent*-minded, I discovered that there is some truth in seeing the human mind as absent from the body, missing in action, lost between bookends. If the mind, ensnared in the illusionary world perpetuated by media, is to become present, inner stillness is essential.

The brain appreciates the "space" of stillness. No longer hemmed in by a flood of incoming stimuli, it is freer to perceive the relationship of stimuli selected for perception. The psyche is also given a sense of regained youth and time: when one does not feel required to comment on all or even any subjects, vistas of observation and hours of reflection become available. Moreover, when one does break the silence, one's few words carry authority. There is much more thought back of each word. Their economy sharply contrasts with filibusters round about. Less is more. *Still* waters run deep.

I am not advocating a world of total silence or speechlessness. Those who have lost their voices or hearing due to accidents point out there is no romance in being deaf or speechless. Beethoven is said to have felt violently frustrated and totally impoverished from his loss of hearing. Too much beautiful poetry, drama and music have been created by every species for me to advocate global earplugs. The point is, rather, that *I* must restrain from contributing to the noise, the redundancies, the jargon, the babble, the stream of non-consciousness, the "people talking without speaking," the information monsoon.

FOCUSED PERCEPTION

When the welter of competing cacophonies is subdued, it is then possible to focus upon sounds and their creation, one at a time. After all, the ear seems designed to fully "understand" one sound at any given instant or orchestrated sound cluster, such as a symphony or chorus, at once. If you disagree, go to a restaurant with a friend, engage in conversation during your meal and determine how many other conversations at neighboring tables you can simultaneously and accurately monitor, for even ten minutes. Several years ago I was alone in the control room of a TV station with a producer. I asked him to turn off the twenty monitors being viewed to keep up with the competition, tape inserts and floor cameras. "That's better," he conceded. "We *can* talk better." "Probably see and listen better, too," I thought to myself. The eye and ear appreciate focus.

When sounds and images may be perceived by choice with selectivity of speed, viewing time, replay, contemplation, silent pauses in between, etc., one at a time at natural speeds, relief comes to the head and nervous system. Indeed some sounds are said to bring healing and therapy if properly chosen and replayed. When monks in Eastern Canada stopped chanting, morale decreased and health problems increased. After months of experimentation—change of diet, workload, etc.—chanting was reinstituted. Health and morale seemed restored.

There are numerous other enhancing sounds—one ancient Japanese Haiku translates "There is nothing so pleasing as the sound of running water." Trying to cash in on this perception, recording studios have released CDs of babbling brooks, ocean waves, waterfalls, aviaries and other soothing sounds for home use. Hospitals, asylums, and related institutions continue to experiment with and employ a variety of sound and music therapies.

While there is much beauty in these sounds, relative to the deafening airport sounds protested by members of suburban neighborhoods, even records of the environment and therapy tapes can become another form of media addiction. Perhaps the greatest use of sound is one's own—in *Anatomy of an Illness* Norman Cousins tells of how the renowned elderly cellist Pablo Casals, arthritic and stooped, became a new man when passionately bowing his cello.

Thousands of amateur singers annually "regain a new lease on life" when singing Handel's *Messiah* or other victorious anthems. My own experience of composing and performing music when fasting from media and speech was elevating and enduring.

Thus the secret of *sound* health may not be so much in the acoustical environment as in ourselves, our ability to personally *sound* a healthy tone and *participate* in harmonious frequencies. My speech fast objective was not to silently condemn speech but, rather, to return to it with more music and less monotone in my voice...and in my living. I was reminded of this recently when a friend commented that many people "die with their music still in them."

Naturally, there are other purposes for a speech fast—to enlarge one's awareness of sound and listening, to learn of and from one's *interior* soundscape, and to discover who is present beneath the mask.

UNMASKING

Talk is usually part of the pretense that prevents us from being ourselves. We become aware of the cover-up at cocktail parties, public ceremonies, and other social events. One learns early in life how to "make talk," "don't let on," "see what you can learn without revealing too much," "tread water," "chat," "schmooze," "gossip," "ham it up," "cover your tracks," "hobnob," "curry favor" and "butter up." At subconscious levels, we may feel discomfort from the subtle dishonesty or flagrant insincerity of such forms of communication.

Once during a conference call this phenomenon was clearly articulated by Peter Russell, author of *The Global Brain*. The call, sponsored by Marc Sarkady's inventive and zany "Gallucci Family" (sort of a cross between the Vienna Circle and Surrealism via teleconferencing), featured many "new thinkers," artists, and Marc's friends worldwide, who took turns leading innovative, upbeat teleconference experiments.

In this case, Marc had asked the participants to, among other things, "envision a positive future worldwide." After novel and uplifting visions were voiced from Germany, the U.S., Canada, etc., it was time to hear from England. Peter Russell, who was online, commented: "My idea of a positive future is very simple. It would be for everyone, everywhere to just *drop it*."

The *global silence* was deafening.

I could envision masks, such as the one Eleanor Rigby wore, dropping in neat little piles on the street corners of London and everywhere. Everyone listening to the teleconference understood Peter's meaning as transcultural. The masks that prevent genuineness are as obvious in the subway in London as in Washington, D.C., or Moscow or Tokyo.

The roles and postures we have been taught to assume to be successful, to blend with social mores, often become so entrenched that we forget we are playing them—like an actress who begins to live the life of her character. Russell's ideal was that everyone would step *out* of character, providing even greater magic than when great actors step into character.

Letting the mask fall can be an adventurous component of our fasting from speech. Although many claim to be threatened by "who might be inside" oneself, beneath the murky second level of self (where many negative feelings and fears are stored) is a third level—as fascinating, expansive and creative as life itself. In my view, this core of being is one's permanent home.

What would happen if the mask did fall worldwide? If everyone felt at home together? If pretenses, defenses and boundaries were viewed as the barriers to genuine dialog, rather than language, custom and weapons? Buber describes what such communication might be like in his essay "Elements of the Inter-human." He invites each of us to be genuine in our dialog, to "behold the other such as the very one we are"; to engage in a "mutual fruitfulness" of discovery and, in short, to trust in the power of communication at an unmasked ball.

Some have claimed that such unmasking leads to the mystical part of self—to the esoteric, the exotic, and even to extraterrestrial awareness. My concern is not so much with the *supernatural* as with noting that the *natural* is *super*. On the other hand, I am not doubting that if Joan of Arc, Mohammed, Moses and others did, as reported, hear other voices, it must have helped for them to have clear receivers; that is, well-tuned inner ears would be required for deeper levels of communication. Such acute listening would be one aspect of a fast of *forty* days and nights, the notable length reported for the "temptation" fast of Jesus.

A close inspection of Jesus' emphasis, if accurately transcribed, suggests that the purpose of abstinence is to fast from *self-centeredness*. It is reported that he said, "When you fast, go into your closet," rather than "show off your self-control, hunger pangs and piety." In that spirit, it would be a sad irony if one developed the *habit* of fasting for self-promotion rather than for a far larger purpose.

Those who become consistent at inner listening have claimed to hear at other levels, such as to hear "the sound of one hand clapping" in Eastern monasteries or, as a Native American healer reported, "to hear the sound of the earth." Psychologists report that "hearing voices" and unexplained sounds is a far wider phenomenon than is admitted or reported. Most people do not wish to be perceived as eccentric or crazy.

Of course *some* such people have gone over the edge and can no longer discern practical reality from inner fiction. From our standpoint what is noteworthy is that *media* fantasies now figure prominently in the hallucinations and imagination of those who are paranoid, schizophrenic, psychotic, and lost in other worlds. People no longer limit their imagination to thinking they are Napoleon or Cleopatra but may as easily assume they are James Bond or Julia Roberts. What is more frightening to some social observers is that *all* media consumers, at one time or another, subconsciously imagine they are Bond, Roberts, or some other celebrity, sports star or newsmaker.

Many of us have this Walter Mitty-style daydream frequently, even to the point of missing our exit on the freeway, assuming we are more attractive or important to others than is realistic, burning the toast, or applying for jobs well beyond our competency. The "other voices" most of us hear and embellish are often from these "inner reruns."

The possibility of hearing the earth's heartbeat is compelling. If all man-made sound were to recede for a decade, what else would we hear? If inner listening were highly developed, what inner frequencies could be tuned in? Often when there is a nocturnal power failure in a large city, observers claim that the sky is flooded with stars. Of course the stars were there all along, merely blotted from view by the halo of urban electric lighting. What sounds are *already* there?

My own purpose for sustained silence was not to discover other voices but, rather, to hear my own more clearly. When one's inner fictions are brought to silence, a still, small voice is heard with increasing clarity. Such a voice is nothing to be feared or viewed as mystical, since it is actually oneself. When I discussed intra-communication (as in "talking to oneself") in class, a student asked me "What inner voice?" He continued: "When you said 'inner voice,' something inside me asked 'What inner voice'?"

"*That* inner voice," I replied.

He smiled.

The phrase used by my student, "Something inside me"—which surfaces throughout pop lyrics and conversation—is one sign of this buried identity. "Something inside me" is a figure of speech closely linked to "Know thyself," "Scratch the inner itch," "Touch bottom inside," and "Come out of hiding." As Cavell, Wittgenstein, Austin and others indicate, our language, despite its tendency to betray us, at other levels reveals us.

I still find Stanley Cavell's question "Must we mean what we say?" invigorating to explore. But after the discoveries of fasting, the next question becomes: "Must **not** we say what we mean?" So long as we say otherwise—whether to bedazzle, deceive, entice or hide—how may we scowl at false advertising? We are its origin.

HOMECOMING

When Kubrick filmed *2001: A Space Odyssey*, the critics gasped and cheered at his innovative use of visual space and motion. Annette Michaelson's essay in *Artforum* was deepest in suggesting why we were *moved* by Kubrick's *movements*—of cameras and content, of visual and galactic space. I was similarly *moved* by the "death" of HAL, the spaceship's command computer "who" maintained all in-flight operations. HAL talked, called crew members by their first names, used emotive vocal inflections, and thus seemed to have latent personality.

When being deprogrammed, HAL slowly lost his memory, his control of the ship and his meaning. His swan song, the singing of "Daisy," finally slowed to a stop, and so too did HAL. For us as human beings, our difference is critical. When *our* programming by media and the environment, of chitchat and camouflage, winds down, there is still someone "at home." Instead of losing memory, control and meaning, these are regained, as if we are patients awakening from amnesia.

Ultimately, HAL can be threatened by attempts to terminate his function. He appears even to feel lonely for companionship and insecure when his competency is in question. He seems *almost* human. But when the programming is gone, so too is HAL. When our programming recedes, another dimension of communication appears. Computers may be trained to duplicate the questions that surface beneath our programming—questions such as "Who am I?" "What has meaning?" "What am I doing?" But artificial intelligence is not driven by an endless compulsion to find the answer, an answer that can neither be fully programmed nor converted to data.

We, conversely, are governed by the quests for meaning, fulfillment, purpose and home. "Fasting" from external stimuli initially seems to be just a novelty or a better means for understanding media's role in our lives. But it may instead lead to a type of "homecoming," a return to reality, depending upon who is involved and with what degree of personal penetration.

Contained within the sounds of silence, freedom from habit, and the authority of firsthand experience, are the seeds of creation. These may not be rented at the nearest video outlet. Nor are they listed in *TV Guide* or the contents guide of the newspaper. One must express life directly, rather than consume it indirectly, to know its meaning and purpose.

However, if someone *is* at home beneath the programming, the sounds of silence, freedom from habituation, and authority of firsthand living may be known in the process of producing or using any mass medium, fast or slow. Indeed, these sounds of silence, freedom from addiction, and authority of firsthand living may enliven all reflection and activity.

Communicators *may* play a valuable part in understanding the state of the planet and providing an alternative. However, one is ill equipped to accurately see the larger picture or do anything about it without authenticity, transcendence, grounding, stillness, observation and sustained listening. It also helps to reduce excessive consumption, waste and their causes. There is a deeper meaning to Simon and Garfunkel's lyrics "Slow down, you move too fast. You got to make the morning last."

CONCLUSIONS

The conclusions of any experiment of this type are personal, and thus *in*conclusive, whatever our attempt to reach scientific closure on the nature of reality. My fasts were deliberately personal, and I encourage those who conduct more clinical research to test larger groups of people from varying backgrounds in control situations.

In this latter context, I am equally interested in our *interior* research conducted in daily living. Feel free to write me, via the publisher, about your breakthroughs and discoveries in personal and mediated communication. Our discovery and contribution are ongoing.

In this sense, the final exam for this book is a *take-home* exam. The most important question, "Who is at home beneath our syrup of media overlay?", might also be worded: "Who is inside the consumer?" Just as the two questions are really one, so too are the two answers: "I am" and "the creator." In short, "I am the creator" is the awareness and attitude which, when activated, motivates the addict to kick the consumer habit and participate fully in the creative process.

Elbert Hubbard, the famous nineteenth-century Roycrofter and author of the world's most widely circulated essay, "A Message to Garcia," wrote the more obscure "Essay on Silence," which was nevertheless translated into dozens of languages without difficulty. The reason for the translator's ease was that Hubbard's essay, following its title page, contained but twelve *blank* pages of paper.

Hubbard did, however, leave one hint at his intended meaning. On the back of his essay are the words "Some things are better left unsaid." So it is with this book and these simple conclusions. Silence is spoken here.

Depending upon whether you are a teacher, group leader, student or general reader, you may wish to consider the suggestions under the two attached appendices if you intend to conduct your own media fast. Of course there is no expectation from me that you will either fast or, if you do, follow these suggestions. In any event, they are simply intended as points of departure.

What seems of greater importance is the awareness that comes, not simply from fasting but from living and thinking more fully. The period of abstinence is only as significant as its silent impact when one returns to full-time interaction with the full spectrum of society. One then asks, "Is my *current* communication more conscious?" "Is it more creative than destructive?" "More perceptive?" "Less conspicuous?" "Less addictive?" "More open?" "More inspiring?" "More effective?" "Is my perception of media more two-way?" "Selective?" "Balanced?" "Focused?" "Understanding?" "Acute?" It seems such questions could be usefully answered at any time, fast or no fast.

In *Amusing Ourselves to Death*, Neil Postman calls our attention to Huxley's warning, rather than Orwell's. Orwell cautioned that we would lose our freedom of thought to some *external* dictatorial omni-media, which monitors and reprograms our every movement. Huxley, instead, warned that we would die of *internal* atrophy, laughing ourselves to death at mindless entertainment, drugged by the "feelies," fiddling while Rome burns. In such conditions our attention span withers, news becomes entertainment, and we live, like Pavlov's dogs, for the bells and whistles of intravenous pleasure. In a society that ingests more television (not to mention newer media) than any other experience, there is no point in arguing with Huxley or Postman.

But there is even a greater danger than that we will all be quickly converted to mental and emotional slush, due to amusement, apathy and

201

anomie. This danger is the mirage of belief. For centuries we have believed that some new technology, some greater education, some omniscient religion or scientific discovery would miraculously counteract the fears of Orwell and Huxley and solve all problems.

Such presumptions have not proven true. As hopes escalated, so too did prices, shortages, populations and early warnings. This hope and conviction that "things will somehow get better" or that "I won't be affected" is what allows us to sustain our mindless amusement.

Moreover, it is but a small step from believing the illusions of our beliefs to accepting the illusions of our media. When once asked to speak to a chapter of the Theosophical Society, I noted their astute motto: "There is no religion higher than truth." As an educator I can think of no philosophy nor pedagogy, no concept of belief, which is higher than truth—education's ultimate goal. Similarly, most of the journalists I know hold to the premise that no news source or institution is higher than truth—journalism's professed destination.

Our deepest danger is that we would ignore truth and not care, that we would persist in belief and hope, and thus avoid evidence. The longing for truth unites the spirit of education, religion, philosophy, science and journalism. If fast media were to *ring* true, not attract through the cosmetic, there would be less need for a media fast. It is to that quest for the ongoing discovery of truth, as best we may determine it, that this book, fast and life are dedicated. One and the truth are a majority.

So one of the deepest purposes of a media fast lies in the pursuit, and even the revelation, of truth. What is the truth of myself beneath my programming? Whatever *your* purpose in a media fast—novelty, learning, meditation, change, retreat, clarity, inventory, education, rest, direction, focus—there is the possibility of pushing your experience further, to life's most important questions. Indeed there is the possibility that, upon reflection, you are one of life's most important answers.

APPENDICES

PERSONAL FASTING

Your Checklist and Options

Since this book is intended for the general reader—not just group leaders, teachers and students—you might discover that you are now ready to conduct your own personal media fast. Teachers, group leaders and students, however, may wish to read the next appendix and Chapter Six before conducting media fasts. Everyone, whether on individual or group fasts, should also refer back to the Introduction and Chapter One to consider your purpose, motivation, ground rules and guidelines.

You may choose a totally different type of experiment than the one I report. For example, you may choose to fast from *electronic* media, rather than *all* media, say for two weeks rather than a month. Or you may wish to try the experiment with a partner or group of friends.

Whatever format you select, this checklist of *practical* questions to ask *prior* to the fast might make it more manageable, consistent and successful by whatever standards you choose.

GENERAL CHECKLIST

1. What *length* will the fast be? Have you checked to see who or what this might influence and advised them of your situation? Have you studied your Day-Timer or calendar to see what events will be influenced, which might commit

you to encountering media? Will this be a *strict* timed fast or might you play it by ear concerning how long it will last?

2. Will any parts of this book guide you about questions you wish to ask or *areas of consideration*? If so, do you wish to mark them or post them, perhaps paraphrased in your own words, to refer to throughout the experience? Are there other questions or concerns that might help guide your thought at various intervals? How will you maintain consistent focus?

3. What *guidelines* and *ground rules* will you set for yourself? Will you include *all* media? Just one to which you think you might be addicted? What will you do if you *have* to read a book, look up Web sites or view a tape for your job? Will you set *strict* ground rules or leave loopholes? Will you fast from speech? How will you note or record thoughts and feelings?

4. With whom should you *communicate* about your fast? Is there anyone you usually attend movies with or who expects you to read job-related articles, etc., whom you should advise of your fast? Would you need permission from anyone to not use media during your fast? Is there anyone you wish to have advise you before or during the fast? to be a sparring partner with you about your ideas? to keep you informed about major news stories?

5. Will you experience a variety of *activities* during the fast? Where? Are there other activities you might add which could prove educational? Are there activities you often experience via mass media (news events, sports, concerts, trials, political rallies, etc.) you might wish to experience firsthand?

6. How will you spend your *time* during the fast, particularly time formerly spent consuming? Are there people or groups you wish to know better or that depend on you for leadership or companionship? Are there hobbies, activities, quiet

times, social times, etc., you wish to explore or instigate? What could you *create* during this time, whether through the arts or with teams of people or in design? cooking? writing? Are there projects you have shelved that you wish to resume? What about nature? culture? other cultures? sports? relationships? religion or spirituality? learning? growth? martial arts? latent interests?

7. Are there ways you wish to be more *responsible* about your communication, which you can apply during the fast? What do you discover about your listening and speaking habits? What about your use of resources and "media waste"—unread newspaper sections, old tapes, back issues of magazines, outdated software, subscriptions you never utilize, and other excess? How do communication, the state of the earth, and your actions during and after the fast relate?

8. How will you follow up *after* the experience? Will you collate and write up your findings? Could these be suitable for publication if you submitted them to online magazines, newspapers, newsletters or other mass media? Will you write me about your highlights and findings? Will you conduct another media fast or lead others in one? What will you continue to create?

9. Finally, what is *most significant* about this book and experience for you? Are there changes you wish to make or thoughts you wish to apply? Are there other thoughts that the book omitted but which you wish to contemplate or raise publicly? Do you have useful feedback for me, your teachers, your group, or for leaders in the media industries that we might find helpful? Never underestimate your influence.

GROUP FASTING

*Thoughts and Assignments for Group
Members and Students*

If you are using this book as part of your course work or group fast, your teacher or group leader will let you know what reading assignments, homework and deadlines are part of your media-fast process. If, however, you are reading this book casually, without academic supervision, say over the summer, please consider yourself a general reader and read Appendix I.

Students who are conducting the fast as part of your course work might be given specific handouts and assignments before, during or after the media fast. However, your teacher may wish for you to *choose* one or more of your assignments, projects or topics for discussion. To help you start the selection process, some questions are listed below. Although you and your teacher might agree that you write on one of these questions, the question might also serve as a catalyst to lead you to discover a better topic or question. Give some thought to the possibilities. Then talk with your instructor.

Depending upon your level of education or type of group, you might be writing a report, essay, diary, term paper, project or dissertation. You might also be asked to present an oral presentation, take one side of a debate, lead a discussion, organize a slide/photo/video show, or present your highlights, breakthroughs or findings in a more original manner.

Whatever approach is appropriate in your situation, discuss possible topic(s) with your leader, instructor or advisor as soon as possible.

Remember, too, that these questions are just a short list of ideas that will serve as points of departure. You may find that discussing these with your leader or instructor or friends may lead to more specific questions, better suited to your current level of study. You might also discover that some of the dozens of questions throughout the book which appear in "question clusters"; that is, in groups of consecutive questions, would be of greater interest to you or of more relevance to your group than the questions below.

1. Is the increasing consumption of media healthy or unhealthy for society? Does this differ according to who is consuming and in which country? Does it depend upon which media or medium they are consuming? Can you back up your thought with logic? evidence? statistics? common sense? quotations from authorities? comparative studies? creative thought? Can you really count the computer and telephone within your study of "media," since they can be personal and two-way?

2. What is the relationship between the critical state of the earth and mediated communication? Can you find evidence about at least one resource; for example, the amount of paper consumed by newspapers or magazines each year? What alternative approach might you attempt? How? Why? Please document. What will happen if the current consumption continues? Quote authorities, footnote findings, and support all conclusions.

3. Are there purposes for silence? for speaking? If so, what? Can we better utilize each of them? How? How does sound differ from noise? Do you advocate making personal or social changes in your use of sound, noise and silence? Substantiate your thoughts with logically developed thought and, if possible, empirical documentation.

4. Now that you have completed your media fast, would you

encourage peers to fast, cut back their consumption, or continue without change? Would you encourage everyone to do the same? Why? If you think that we should cut back our consumption, how do you know by how much? Would your thought hold true for all countries or just yours? If you do not know, how could you find out? Will you fast or cut back consumption in the future? Why? If so, how much? Why?

5. If you are trained in research methods, why not devise a questionnaire that would help determine if your classmates or group changed attitudes or habits during or after the fast? Discuss with your teacher or leader what types of data and methods would be most useful. Using this information as a rough tentative indicator, what patterns do you see? What problems with the validity and reliability of your data do you perceive? What have you learned from your tabulations? Would you expect to find similar patterns with larger samples of people, whether of your age, younger or older? Why or why not?

6. During the fast, what is your *personal* experience of media residue and afterimages? What is your personal experience of discovering addictions or habituation to specific media? genres? subjects (sports, weather, news, sex, violence, celebrities, etc.)? What media-related time habits have you discovered, if any? If you have addictions or habits, did you at least temporarily break them? With what difficulty? Do you better "know yourself" in the manner Socrates taught?

7. What is original thought? Does it really exist? Do you think media obliterate or dilute personal thoughts and the amount of creative thinking that is possible?

8. How does the world differ for heavy media users and those who abstain? What research literature is available, demonstrating how heavy media users view the world differently from nonusers? Does the research appear to be valid and reliable? How could you find out? If media

consumption continues to increase, how will our perceptions of our neighbors and of the world change? Although you are aware that this latter question is speculative, can you give evidence to support the projected directions you have chosen?

9. Is *freedom* of thought and action truly possible? Is one ever free of secondhand experience? Is media programming an enslaving force that destroys free thought and action? How could you find out? If freedom of thought is no longer possible, then *your* thought at this moment is currently restricting your interpretation of this question. Do you think that you *are* controlled by subconscious programming? To what degree? If so, what could you do about it? What could others do?

10. If you were to choose a career in communication, what could you do to make people more aware of media control, addiction, waste, stereotyping, and some of the other concerns raised in this book? What could you do if you chose to become a teacher? What can you do now as a citizen? How? Pin down your ideas with specific steps and concrete means of implementation.

11. Plato suggested that writing would be dangerous because we would substitute reading about an experience for the experience itself. Do you agree? How much of your experience is secondhand? In your observation of those around you, how direct is their experience? How do you evaluate a society so dependent upon secondhand knowledge and substitute experiences?

12. Are interpersonal relationships truly changing by virtue of our increased media consumption? If so, how? Is such change healthy or unhealthy for society at large? Why? What effects might further change bring? Would collective fasting have an impact on this change? What type of change?

13. Are media truly useful to society or do they serve as what

Pascal called our greatest human problem—distraction? Why? If they are useful, to what degree? Could you debate either side of the resolution: "If global citizens voted to stop using all forms of media, society would gain more than it loses"?

14. In every chapter of the text, I quoted from or alluded to thinkers, leaders and scholars whose reflections seem important to me. Do you wish to read a book or essay—for example by Aristotle, Buber, Exeter, Gerbner, Heidegger, Heinberg, Huxley, Meyrowitz, Orwell, Pascal, Postman or Sartre—to develop and examine ideas we merely touched?

15. What questions can *you* devise that could sharpen our discussion and your education, based upon your fasting and group experience? If given total freedom in devising your essay, paper or dissertation, what topic would you choose? Why? Is its scope feasible? Is there sufficient reliable research literature available to survey the question intelligently? If little research exists on the topic, can you develop a more philosophical answer substantiated by a well-developed line of argumentation? What would you better understand, if not know, by attempting to answer this question in depth?

Remember to consult your teacher or leader before choosing or designing your project and precisely wording your topic. Education, whether within or beyond school, can be extremely fascinating, so remember to let this experience be creative and adventurous. Choose a topic you can sink your teeth into and by which you hope to experience *le gai savoir*, the joy of learning.

Your work has worth and could be of interest to many. I, for one, would love to hear what you have learned, what feedback you have about how we might improve this educational experience. If you have the time and interest, please let me know what changes you intend to make, if any, in your relationship with media and in your living.

INDEX

Y

Z

ABOUT THE AUTHOR

Dr. Thomas Cooper is a tenured Professor of Visual and Media Arts at Emerson College, and was recently guest Professor at the University of Edinburgh, Scotland, and Union University. His most recent research was at Oxford, Cambridge, Harvard, Princeton, Yale, and five other leading universities. He has taught at Harvard University, the University of Hawaii, the University of Maryland, Middle Tennessee State University and Temple University. As founder and co-publisher of *Media Ethics* magazine, author of seven books and over one hundred and twenty other publications, Dr. Cooper actively addresses topics in new media, communications, journalism, speech, ethics, and the arts. Tom was an assistant speechwriter in the White House and was one of the first producers of audio spacebridges among U.S. and Soviet communication professionals. As a graduate student at the University of Toronto, Tom was mentored by Marshall McLuhan and served as one of his assistants. With Dr. Clifford Christians, Dr. Cooper co-convened the first Media Ethics Summit Conference in 1987 and the second Media Ethics Summit Conference in 2007. Cooper has won or raised nearly one million dollars in awards, grants and fellowships, and has been selected a King, East/ West, Massey, and Young Fellow. He received his B.A. (magna cum laude) from Harvard and his M.A. and Ph.D. from the University of Toronto. An international speaker at the University of Moscow, Oxford, Harvard and other leading institutions, he is also a musician, poet, playwright and Black Belt who founded the Association for Responsible Communication, which was nominated for the Nobel Peace Prize.

OTHER PUBLICATIONS FROM GAETA PRESS

By Dr. Michael Gaeta

Home Learning Programs on Wholistic Health
- Understanding Whole Food Nutrition: Natural vs. Synthetic, Whole Foods Diet
- A Wholistic Approach to Detoxification & Lasting Weight Loss
- Ten Essential Western Botanicals
- Vaccination Alternatives and Effective Immune Support
- A Wholistic Approach to Improving Cardiovascular Health
- Cancer Support and Prevention
- Healing the Center: Improving Gastrointestinal Health
- Protomorphogens & Autoimmune Disease
- The Triad of Endocrine Health

Love, Serve & Succeed®: Connecting Spirit to Success™ for Health Professionals
Home Learning Programs
- Module One: Spiritual Mastery & the Healing Relationship: The Essential Foundation
- Module Two: Starting Up Right: Preparing to Create a Strong Practice
- Module Three: Legal Issues and Asset Protection (created with Deanna Waldron, Esq.)
- Module Four: Effective Marketing on a Shoestring: What Works & Doesn't Cost a Lot
- Module Five: Growing a Thriving Practice: How to Run a Thriving Practice (office systems)
- Module Six: Building & Preserving Wealth: Money Smarts, Getting Out of Your Own Way

- Module Seven: Integrity in the Healing Relationship: Ethics for Health Professionals

E-Books
- Love, Serve & Succeed: Connecting Spirit to Success for Health Professionals
- You Can Create Cardiovascular Health: Seeing Through the Cholesterol Myths
- The Vaccination Myths
- Detoxification and Lasting Weight Loss

DVD
Heaven in My Hands: An Introduction to Attunement

Recorded Webinars
- The Core: Natural vs. Synthetic, and Essential Nutritional Support for Everyone
- Autoimmune Disease and Protomorphogens
- The Triad of Endocrine Health: Essential Support for Hormonal Wellness
- Hair Mineral Analysis and Natural Medicine
- Optimal Reproductive Health for Men and Women
- Chinese Medicine Energetics of Whole Food Supplements
- How to Buy or Sell a Healthcare Practice
- Nutrition with the Seasons (audio only)

Audio Programs
Interviews with the Experts on Wellness, Healing and Nutrition, including Bob Duggan, MAc; Kim John Payne, M.Ed; Stuart White, DC; Duane Graveline, MD; Bernie Siegel, MD; William Lee, MD; and many others.

Music
Open Green, with Joyce Karchere, voice. Uplifting original acoustic music.

By David Lesser, MBA, Executive Coach

Interviews with the Experts on Business Success, Leadership & Growth
Audio recording and complete transcript.

- Leo Hindery, MBA   Topic: It's Time to Lead with Integrity

- Michael Gerber   Topic: Awakening the Entrepreneur Within

- Jim Warner   Topic: When Having It All Isn't Enough

- Cliff Barry   Topic: Bring Your True Self Out of Shadow

- Russ Hudson   Topic: The Power of Understanding Your Personality Type

- Jim Kochalka, PhD   Topic: The Psychology of Leadership

- James Flaherty   Topic: Being True to Ourselves in the World of Commerce

- Raz Ingrasci   Topic: When You Are Serious About Change

- Byron Katie   Topic: Your Personal Turnaround

- Joan Borysenko, MD   Topic: Tired No More

- Kausik Rajgopal, MBA   Topic: A Comprehensive Approach to Executive Development

- John Carver   Topic: Reinventing Your Board

- Bill Isaacs, PhD, & DeLynn Copley   Topic: Couples in Transition/Systems in Transition

E-Book
- Writings on Success, Leadership & Growth

Please see gaetacommunications.com for a complete listing, or call 646 705 4855. For individual coaching and Board/group facilitation by David Lesser, please visit executiveconfidant.com.

****

*To order these and other publications, and for live presentations with **Dr. Thomas Cooper** or **Dr. Michael Gaeta**, please visit gaetacommunications. com. For telephone consultations with Dr. Gaeta, please visit the website or call 646 705 4855.*

Dr. Gaeta offers a guided three-week transformational detoxification and cleansing program which incorporates the media fast elaborated by Dr. Cooper in this book.

****

CPSIA information can be obtained at www.ICGtesting.com
Printed in the USA
BVOW04s0026100816

458488BV00001B/17/P